AFRICAN REFORMATION

AFRICAN REFORMATION
AFRICAN INITIATED CHRISTIANITY
IN
THE 20TH CENTURY

ALLAN ANDERSON

Africa World Press, Inc.

P.O. Box 1892
Trenton, NJ 08607

P.O. Box 48
Asmara, ERITREA

Africa World Press, Inc.

P.O. Box 1892   P.O. Box 48
Trenton, NJ 08607   Asmara, ERITREA

Cover design: Ashraful Haque

Library of Congress Cataloging-in-Publication Data

Anderson, Allan.
    African reformation : African initiated Christianity in the 20th century / Allan H. Anderson
        p. cm.
Includes Bibliographical references and index.
    ISBN 0-86543-883-8 -- ISBN 0-86543-884-6 (pbk.)
    1. Africa, Sub-Saharan--Church history--20th century. I. Title.
    BR1430 .A765 2001
    289.9'3--dc21
                        2001003383

CONTENTS

Foreword

John Pobee

It is a contemporary mantra of the study of Church History and Missiology that the Centre of gravity of world Christianity has shifted from the North Atlantic to the South, with Africa, Asia, Latin America and the Pacific as the new heartlands of Christianity. The cutting and dynamic edge in the new shift is represented by the phenomenon variously described and which for our purposes here shall be designated "African Initiated Christianity" (AIC), the sub-title of this new book. At the beginning of the last century of the twentieth century, they constituted an All-Africa population of 42,000. By 1983 they were 29 million, i.e. 12% of the Christian population of Africa. In the year 2000 they were estimated at 54 million, i.e. 14% of the Christian population of the whole of Africa.

Their significance is not only due to their increasing numbers but also because their growth in many cases has been at the expense of the so-called historic Churches. Besides, even when they have departed from the historic Churches, they continue to grow. Thus they cannot be said to be only protest movement but are on to something that the historic churches have not discovered, which speaks to epistemology and ontology, the questioning, the hopes and fears of Homo Africanus. Equally striking and significant is it that these representatives of African Initiated Christianity have now appeared in Europe: the United Kingdom, France, Belgium, Germany and Holland. Africans are not only missionaries to themselves but also missionaries to Europe, thus in their own way reversing the historic missions from North to South. This story warns against the common distinction between "mainline churches" (i.e. historic churches and "sects" i.e. AIC (p.121).

The picture painted above should prepare us to be least surprised that this genre of Christianity has become a subject of much research and study by several disciplines, including sociology. This volume for which this foreword is written is by a missiologist. Missiology, of course is concerned among other things, with processes of growth and transformation. Therefore, this volume endeavours to throw some light on the factors conducive to their growth in breadth and depth, from which the historic churches in their phase of decline will do well to learn for their revival and renewal.

Of the phenomenon of AIC, various words have been used, i.e. revolution, schism, renewal, etc. Allan Anderson is putting on the scholarly scene a new volume *African Reformation. African Initiated Christianity in the Twentieth Century.* AIC is an African Reformation. But it is not as if they represent either a reformation or a revolution, or renewal in isolation. Anderson writes "the fact is that a religious revolution, an African reformation, has been going on in southern Africa for many years, and Christianity has been irrevocably changed in the process" (p.120).

This study is unique in its own way. First, whereas earlier studies were done largely by non-adherents of AICs, this study is done by a self-styled "Pentecostal"—not to be confused with most Western forms of Pentecostalism—having for years worked and worshipped in Praise Tabernacle Church led by Victor Mokgotlhoa. He writes then as an "insider"—his knowledge is not only academic but also the experience of an insider, even if subjected to the rigors of academic discipline. Equally interesting is it that the author is Caucasian African who has as much claim to Africanness as Negroid Africans.

Anderson's study puts several red warning lights on the road as we study AICs. For some time now, such studies have been beholden to typology. Anderson warns that the much appreciated typology of AIC is not always helpful because AIC are dynamic and under constant process of change (p.94). In any case, they represent a tremendous great variety; they are neither a monolithic nor a homogenous entity. One so-called "type" may embrace varied elements from other "types". An AIC can at one and the same time represent socio-political protest and cultural resistance. The Lumpa "sect" of Alice Lenshina from Zambia, for example, got into a political struggle with the nationalist government of Kenneth Kaunda and also rejected traditional rituals, adultery, divorce, polygamy, tobacco and alcohol. That "church" shunned the sacrament of Holy Communion because it was regarded as ancestral rite—their understanding of the theme of "memorial" attaching to the Eucharistic rite. So there is warning against wrong conclusions drawn from superficial observation (p.232). Thus the earlier studies of the "missiological saint", Bengt Sundkler, Marie-Louise Martin, and G.C. Oosthuizen are not to be taken as the last word on the subject, especially as they themselves revised some of their earlier judgement. At least for these warnings, Anderson's new book must be compulsory reading for the students of AICs.

The bottom line issue of AIC boils down to such phrases as inculturation, indigenization, contextualization and innovative approaches in mission. As such AIC represents one style of African theology, which, though not taking the prepositional, literary style is nevertheless African narrative theology. Theology is formed in the relevance to the felt needs and questionings of people. As such, AIC and Anderson's book *African Reformation* throw light on the relationship between gospel and culture, the contextualization of Christianity, new forms of mission strategy, a radicalized experiment of an indigenized Christianity, intercultural communication of the Christian gospel, the encounter between Christianity and another living religion. In Anderson's own words, he attempts to demonstrate "the importance of this African form of spirituality to the proclamation of the gospel in the mission of the universal church" (p.8).

Let me mention two areas in connection with this study, partly because of my own biography—theology being also biography. First, AIC represents a challenge to ecumenism and ecumenical movement. Of course, there are ecumenical trends in the AIC represented not only by the fact that some from that genre have joined in the multilateral ecumenism expressed by the World Council of Churches, but also intra-AIC institutions such as the Pentecostal Association of Ghana founded in 1962 (pp.80, 84), the Council of Independent Churches in Ghana, the Association of Aladura churches, and the Organization of African Instituted Churches. On the other hand, AIC has a fissiparous tendency. For one thing, a sense of divine call and commission often leads to or heightens the tendency to fission. For another thing, charismatic authority militates against stable institutionalization. Besides, from a Christian theological perspective, the teachings of some groups are suspect, e.g. the Mai-Chaza Church or Guta ra Jehova has replaced the New Testament with a Guta ra Jehova Bible which are the words and deeds of Mai Chaza. The challenge to the ecumenical consensus of the scriptures of the Old and New Testaments as common patrimony of all in the body of Christ is obvious. Anderson has a thought worth exploring—the experience of the Holy Spirit as the unifying factor in a global Christianity that is still divided, and as a catalyst in the emergence of a new society where there is justice and hope for despairing people (p.259).

In other words, the emergence of AIC is asking us to review our time-honoured marks of the Church, be it "One, holy, catholic apostolic church" or the place where the Gospel is preached and the sacraments of baptism and Eucharist are celebrated. Can ecumenical convergence be reach via the pneumatology route? I suspect a developed Trinitarian, rather than Christological emphasis as basis of ecumenism can be a viable route to ecumenical agreement. I guess the ecumenical vision needs to translate as radical openness to the movement of the Holy Spirit as He/She leads and points the way to new frontiers of mission.

The other significant thing about AIC is its pivotal role in the formation of a contextualized African theology. Theology for too long has been the preserve of the elite few (pp.242, 251), because the church's cultural dimensions are marked by its Greco heritage and its presuppositions of *Logos* and *ratio*. As such, theology has been alien to the majority of the faithful in Africa. AIC reminds us of the need to democratize theology and church and Christianity. Theology is the duty and responsibility of all the faithful. This is in tune with the WCC process in the 1980s called "theology by the people". Further, relevance is the test of good and sound theology. From the AICs we learn that the experience of people is the hermeneutic for understanding and ensuring the relevance of a religion.

Finally, AIC is gripping people, because its theology is marked by holism. Theology that will hold people must address the physical, emotional, mental, social and personal needs of people. In this context they present soteriology or theology of salvation (p. 235), which is described as pneumatological soteriology (p.236). Emotion, like rationality, must be a mark of vibrant theology.

This is a careful, well-researched, well-documented study. It gives us exposure to select AICs in Eastern, Central, Western and Southern Africa, again rather unusual. This is recommended necessary reading for all who would study AIC.

Rev. Canon Prof. Emeritus John S. Pobee

Accra, Ghana

December 2000

Acknowledgements

This book was first conceived in the preparation and delivery of lectures from 1996 to 2000 to a post-graduate Master of Arts class at the Centre for Missiology and World Christianity, formerly Selly Oak Colleges, now part of the Department of Theology, University of Birmingham, England. Since 1995, I have been Director of the Research Unit for New Religions and Churches at Selly Oak, where I was given every opportunity and encouragement to develop a course entitled "African Initiated Churches". I had access at Selly Oak to that wonderful treasure-house of information, the Harold Turner Collection, and am immensely grateful to Harold Turner for creating it, and to my predecessors Jack Thompson, Stan Nussbaum and my elder colleague Father Ralph Woodhall for developing it. Although I now work at a British "secular" university, the majority of the students I interact with are mature Christian ministers from the continents of Africa and Asia. Many of these are from churches founded in Africa by British missionaries. My rather limited and regional knowledge and experience of the AIC movement was greatly stimulated and expanded during preparation for lectures, through class discussions, and in evaluating essays and theses. I am very appreciative of all those who participated in this process from all over Africa as well as from other parts of the world.

A period of study leave in 1999 enabled me to do the enormous amount of reading and research required for the completion of this book. Andrew Kirk, director of the Centre for Missiology and World Christianity, Werner Ustorf, Professor of Mission at the University of Birmingham and friend and colleague "Sugi" Sugirtharajah have contributed enormously to a stimulating environment. Chris Oshun from Nigeria and John Padwick from Kenya read through an early draft and made valuable suggestions for two of the chapters. John Pobee, ecumenical African theologian *par excellence*, agreed to do the Foreword at short notice.

Kassahun Checole of Africa World Press accepted the book for publication with no hassle—truly an author's dream!

My octogenarian parents, Keith and Gwenyth Anderson, who served the African church in Zimbabwe, Zambia and South Africa for half a century, have given me a wonderful example of Christian commitment and their own personal support. My beloved wife and children Olwen, Matthew and Tami have endured a husband and father who was often less available and more irritable than usual.

My heartfelt thanks go to all these and above all, to my Creator and Sovereign Lord, who made the study possible. This book is dedicated to all the Christians of Africa who have so inspired me with their faith and creativity.

God bless Africa and all her peoples with peace.

Selly Oak, Birmingham, England
June 2001

Part One

CONTEXT

1

OVERVIEW

I was raised in Zimbabwe (my father's birthplace), but have spent most of my adult life (1971-1995) in South Africa. I'm a 'missionaries kid', son of Salvation Army officers and the sixth generation of church ministers in Southern Africa. My forefather, William Anderson, one of the early LMS missionaries, arrived in Cape Town from London in 1800 to work beyond the reaches of the Cape Colony. I've spent most of my life living and working in African communities that I've tried to identify with and understand. During the last seven years in South Africa (1988-1995), my family and I lived in a "township" community in Soshanguve, near Pretoria, during apartheid's final years. During that time there we worshiped and worked in an African independent Charismatic church, Praise Tabernacle Church led by Victor Mokgotlhoa. Altogether, I have spent twenty-four years fully involved in African Pentecostalism. These experiences have taught me many lessons about African Christianity, some of which will be reflected here. I consider myself "Pentecostal" because of my experience of the working of the Holy Spirit, although I don't identify with many western forms of Pentecostalism. The central thesis of this book is that Africa has had a reformation of the Spirit that has revolutionized the face of Christianity. This is no "impartial spectator", for I am a sympathetic participant observer who has been fully involved in an enthusiastic, lively, and "non-formal", spiritual African Christianity freed from many "foreign" constraints. I'm a perpetual "non-conformist", but this also makes me critical of my own cultural and religious traditions. Nevertheless, this book emphasizes the role of African "Spirit inspired" initiatives in this twentieth century transformation of Christianity. These are my roots, and these undoubtedly will help readers understand any presuppositions that inevitably will appear.

The Research Unit for New Religions and Churches at Selly Oak,[1] Birmingham, England administers the internationally acclaimed Harold Turner Collection of over 25,000 documents, focusing on those Christian movements in the Third World demonstrating the interaction between Christianity and "indigenous" or so-called "primal" religions. About half of the documents pertain to Africa and the phenomenon of African Independent Churches or, as I prefer to call them here, African Initiated Churches (henceforth, AICs).[2] During my six years at Selly Oak, I have come to a greater realization of the continental and, indeed, international implications and importance of this "African Reformation". The subject of this book is a phenomenon of such momentous significance that it can truly be called the "African Reformation", which must be taken seriously by anyone interested in African Christianity and the globalization of Christianity. Observers of the African Initiated Church (AIC) movement have long recognized the fact that this was a fundamental reformation of African Christianity. James Webster spoke of the rise of "African" churches in the period 1888-1922 as an "African Reformation".[3] David Barrett's groundbreaking *Schism and Renewal in Africa* makes a cogent case for seeing "independency" as a manifestation of "a vast movement of reform of the Christian community" that is not restricted to AICs alone.[4] He considers there to be "a striking number of parallels" between the history of AICs and that of the European Reformation. He describes the AIC movement as one with a "radical mission of renewal and reformation" and says that AICs constantly refer to themselves as "a reformation of over-Europeanized Christianity" and "are conscious of a reforming mission". He says that the entire AIC movement "has discovered and implemented some of the major theological concerns being expressed elsewhere in the world concerning a reformation of the Christian community". This reformation had occurred in the context of Africa itself, spurred on by the vernacular translations of the Bible, as was also the case with "numerous earlier reformations and theological renewals in history".[5] Similarly, Hans-Jürgen Becken called the AIC movement in South Africa an "African Reformation" of Christianity, which he described as "similar" to the Protestant Reformation in northern Europe.[6] This book will attempt to show how the entire AIC movement in all its many forms throughout the continent, but particularly in its most prominent pentecostal-type churches, represents such an indigenous Reformation and transformation of Christianity on a continental scale unprecedented in the history of the worldwide church.

This book is not an attempt to romanticize the AIC movement or portray it as a paragon of African virtue or "indigenous church"—although I do think that the AIC movement has something distinctive that is quite unlike other forms of African Christianity.[7] There are many forms of Christianity on the continent, which all express various degrees of interaction within different African contexts. It's hoped that this introductory study will also delicately unravel the weal and woe of the AIC movement whilst pointing to many positive lessons for the universal church. Sensitive and sympathetic studies of this section of African Christianity have enriched the church throughout the world and have irrevocably challenged the earlier western hegemony of Christianity in Africa. Indeed, the many lessons learned from this movement touch the very nature of Christianity itself.

Much of the extensive literature that has appeared on the AIC movement was written by European missionaries in Africa and more recently (thankfully) by African scholars—but unfortunately, only a little has yet been written by scholars within the AIC movement itself. Many existing studies deal with one specific movement or those found in one country or region. Although several studies have been conducted over fifty years on particular AICs in different regions, no contemporary and introductory study of the movement as a continental phenomenon exists, particularly as it has continued to develop and change rapidly. One of the first attempts at an introduction was Victor Hayward's edited collection for the World Council of Churches in 1963, entitled *African Independent Church Movements*. The contributions from leading missionary scholars unfortunately reflected some of the prejudices and the paternalism of the time.[8] Barrett lamented over thirty years ago of "the paucity of studies attempting to deal with the movement as a whole". His 1968 publication *Schism and Renewal in Africa* went a long way towards supplying that lack, but was mainly a comprehensive and informative discussion of causative factors.[9] *Schism and Renewal*, followed more recently by Barrett and Padwick's 1989 publication *Rise Up and Walk!* and M.L. (Inus) Daneel's *Quest for Belonging* in 1987 also dealt with the AIC movement as a whole, but these all had somewhat of a regional focus, the former two largely concentrating on Kenya and the latter focusing mainly on Zimbabwe.[10] The first two publications from within the AIC movement itself came from South Africa and were limited by their unavoidable lack of contact with the wider context: *Speaking for Ourselves* (1985) and Paul Makhubu's *Who are the Independent Churches?* (1989).[11] Adrian Hastings, in his two comprehensive volumes on the history of African Christianity, has dealt with "independency" continentally as separate and prominent sections of his studies, but these books have much wider interests than AICs alone.[12] Most recently, introductory books on AICs by African theologians have appeared: Ayegboyin and Ishola's *African Indigenous Churches* (1997) and Pobee and Ositelu's *African Initiatives in Christianity* (1998). Although brief, these are refreshing studies by West Africans with participation (in Ositelu's case) from an AIC leader himself, but the former tends to focus on West African churches and, in places, makes some unsubstantiated and polemical generalizations against them, while the latter is a short introduction of the AICs to the ecumenical movement.[13] The present book doesn't pretend to improve on all the earlier studies, but tries to provide an up-to-date and comprehensive textbook for students of Christianity and religion in Africa. By focusing on the history, contemporary practices and theology of the AICs as a reformation movement on a continental scale, it points to possible lessons for world Christianity. This is admittedly an introductory study with mainly theological interests. Many detailed regional studies and those pertaining to particular movements have appeared over the years, but the hope is that this study has a sufficiently wide sweep to embrace the whole movement. The reader will be referred to some of the particular studies in the footnotes and references cited to stimulate further reading and research.

In most countries of the sub-Sahara, no one can engage in Christian work without encountering this vast phenomenon. Although there are inevitable difficulties with statistics in Africa, Barrett and Padwick estimated that from a total of about 42,000 AIC members in 1900, there were some 29 million or 12% of the total Christian population of Africa in 1985. This figure was projected to rise to 54 million or 14% by 2000.[14] The *World Christian Encyclopedia* estimates 83 million "Independents" and 126 million "Pentecostals/Charismatics" in Africa in 2000, about 20% of all Christians.[15] About two-thirds of AIC members are found in the three countries of South Africa, the Congo (Kinshasa) and Nigeria, where the proportion of AICs to the total Christian population is much higher than in other countries, with the possible exception of Swaziland, Zimbabwe, Kenya and Ghana. Whatever the accuracy of the statistics, AICs are undoubtedly a major force in African Christianity today, one manifestation of the shifting of the center of gravity of Christianity in the twentieth century from the North to the South. To the consternation of some, this astonishing growth has sometimes been at the expense of older European mission-founded churches. Christianity, which commenced in the Third World, is returning to its roots. There are ways of expressing theology other than those familiar to westerners. The AICs illustrate theology in oral narrative and experience, and those who are seeking a meaningful African theology that takes seriously the African worldview must examine this contribution. Important lessons about the relationship between the gospel and culture, the contextualization of Christianity, and new forms of mission strategy in Africa are taught. Living, radical experiments of an indigenized Christianity that has consciously rejected western ecclesiastical models and forms of being Christian are here provided. Barrett described this process as "the product of African spirituality stripped of support from other cultures". He said that the AIC movement had "grown in the teeth of the anathemas of the vastly richer mission churches, with, in most cases, no help from outside."[16] This is also, therefore, a missiological study, not just because I am a missiologist, but because AICs provide valuable insights into many aspects of missiology, such as the intercultural communication of the Christian gospel and the encounter between Christianity and another living religion. I hope to demonstrate throughout this study the importance of this African form of spirituality to the proclamation of the gospel in the mission of the universal church.

This book tries to give an overview of AICs in different parts of the Sub-Sahara, examining the reasons for the historical emergence and growth of churches that have resulted from the interaction between Christianity and African pre-Christian religions. It will describe the characteristics of different types of churches and the lessons they teach the universal church. We will examine brief histories, teachings, beliefs, and practices of a selection of representative churches in different African countries and their significance for world Christianity. Throughout the book, post-independence names of African nations will usually be used rather than colonial ones to avoid confusion, even when events being described belong to the colonial era.

This chapter introduces the subject and in the next section, discusses different kinds of African initiated churches, from the earliest "Ethiopian" and "African" churches that emerged at the end of the nineteenth century to the later, more prolific "prophet-healing" and "spiritual" churches, the main focus. The most recent "new Pentecostal" or "Charismatic" churches that have developed since 1970 are also described. The second chapter pauses to consider the reasons for the emergence, development, and growth of AICs in the twentieth century. The next seven chapters are mainly historical. Chapter 3 looks at the ancient Ethiopian church, Kimpa Vita (Dona Beatrice) and the birth of the AIC movement in the Kongo Kingdom, and early movements in West Africa and South Africa at the end of the nineteenth century. The following five chapters consider AICs in different regions. Chapter 4 considers the fascinating story of the Liberian prophet William Wade Harris and the Harrist movement that emerged from his remarkable ministry, their influence on AICs throughout West Africa, the rise of "spiritual churches" in Ghana, and "Aladura" (praying) churches in Nigeria. The chapter concludes with a brief survey of a more recent phenomenon, the transplanting and development of AICs in Britain and other parts of Europe since the 1960s. The fifth chapter deals with parallel developments in AICs south of the Zambezi, with particular focus on Zimbabwe and South Africa, where the greatest proliferation of AICs in the continent is to be found. Zionist and Apostolic movements in Southern Africa are discussed, the largest of which is the Zion Christian Church founded by Engenas Lekganyane, and the more unusual but equally significant Zulu movement of Isaiah Shembe, the Nazareth Baptist Church better known by its Zulu term "amaNazaretha". Chapter 6 focuses on the area from the Congo Basin to the Zambezi, with the moving story of Simon Kimbangu and Kimbanguism in the Congo (possibly the largest AIC in the continent), the rise of Ngunzism, and the tragic episode of Alice Lenshina and the Lumpa movement in Zambia. Chapter Seven moves to East Africa and particularly to Kenya, where AICs have proliferated, discussing some of the particular churches unique to that region. Chapter Eight looks at the more recent development of the "new Pentecostals" that have arisen in different parts of the continent in the last three decades of the twentieth century, revivalist, and rapidly growing independent Pentecostal or Charismatic churches and the challenges these present to the church in Africa today.

The final three chapters look more specifically at the contribution these different churches make to the mission and theology of the church in Africa. Chapter 9 deals with the innovative adaptations these churches make and their attitudes to older African religious beliefs, such as their attitudes to ancestors, divination, and traditional medicine and healing. Chapter 10 considers the contribution made by AICs to an "enacted" and contextualized African theology, particularly in the realms of pneumatology, Christology, and soteriology. The hermeneutical perspectives of AICs and the important role of African prophets are discussed. The final chapter focuses on the reforming initiatives of AICs and their challenges to the universal church. The contribution of AICs to understanding issues like contextualization, inculturation, syncretism, and how the gospel relates to culture are considered. This contribution is so far-reaching that we may really consider this to be a reformation of at least the magnitude of the Protestant Reformation in Europe, and we may be excused for concluding that this was perhaps a more profound Reformation than the European one ever was.

Types and Terms

The many thousands of AICs today, including the most recent varieties, have become the dominant and fastest growing expression of Christianity on the continent. After the European colonization of Africa, a process of religious acculturation took place as older African religious and social traditions were threatened and partially replaced by new ones. The creative independent African Christian churches that began to emerge at the turn of the twentieth century were initially snubbed. Western mission church leaders and other observers labeled them "sects" and "nativistic", "messianic", "separatist", and "syncretist" movements. The term "African independent churches" was probably the first acceptable, neutral phrase used for these new movements. Harold Turner defined "African independent church" as "a church which has been founded in Africa, by Africans, and primarily for Africans".[17] Later, many African churches founded by European missionaries became "independent" of European control, and the term "African indigenous churches" was proposed to distinguish between the newly independent churches in Africa and those that had formed autonomous churches decades before. After the African states began to emerge one by one from colonial domination in the fifties and sixties, there was new impetus towards the "Africanization" of Christianity. Many European mission-founded churches began to talk about and move towards inculturation and seek to be seen as "indigenous". The term "African indigenous churches" has therefore also become somewhat inadequate, particularly because most AICs are not completely free from "foreign" influence and can't be regarded as "indigenous" in any normative sense. "African initiated churches" and "African instituted churches" are terms more recently deployed which avoid these difficulties by simply indicating that these churches were initiated by Africans, and not by western missionaries. Pobee and Ositelu have recently used the term "African Initiatives in Christianity", saying that the term "independent" no longer describes the uniqueness of AICs, which is seen in "their character as African initiatives and, therefore, in accordance with the African genius and culture and ethos".[18] In my opting for the term "African initiated churches", the fact of their "independent" and "indigenous" character isn't questioned, but neither is it presupposed. This is the terminology I will follow here, but the use of the acronym "AIC" from now on will in any case satisfy most readers.

AICs have usually flourished most, but not exclusively, in areas where Protestant missions have been longest. This is particularly the case in Southern Africa, the Congo Basin, central Kenya, and near the West African coast. There also seems to be a connection between the number of different Protestant missions in a particular region and the emergence of AICs there. We look specifically in this book at those movements that regard themselves as Christian churches. There are a small number of religious movements in Africa that don't see themselves as Christian, some of which Harold Turner has defined in an essay about new religious movements in so-called "primal" societies as a global phenomenon. He labels as *revitalization* or *neo-primal* movements those that have deliberately sought to revive traditional religious practices, such as the Church of the Ancestors in Malawi, the Herero Church in Namibia, the Dini ya Msambwa in Kenya, and the Afrikania movement in Ghana. He refers to another type of movement as *syncretist*, later *synthetist,* movements that deliberately take their content from both the traditional African and Christian sources.[19] An example of this might be the Nomiya Luo church of western Kenya. Some African movements have also arisen in Islamic contexts, like the Mahdiyya movements in West Africa that have declared an African Mahdi as the return of the Twelfth Iman.[20] Others Turner terms *Hebraist*, because they consider themselves to be the Old Testament people of God but are not predominantly Christian.[21] The difficulty with what are sometimes arbitrary classifications of these movements is that some classified "not Christian" *do* consider themselves Christian, and one is left wondering by what criteria they were categorized in the first place. Those African movements that do not claim to be Christian are beyond the scope of this study, however.

In discussing any typology, we must avoid making hasty generalizations or overlooking obvious differences, and we must appreciate the distinctive liturgies, healing practices, and particularly the different approaches to African religion and the unique contribution to Christianity in a broader African context of the different AICs. It is important to remember at the outset that European researchers and outsiders coined the many terms used to describe AICs, which are not terms familiar to or always acknowledged by the vast majority of AICs themselves, although some may have accepted them for their own purposes. One of the more perceptive and sensitive of the earlier observers, Harold Turner, has reminded us that a typology can be no more than a hypothesis that depends on further research for its confirmation or correction. A typology may overlook the complexities of the subject or may even distort our understanding of it. Turner's sage advice is that "it is probably wiser to think of a typology of *tendencies and emphases* rather than of individual religious bodies and movements".[22] He suggests that "the only safe course is to proceed to construct an African typology based on the ways in which the phenomena tend to be grouped".[23]

Although there has been extensive literature on AICs over the years, the first systematic and comprehensive regional study appeared in 1948, with the appearance of Swedish Lutheran missionary Bengt Sundker's *Bantu Prophets in South Africa*.[24] This landmark publication set the standard for the flood of literature that followed and few were to attain it.[25] Sundkler's own research on which the book was based was conducted in rural Zululand (now, KwaZulu Natal) during the mid-forties. He identified two main types of AICs in South Africa: "Ethiopian" and "Zionist" churches.[26] Several scholars of the movement during the next forty years followed Sundkler's basic dual typology.[27] These researchers placed the many different kinds of AICs from all over the continent into the two broad categories of "Ethiopian" or "African" churches, and "Zionist" or "spiritual" churches. In West Africa, Harold Turner followed this two-fold distinction between "Ethiopian type" and "prophet-healing type", and Zimbabwean-born M.L. (Inus) Daneel made the same distinction between "Spirit-type" and "Ethiopian-type" churches.[28] "Zionist" or "Spirit-type" is the Southern African equivalent of the more appropriate continental terms "prophet-healing" and "spiritual", and distinguishes "prophetic movements that emphasize the inspiration and revelation of the Holy Spirit from the non-prophetic church groups". The differences between these two types were "religious and organizational rather than socio-political", said Daneel.[29] Hastings remarks, however, that this dual typology is "an external, white imposition—and one chiefly belonging to Southern Africa".[30] It is probably true to say that the dual typology no longer applies to Southern African churches, let alone those in the rest of Africa. But it will help us to understand the reasons for Sundkler's two-fold classification at the time.

South African anthropologist Martin West summarized the difference between Sundkler's two AIC types by saying that "Ethiopian churches" were those that had seceded from mission churches for political reasons, and which "remained patterned on their parent churches". He said that "Zionists" were "a Pentecostal, apostolic movement, stressing the influence of the Holy Spirit and of divine healing, and combining both African and European cultural elements". West doubts whether the categories have added much to our knowledge of the movement, and says that typologies are often like "butterfly-collecting, where information is pigeon-holed and the terms of reference are inadequately explained".[31] In an earlier publication, I suggested that Daneel's term "Spirit-type" might also be termed "Pentecostal-type", because of the common historical, liturgical/ phenomenological, and theological features of these churches and western Pentecostalism, which common features are quite considerable.[32] The term "pentecostal" is often used by observers to describe these particular churches, but suffers from identification with western Pentecostalism. Turner's term "prophet-healing" is possibly a description that can be used continentally for these churches, rather than others that have been suggested with more regional relevance.[33]

Nevertheless, in the use of any terms at all, it is important to remember that there are many more "types" of churches than those proposed by researchers and that often, the churches themselves don't recognize the categories given them by outsiders. Furthermore, within every "type" there are exceptions to the general characteristics—so we have to constantly use terms like "generally" or "usually" in defining them. Despite my attempts to enter this debate in the past, I am no longer convinced that dividing AICs into types is particularly helpful. What is offered here is a very brief outline of an extremely complicated subject that is only of passing academic interest. Types are described here to facilitate understanding the broad differences between the movements, but such categorization does not do justice to their diversity. Placing AICs into categories results in generalizations that don't accurately reflect the true nature of each particular church, and this is not an African concern anyway. Today there are so many recognized exceptions to the "types" and so many new churches being created, that any typology can only outline some of the common characteristics of different "types" in at attempt to make this vast multifarious movement more understandable to the outsider. Hastings makes the point:

> It is rather that there is such a rich spectrum of diversity and that any consistent categorization is either too complex to fulfill its purpose or simply misleading in being based on a too selective approach to the characteristic forms of church life.

He further points out that even the terms "Zion" and

"Ethiopia" aren't mutually exclusive: "Zion is of course Jerusalem, but it is a Jerusalem somehow realized here in Africa, and what is Ethiopia but *par excellence* such a Zion?"[34] Harold Turner suggested that such a "common framework and language" was necessary both for "comparative purposes" and "in order to distinguish the essential features" of African religious movements.[35] The "types" are not intended to be definitive, however, especially as the movements they describe are dynamic churches under a constant process of change.

African/ Ethiopian Churches

AICs that do not claim to be prophetic or to have special manifestations of the Holy Spirit, and which have modeled themselves to a large extent on the European mission churches from which they seceded, have been called "Ethiopian" or "Ethiopian-type" churches in Southern Africa,[36] and "African" churches in Nigeria.[37] These were usually the first AICs to emerge. However, the term "Ethiopian" or "African" is not used or recognized by all churches in this category. In Kenya, for example, the terms aren't used at all for many AICs there which would be very similar in character to this type. The largest of these AICs is the African Independent Pentecostal Church, which further complicates the typology. Jean Comaroff prefers the term "Independent" to describe these churches, but this may add to the confusion.[38] Nevertheless, the terms "Ethiopian" and "African" are used here for want of better ones. These churches are generally earlier in origin than the other two types described below, and arose primarily as political and administrative reactions to European mission-founded churches. For this reason, "African" churches are very similar to the churches from which they emerged. They usually practice infant baptism, read liturgies, sing translated European hymns, wear European-type clerical vestments (often black) and are less enthusiastic or emotional in their services than are the "prophet-healing" churches. They tend to be less prescriptive than other AICs regarding food taboos like eating pork, the use of medicine, and the consumption of alcohol. Most often not named "Ethiopian" or "African", they originated in secessions from mission-founded churches on racial and political grounds. They were formed as a reaction to the white mission's conquest of African peoples; although as Sundkler pointed out, the "church organization and Bible interpretation are largely copied from the patterns of the Protestant Mission Churches from which they have seceded".[39] Sometimes they even include the church's generic name in the church title: "Methodist", "Presbyterian", "Congregational", "Lutheran", and so on.[40]

In Southern Africa, the word "Ethiopian" in the church name is more common and had special significance in these countries more heavily colonized than the rest of Africa. Ethiopia, the only African nation that had successfully resisted European colonialism by defeating Italy in war, is mentioned in the Bible as a nation that "stretches out her hands to God" (Psalm 68:31). This verse and the conversion of the Ethiopian court official (Acts 8) formed the basis of the "Ethiopian" ideology that spread in South Africa and Nigeria in the 1890s and may have affected the establishment of these AICs elsewhere. Africans had received Christianity before Europeans had, and therefore had a special place in God's plan of salvation and at least as much right to being missionaries of the gospel as Europeans. The "African" and "Ethiopian" churches have declined in the past fifty years and have been somewhat eclipsed by the other, more enthusiastic pentecostal-type churches. Comaroff suggests that this is because they occupy the middle ground in an increasingly polarized society and do not offer radical alternatives.[41] The history of these churches will be traced in Chapter 3.

Prophet-Healing/ Spiritual Churches

The "prophet-healing" or "spiritual" churches are churches that emphasize spiritual power. They are independent African churches with historical and theological roots in the Pentecostal movement, although they have moved in their own direction away from western forms of Pentecostalism in several respects over the years, and may not be regarded as "Pentecostal" without further qualification.[42] Like western Pentecostals, however, they are churches that emphasize—usually in contrast to "Ethiopian" and "African" churches—the working of the power of the Spirit in the church. Pobee and Ositelu call these "Pentecostal churches in Africa" which do not originate in Europe or North America.[43]

This is the largest and most significant grouping of AICs, and therefore will occupy the major part of this study. This is a particularly difficult type to describe, for it includes a vast variety of some of the biggest of all churches in Africa—the Kimbanguist church and the African Apostolic Church in Central Africa, the Christ Apostolic Church, the Aladura and the Harrist churches in West Africa, and the Zion Christian Church and the *Amanazaretha* in Southern Africa. These are all churches with hundreds of thousands of members, and in at least two cases (Kimbanguists and Zionists) there are millions. Some of these churches are now members of ecumenical bodies like the different national councils of churches, the continental All Africa Council of Churches, and the World Council of Churches. In the eyes of those who consider these councils as offering some measure of respectability, these moves are welcomed and give the AICs legitimacy denied them by European churches and colonial powers for so long. But most AICs are not members of ecumenical bodies and are not clamoring to be so. Their legitimacy hails from a belief in divinely appointed leaders who don't need to seek human recognition, and from their time-tested strengths as major denominations in their own right.

Because written theology is not a priority and is generally less precisely formulated in these churches than in European instituted churches, the differences in belief systems, liturgy, and prophetic healing practices are considerable. Foundational to these churches are definite theological presuppositions, found more in the practice of their Christianity than in formal dogma. Like the new Pentecostal and Charismatic churches described below, there is an emphasis on healing, although the methods of obtaining healing differ. Whereas other Pentecostals generally will practice "laying on hands" or prayer for the sick, this will often be accompanied in prophet-healing churches by the use of various symbolic objects such as blessed water, ropes, staffs, papers, ash, and so on. This constitutes one of the more obvious differences between other Pentecostals and these churches. There are also strong taboos for members prohibiting alcohol, tobacco, and pork. The attitude to traditional religious practices is generally more ambivalent than in the new Pentecostal churches, particularly when it comes to ancestor rituals, and some of these churches also allow polygyny.[44] But for the majority of these churches across Africa, a clear stand is taken against certain traditional practices like witchcraft and spirit possession.

For the outside observer, the biggest distinguishing feature of these churches in most parts of Africa is the almost universal use of uniforms for members, which are often white robes with sashes and in some cases, military-like khaki. These obviously non-African accretions notwithstanding, these churches have possibly adapted themselves to and addressed the popular African worldview more substantially than other types of church have, and this is their unique contribution towards understanding Christianity in Africa. It is in fact this adaptation to and confrontation with African tradition that constitutes at the same time both the challenge and the problem of these AICs to a contextual African theology, particularly when African theologians have taken on board the entire spectrum of African traditional religion without question. This subject will be further discussed in Chapter 10.

Pentecostal/Charismatic Churches

The term "Pentecostal" is taken from the Day of Pentecost experience of the second chapter of Acts,[45] and although prophet-healing churches differ fundamentally from western Pentecostal churches, they too emphasize the centrality of the Holy Spirit in faith and (especially) in practice, and can therefore also be termed "African Pentecostal". Three decades ago, Swiss theologian Walter Hollenweger employed this broad use of the term "Pentecostal" to refer to prophet-healing churches, and more recently, Harvey Cox referred to them as "the African expression of the worldwide Pentecostal movement".[46] But although there are definite links with and similarities to Pentecostalism,[47] a consistent distinction between "prophet-healing" and "Pentecostal/ Charismatic" churches in Africa is made to avoid confusion.

The Pentecostal or Charismatic churches and "ministries" are of more recent origin, and may be regarded as "Pentecostal" movements because they too emphasize the power and the gifts of the Holy Spirit.[48] They vary in size from small independent house churches to rapidly growing and large organizations, such as the Deeper Life Church in Nigeria under William Kumuyi,[49] the Zimbabwe Assemblies of God African of Ezekiel Guti,[50] and Grace Bible Church under Mosa Sono in South Africa,[51] to name a few. Despite their recent origins, some of these churches are already among the largest and most influential denominations in their respective countries, especially in West Africa. The growth of these churches over the past two decades indicates that a significant number of their members come from older European mission-founded churches and from prophet-healing churches. There is a western, especially North American, Pentecostal influence in many of these churches both in liturgy and in leadership patterns, and North American "prosperity" preachers are sometimes promoted.[52] The difference between these churches and Pentecostal and Charismatic churches in the West is difficult to discern on the surface, except that leadership is entirely African and more of a local, autonomous nature. Their founders are generally charismatic and younger men and women who are respected for their preaching and leadership abilities, and who are relatively well educated, though not necessarily in theology. These churches tend to be more sharply opposed to several traditional practices than is the case with prophet-healing churches, and they often ban alcohol and tobacco, the use of symbolic healing objects, and the wearing of uniforms. The membership tends to consist of younger, less economically deprived, and more formally educated people. They are often seen, particularly by the older AICs, as mounting a sustained attack on traditional African values.

These are three of the ways in which AICs can be described, but these "types" are by no means the only ones, nor is this the only way a typology could be suggested. There are hundreds of AICs that don't neatly fit into any of these three "types" and probably wouldn't wish to do so either. Deciding on types is so often determined by the criteria used and by whom. What is important is how the churches see themselves. The tremendously rich diversity and creativity of the AIC movement will be illustrated in the chapters that follow, and this discussion of typology is merely intended as an admittedly superficial introduction to the subject. Hopefully, the reader will be able to make evaluations about the complexity of the AIC movement later, on the basis of the internal evidence from the churches themselves.

Notes

[1] Previously in the School of Mission and World Christianity, Selly Oak Colleges, from August 1999 the Unit has been attached to the newly named Centre for Missiology and World Christianity, Graduate Institute for Theology and Religion, University of Birmingham, England.

[2] The use of this term is discussed in this chapter later.

[3] James B. Webster, *The African Churches among the Yoruba 1888-1922*, Oxford, 1964, 190.

[4] David B. Barrrett, *Schism and Renewal in Africa*, Nairobi, 1968, 186.

[5] Ibid., 161-2, 173-4.

[6] Hans-Jürgen Becken, in Irving Hexham & G.C. Oosthuizen (eds.), *The Story of Isaiah Shembe*, Lewiston, 1996, ix.

[7] David Barrett & T. John Padwick, *Rise Up and Walk!*, Nairobi, 1989, i, describe it as "in fact a movement unique in extent and magnitude in the 20 centuries of Christian history".

[8] Victor E.W. Hayward (ed.), *African Independent Church Movements*, London, 1963.

[9] Barrett, *Schism*, 4. The extensive literature on the subject written before 1977 is listed in Harold W. Turner, *Bibliography of New Religious Movements in Primal Societies. Vol. I: Black Africa*, Boston, 1977.

[10] Barrett and Padwick; M. L. (Inus) Daneel, *Quest for Belonging*, Gweru, Zimbabwe, 1987.

[11] Institute for Contextual Theology, *Speaking for Ourselves*. Johannesburg, 1985; Paul Makhubu, *Who are the Independent Churches?*, Johannesburg, 1988.

[12] Adrian Hastings, *A History of African Christianity 1950-1975*, Cambridge, 1979; id., *The Church in Africa 1450-1950*, Oxford, 1994.

[13] Deji Ayegboyin & S. Ademola Ishola, *African Indigenous Churches: An Historical Perspective*, Lagos, 1997 (see especially pp. 153-8); John S. Pobee & Gabriel Ositelu II, *African Initiatives in Christianity: The Growth, Gifts and Diversities of Indigenous African Churches — A Challenge to the Ecumenical Movement*, Geneva, 1998.

[14] Barrett & Padwick, 9.

[15] David B. Barrett, George T. Kurian & Todd M. Johnson (eds.), *World Christian Encyclopedia*, 2nd Ed, 2 vols, Oxford & New York, 2001, 1:13.

[16] Barrett, *Schism*, 163.

[17] Turner, *Religious Innovation*, 92.

[18] Pobee & Ositelu, 4.

[19] Ibid., 8.

[20] Peter Clarke, *Mahdism in West Africa: The Ijebu Mahdiyya Movement*. London, 1995, 111.

[21] Turner, *Religious Innovation*, 83-6.

[22] Harold W. Turner, *Religious Innovation in Africa*, Boston, 1979, 80 (emphasis mine).

[23] Ibid, 82.

[24] Bengt G.M. Sundkler, *Bantu Prophets in South Africa*, London, 1948, 1961.

[25] See Barrett's assessment of the literature in *Schism*, 37-43.

[26] Sundkler, *Bantu Prophets*, 53.

[27] Allan Anderson, *Bazalwane: African Pentecostals in South Africa*, Pretoria, 1992, 56-8; Jean Comaroff, *Body of Power, Spirit of Resistance: The Culture and History of a South African People*, Chicago & London, 1985, 272-3, n. 11, n. 14.

[28] Turner, *Religious Innovation*, 94-101; M. L. Daneel, *Old and New in Southern Shona Independent Churches. Vol 1*. The Hague, 1971, 285.

[29] Daneel, *Old and New 1*, 350.

[30] Hastings, *History*, 69.

[31] Martin West, *Bishops and Prophets in a Black City*, Cape Town, 1975, 16-7.

32 Anderson, *Bazalwane*, 59.

33 Turner, *Religious Innovation*, 94-101.

34 Hastings, *History*, 69.

35 Turner, *Religious Innovation*, 79.

36 M. L. Daneel, *Quest*, 38.

37 Turner, *Religious Innovation*, 95.

38 Comaroff, 272, n.11.

39 Sundkler, *Bantu Prophets*, 54.

40 Examples of this are given in the list of church names in Anderson, *Bazalwane*, 126-7.

41 Comaroff, 192.

42 See Allan Anderson, *Zion and Pentecost: The Spirituality and Experience of Pentecostal and Zionist/ Apostolic Churches in South Africa*, Pretoria, 2000, Chapter 2.

43 Pobee & Ositelu, 34.

44 The term "polygyny" ("many wives") is used in this book in preference to "polygamy" ("many marriages"), because polygyny is the only form of polygamy practised in Africa.

45 Anderson, *Bazalwane*, 2-6.

46 Walter J. Hollenweger, *The Pentecostals*, London, 1972, 149; Harvey Cox, *Fire From Heaven: The Rise of Pentecostal Spirituality and the Reshaping of Religion in the Twenty-first Century*, London, 1996, 246.

47 Anderson, *Bazalwane*, 28-31.

48 Many of these churches, however, don't always regard themselves as "Pentecostal" and in some cases prefer terms like "Charismatic" and "evangelical".

49 Matthews A. Ojo, "Deeper Life Bible Church of Nigeria", Nairobi, 1992, 135.

50 David Maxwell, "'Delivered from the Spirit of Poverty': Pentecostalism, Prosperity and Modernity in Zimbabwe" *Journal of Religion in Africa* 28:3, 1998, 350-73.

51 Anderson, *Bazalwane*, 53-5.

52 Allan Anderson, "The prosperity message in the eschatology of some new charismatic churches", *Missionalia* 15:2, 1987, 72-83.

2

ORIGINS AND CAUSES

Since the first academic studies on African Initiated Churches, writers have speculated on the causes for their emergence and growth. A great number and variety of opinions on the subject often tend to be highly selective, subjective and reductionist, depending on what particular interest or experience they reflect.[1] In discussing the question of causation, we ought to remember that the many different factors that might account for the *origins* of AICs must always be distinguished from those that might explain their subsequent *growth*, as they're not necessarily or even usually the same. We might think, for example, that the earliest movements seceded because they reacted to the dry formalism and rationalism in the European mission churches. This might account partly for their origins, but doesn't explain why some of these movements continue to grow profusely among those who have never belonged to any mission church at all. None of the causative factors highlighted by researchers can be isolated from the others, as a wide number of different causes can result in the emergence of a particular AIC, and equally as many reasons exist for its subsequent growth. We must see the whole question of causation within the macro-context of Africa during the late nineteenth century and throughout the twentieth century. Furthermore, each AIC has its peculiar causes or combination of causes. We'd be guilty of the gravest reductionism if we thought that these causes could be universalized to apply to all AICs. Furthermore, it's not always easy to distinguish between what might be considered "background" factors from the more proximate "immediate" causes. Nevertheless, there are some underlying factors that can be applied to many, but by no means all, of these movements. Here is a brief discussion of six of the more important ones.[2]

Social and Political Factors

Africa has witnessed a century of rapid social change with its accompanying industrialization and urbanization, as well as a transition from a pre-colonial through a traumatic colonial to an equally traumatic post-colonial political order. These factors have affected the formation of new religious movements all over the world, and those in Africa are no exception. The situation was particularly aggravated in colonial Africa with the imposition of discriminatory laws that created migratory labor, the loss of land, alienation, and impersonal mass housing. The full impact of colonialism was often only felt in the latter half of the twentieth century, resulting in a sense of oppression, disorientation, and marginalization that left people seeking to form new relationships in smaller social groups, where they could really belong and regain some human dignity. The AICs thus provided what has been described as a "place to feel at home".[3] Although most noticeable in South Africa, with the largest settler community on the continent and the deliberate social engineering of apartheid, during European colonization throughout Africa, residential, educational, and social segregation existed almost everywhere, to make Africans second-class citizens in their own countries. Worse, this discrimination and segregation extended to the churches too, most of whose white leaders accepted uncritically the socio-political status quo and the paradigms of colonialism. As a result, little attempt was made to give African church leaders any real authority. Social anthropologist Jean Comaroff describes the white Protestant leaders in South Africa who retained "strict paternalistic control over black congregations" which was "paradigmatic of hierarchical state structures at large".[4] This was indeed a significant factor in the formation of AICs, as we'll see particularly in the case of the first AICs to be formed, described in the next chapter. Adrian Hastings writes of the racism present in the mission churches, where "even able and experienced ministers remained second-class members of the Church, always inferior to the most junior missionary recently arrived from Britain".[5] Although this racism seldom directly produced secession, it was a major catalyst for a fire that needed only a spark to set it ablaze. The earliest AICs in Nigeria, Ghana, and South Africa arose at least partly because of nationalist feelings and a desire for African self-expression and freedom from missionary control.[6] More than sixty years ago, Efraim Andersson saw the phenomenon of AICs in the Congo as evidence of the African desire for political independence.[7] Bengt Sundkler, writing about South African movements in the 1940s, saw "the colour bar within the Christian Church" and "the general aversion to the White man's Christianity" as the reason for the emergence of AICs. Later, he suggests that further research would reveal "a morphological correspondence between the "pattern" of a tribal culture and the type, or types, of Christianized prophetic movements which it tends to produce."[8] The idea that the structure of particular African societies favored the emergence of these movements was put forward by several writers and was pursued more rigorously by David Barrett, as we shall see later in this chapter.[9]

Comaroff praises Sundker's sensitivity to the broad structural significance of the AICs and their character as complex symbolic systems, which sensitivity much of the subsequent study on AICs has failed to equal.[10] This becomes the dominant theme of Comaroff's own analysis of AICs in a South African society in the North West Province. She says that AICs were an expression of cultural protest and resistance to colonial domination. The Tshidi, a Barolong (Tswana) people, lacked the power to directly change the social oppression that manifested itself not only in the absence of political power, but also in the limited leadership opportunities offered them by European mission founded churches, which "seemed securely in the hands of the educated elite and were carefully set off from macropolitical concerns". As a result, they turned to "the less orthodox forms of the Western Protestant tradition" to provide the basis for the AICs to emerge as "a more radical expression of cultural resistance".[11] The oppressed people directed their frustrated disaffection against the more tangible colonialism of the mission churches. Repudiating the established churches was also a symbolic rejection of the larger social system. But the first "Independent" AICs in South Africa didn't seriously contest the socio-cultural order of white domination. The prophet-healing churches, the Zionists, were to do this more fundamentally. Comaroff says that the Zionists, through their non-dualistic, "key metaphor" of healing, emphasized "the reintegration of matter and spirit, the practical agency of divine force, and the social relocation of the displaced". The outcome of this was that these movements had drawn together "everything that had been set apart in the black experience of colonialization and wage labor". These AICs became a systematic counterculture attempting to encompass and transform alienating structures of power and control.[12]

Harold Turner sees the prophetic-healing churches as a creative response to the breakdown of traditional African society, providing security and order in new social groupings.[13] Similarly, Inus Daneel says that the development of leadership in the AICs served as a safety valve, a "surrogate" for the development of leadership in other spheres of society.[14] As Pobee and Ositelu observe, all religious movements have political implications because "no matter what their purpose, they affect the allocation of power and influence within a community".[15] And Comaroff points out that AICs are indeed embedded in total socio-political and cultural systems, which must be given due analytical weight in our assessment of causation.[16] So, in viewing the AICs as an

African reformation of Christianity, we must reckon with the importance of the socio-political macro-dimensions in the rise of this movement.

Reaction to European Missions

A variant of the socio-political factors outlined above is the view that the rise of AICs can be seen primarily as a reaction to European missions. This factor is treated separately here because of its prominence in missiological writings. Former CMS missionary in East Africa and now a prominent statistician of world Christianity, David Barrett, has discussed the causes for the rise of AICs in different African societies all over the continent in probably more detail than anyone else. He may be the chief exponent of the "reaction" view, but he is by no means alone. Barrett thinks that the main cause for the rise of the AIC movement is socio-political, for he sees AICs as one manifestation of many African protest and resistance movements. He says that the "common root cause" for the whole AIC movement is a reaction to European missions, which had exhibited a "failure in love" in their attitudes to African people.[17] On the basis of eighteen background factors ascertained by statistical tests that he applied to different ethnic units, Barrett constructed a "Tribal *Zeitgeist*", or a climate of opinion, for measuring the scale of religious tension in these units. The more the different factors are present in a given ethnic group, the more the likelihood of schism. Barrett takes the position that sometimes the traditional social structures of a people, the "Tribal *Zeitgeist*" or atmosphere of discontent, either favor or discourage the formation of AICs. Where there is a centralized hierarchy, as for example among the Baganda, there is less likelihood of religious schism. But where this central structure is absent and people are organized in smaller independent groups, as among the Luo of western Kenya or the peoples of Southern Africa, the possibility of schism increases enormously.[18]

Barrett's "tribal zeitgeist" theory, however, based on somewhat outdated anthropological presuppositions, hasn't found much support in recent scholarship. Unfortunately, his book is now outdated and his sometimes politically incorrect terminology, such as the frequent use of "tribe", detracts from an otherwise helpful and comprehensive analysis. But what he later identifies as the "common root cause" is more illuminating, in that it reveals his belief in AICs as a social reaction to European missions. He says that AICs were a reaction to a situation where the missionaries "were believed to be illegitimately mounting an attack against African traditional society and in particular its basic unit, the family."[19] In this regard, the issues of polygyny, witchcraft, and the ancestors were matters in which missionaries were particularly insensitive. Barrett points out that in spite of exceptions, the "failure in love" consisted of a failure to understand African society and culture, and a missionary paternalism which bred untold resentment. He calls the lack of sympathy and social contact on the part of missionaries an absence of "brotherly love", which in turn led to a failure to understand "Africanism" and a failure to distinguish the good elements in African religions and culture from the bad. This "failure in love" Barrett sees as the "root cause common to the whole movement".[20] Worst of all, this led to the inability to see any parallel between African society and biblical faith. All these factors resulted in poor communication between Africans and western missionaries, who couldn't accept that African Christianity would have to be very different from Christianity in Europe, and stifled any African attempts to express that difference. And so, Barrett makes the case that "the entire complex" of the thousands of AICs throughout the continent "takes on the same appearance of a spontaneous reaction to mission and reformation of over-Europeanized or over-institutionalized Christianity".[21]

Barrett's concept of AICs as primarily a reaction to European missions has been restated time and again by writers on the AICs, most recently by Ayegboyin and Ishola. They say that, amongst other reasons, AICs arose out of a desire to indigenize

Christianity, a passion for a purer form of Christianity, and freedom to exercise gifts of leadership.[22] Similarly, Pobee and Ositelu say that AICs are a protest movement, protesting against the "North Atlantic and Western captivity of the gospel as represented by the historic churches."[23] Adrian Hastings speaks of the underlying cause of the first secessions as being the tension between the established African Christianity at the end of the nineteenth century and "the quickly expanding number of white missionaries sharing in the expansionist self-confidence of Europe".[24] The missionaries withheld independence from the African churches they controlled. Hastings regards the pressure of African religion and culture on the churches, and the corresponding failure of the European missionaries to understand the appropriation of the gospel by African Christians within their own thought forms, to be a significant factor in the rise of the AICs.[25] The use of these and similar phrases implies a belief that AICs are a reaction to European missionary Christianity. As we shall see, the main weakness of the "reaction" theory is that it creates the mistaken impression that all AICs were founded by former members of European mission churches. The majority of AICs today did not begin in secessions from European missionary churches, although this may be true of the earliest churches.

Protestant Denominationalism

When European missionaries came to Africa, they not only reproduced the many denominations of Europe, but also in some cases, they created separate denominations according to different mission societies of the same European church. This was particularly and glaringly obvious in South Africa, where almost every Protestant missionary group from the West established itself and no comity agreements were observed. Various mission groups competed with and even slandered one another, had different qualifications for membership and leadership, and different disciplinary regulations.[26] Consequently, it was easy to switch membership from one denomination to another. Some of the new North American and European missions from which AICs emerged, such as the Zionists, the Pentecostals, and the Faith Tabernacle, were themselves undergoing a process of fission, inherent in the ecclesiological structures of these groups. In fact, as Hastings points out, secession is not a particularly African phenomenon—it is endemic to Anglo-Saxon Protestantism, particularly after it ceased to be a state church.[27] The result was considerable confusion, so that the new African Christians saw a multiplicity of denominations as the norm, and the creation of many more new ones a natural consequence. Hastings considers the entire AIC movement to be "clearly a very Protestant movement" emerging and continuing from a string of denominations and secessions in Britain and the USA. Of all the factors he mentions, Protestant denominationalism seems to be, for this Catholic writer, the most significant.[28] Barrett concludes, "Separatism therefore arises out of a Protestant climate".[29]

It is true that in countries where Catholics were a majority, this proliferation of new churches may not have been as frequent. There are, however, several notable exceptions to this trend, in AICs that seceded from the Catholic Church in Zambia, the Congo, and Kenya. It must also be remembered that some AICs have recruited large numbers of members from the Catholic Church, as in the case of the Harrist movement in the Ivory Coast, the Tocoist movement in Angola, and the Lumpa Church in Zambia. Nevertheless, the tendency for Catholics to be more resistant to schism may be attributed partly on the one hand to their rigid central hierarchical system that did not favor the ideal of an "indigenous church", at least before Vatican II. On the other hand, their different attitude towards the Bible, which for them doesn't exist as an independent source of authority apart from the church and therefore doesn't exist apart from the European missionary priest, may also explain this tendency. The Catholic missionary priest had generally much greater authority and higher qualifications than had the Protestant missionary. The high entrance requirements and commitment, including celibacy, expected of Catholic priests tended to insulate them from the possibility of rival authorities. In contrast, Protestant churches encouraged an indigenous ministry with only a minimum of theological training required for their ministers. This was to favor the emergence of indigenous churches. In addition, the greater emphasis placed by Catholics on ritual made their form of Christianity attractive to many Africans whose customary religions abounded in many different kinds of rituals. AICs seceding from Protestant churches often became more like Catholics in their emphasis on ritual, as well as in the episcopal ecclesiology than often emerged. But even more important is the fact that Catholic missionaries were more accommodating toward African customs (including ancestor rituals), which often were assimilated into the church in modified forms, whereas Protestant missionaries tended to confront and reject what they saw as "pagan" customs. Daneel thinks that this has to do with different theological approaches, the "natural theology" of the Catholics with its greater flexibility versus the emphasis on "the total corruption" of human nature of the Protestants, with its accompanying stress on making a "radical break with paganism and hence with traditional values".[30]

Bible Translations

The translation of the Scriptures was often the first literature to appear in an African language. For many years, the primary objective of the mission schools was to enable people to read the Bible in their own language. Great authority was thereby given to the printed word, and Africans were now able to distinguish between what the missionaries had said (or hadn't said) and what the Bible said (or didn't say). The Bible became an independent source of authority apart from the European missionaries. As Hastings observes, although western missionaries believed wholeheartedly in the *content* of the Bible, they didn't usually see any *continuity* or connection between the biblical context and the present African one. This was a feature that Africans were quick to discover and proclaim, especially after the translation of the Bible into the vernacular. As a result,

Africans were soon to criticize the missionaries for not being biblical enough.[31]

Because of the authority given to the vernacular Bible in all areas of life, most AICs interpreted it in a very literal and fundamentalist way. The Bible was usually central to their faith, and some felt that missionaries had concealed or at least had misunderstood the truth. This was particularly so when the Bible seemed to support several African customs that the missionaries condemned, like the practices of the transfer of marriage goods ("lobola") and polygyny. Even the honor given to departed relatives was found to be a prominent part of the Old Testament commands and in close keeping with African spirituality. Sometimes the conflict between Africans and European missionaries on these subjects had been extensive, particularly in the case of polygyny, which missionaries sought to eradicate by imposing strict prohibitions for members.[32] Africans saw practices or customs in the Bible closely resembling their own, and it seemed to them that the Bible was much more sympathetic to African traditions than the missionaries had led them to believe. The Bible had many examples of polygyny practiced by its heroes that were never disapproved of, and the long lists of ancestors seemed to legitimate the Africans' concern that the "living-dead" continue to be honored. Many AICs allowed polygyny because they saw it as a fundamental feature of African marriage. There were, however, some notable exceptions like the Kimbanguists in the Congo and the Lumpa Church in Zambia, who retained the prohibition of polygyny for church members. A few AICs continued some ancestor rituals, reasserting their importance in African religion.[33] The new churches used Bible verses to justify their practices, and found new prohibitions there that were taken literally, from the Old Testament in particular. For this reason too, AICs often rejected witchcraft and magic, and sometimes ancestor veneration, as a means of solving problems.

Western missionaries had also rejected these rituals, but for quite different reasons. Whereas their western worldview saw these practices as "ignorant superstitions" to be systematically obliterated by education, Africans saw them as real social problems that were manifestations of evil spirits and sorcery, and they proclaimed a more radical solution. In this they appealed to the Bible, and created what Adrian Hastings suggests amounted to "a sort of biblical-African alliance" against the more rationalistic and inflexible western Christianity.[34] Through the vernacular Bible, Africans had an independent source of authority abounding in symbolic healing practices and exorcisms not unlike their own. The Bible seemed to lend much more support to traditional African customs than to the imported cultural customs of the European missionaries.

Religious Factors

The causative factors outlined above may create the impression that AICs are to be regarded primarily as protest or resistance movements reacting to western missions and colonialism. This theory has some validity, particularly in the case of the first "Ethiopian" or "African" movements, but isn't altogether satisfactory, for a number of reasons. It does directly relate to the *origins* of the first AIC movements, which were secessions from mission churches. But the theory doesn't explain the ongoing growth of AICs long after mission connections had been broken, nor does it account for the fact that the majority of AIC members have never had any mission church connection at all. AICs are probably best regarded as an *indirect*, incidental, and largely subconscious reaction to colonialism and western missions. The theory does explain why some people prefer to join AICs rather than older mission churches. Once people have joined the AICs, they sometimes become critical of the mission churches, particularly the perceived "absence" of the Holy Spirit in these churches.[35] According to Daneel, the main criticism made by "Spirit-type" (pentecostal) AICs in Zimbabwe against mission churches was what they saw as the neglect of the Holy Spirit,[36] and that some Apostolic leaders in particular accused the mission churches of actually suppressing the work of the Spirit.

The reaction theory does not sufficiently recognize the creative and innovative endeavors of African missionaries in the AICs, who crossed national and ethnic boundaries in order to proclaim their new message. The growth of these AICs should also be seen as the result of a proclamation of a relevant message, an authentically indigenous response to the Bible, rather than emphasizing its cause as a negative reaction to western missions and colonialism. Instead of being the *objects* of European mission reacting to that mission, AIC leaders were in fact the *subjects* of their own mission, actively involved in truly African mission initiatives. Hastings says that AICs should actually be seen in a continuous rather than a discontinuous relationship with missionary churches, because African prophets sought to reproduce what they saw as important in missionary Christianity. The process was primarily one of conversion, not of secession.[37] Although this is certainly an important observation, it should not detract from the fact that the AICs introduced many innovations to Christianity that the European missionaries had been unable to do within the confines of their western cultural paradigms.

Among the many contributing causes to the emergence and growth of the AIC movement, the religious factors were possibly the most significant ones. Harold Turner says that the prophet movements are fundamentally spiritual and religious movements and thus should be studied and evaluated in religious terms.[38] This may be stating the obvious, but as Daneel observes:

> Their interpretations of the Bible, distinctive forms of worship, and modified rites are part of an authentic, indigenous reaction to the gospel, an independent momentum free of European supervision and of the radical spirit which would have characterized a real reaction to mission.[39]

Although we may not make an arbitrary distinction between religious and non-religious factors, remembering that AICs are *religious* movements will help us understand that many factors accounting for both their emergence and their continuing growth are also primarily religious. This is especially the case with the pentecostal, prophet-healing, and "spiritual" churches that have dominated the AIC scene in the twentieth century. David Bosch speaks of the "superficial, impoverished gospel" preached by western missionaries that "did not even touch on many facets of the life or struggle of the African" and answered questions that Africans weren't even asking. "Salvation" was seen exclusively as the "saving of souls" from moral sins, so that Christianity was perceived as a religion with a list of taboos. As he points out, this inability to be relevant to the daily struggles of African people, especially in the area of sickness and healing where "the church simply had no message", created a vacuum that was later filled by the prophetic and pentecostal movements.[40] This resulted in profound disillusionment with the form of Christianity Africans had embraced after forsaking their traditional religions. No solution was given to the problem of sickness, and even the advent of medical missions tended to secularize healing to the realm of western medical expertise and outside the sphere of religion.[41] In African communities, however, religion could not be separated from the whole of life's experiences, and sickness and affliction were also religious experiences. Healing and protection from evil are the most prominent practices in the liturgy of many AICs and are probably the most important elements in their evangelism and church recruitment, especially in the early stages of their development. Traditional African communities to a large extent were health-orientated communities and in African traditional religions, rituals for healing and protection were the most prominent ones. The AICs both continue this tradition and transform the familiar symbols with new meanings.

AIC leaders responded to what they experienced as a void left by a rationalistic, western form of Christianity, which had unwittingly initiated what amounted to the destruction of African spiritual values. Pobee and Ositelu say that "Pentecostal" AICs "reflect an African dissatisfaction with a Christianity that is too cerebral and does not manifest itself in acts of power in the Spirit and Spirit possession." [42] They describe the main characteristics of AICs as being their emphases on receiving a conscious experience of the Holy Spirit, healing and exorcism, their insistence on personal testimony, and their function as a "protest movement" against "the North Atlantic captivity of the Christian faith".[43] African missionaries proclaimed that God is not only in the business of "saving souls", but he also heals physical affliction and delivers from all kinds of oppressive forces and structures, and provides answers to felt human needs.[44] South African black theologian Simon Maimela remarked that many African Christians felt that the church was not interested in their daily misfortunes and concrete problems. He suggested that the greatest attraction of AICs lay in their open invitation to Africans to bring their anxieties about witches, sorcerers, bad luck, poverty, illness and other kinds of misfortune to the church leaders.[45] The major thrust of Daneel's research amongst Shona AICs in Zimbabwe was to demonstrate the predominance of religious factors in accounting for the appeal of these movements. He highlights these factors to include adaptations to traditional rituals and customs, prophetic practices in detecting and removing malignant medicines and wizardry, and especially the role of healing and exorcism.[46] The message of deliverance from sickness and from the oppression of evil spirits, and the message of receiving the power of the Spirit enabling one to cope in a hostile spirit world, was good news. This was a religion that offered solutions to all of life's problems, and not only the so-called "spiritual" ones. Ayegboyin and Ishola say that the AICs arose "to correct the foreignness of the Church" and they "felt that any religious institution, which didn't meet the African daily life's experience, would create spiritual hunger." This was also, they said, caused by a "passion for a purer form of Christianity".[47]

Powerful people—charismatic leaders who attracted followers through their preaching and healing attributed to the power of the Holy Spirit—founded many AICs. This concept of a man or woman "of the Spirit" was a leading factor in the origin and growth of AICs.[48] Some of these leaders, like Garrick Braide in Nigeria, Wade Harris on the coast of Ghana and the Ivory Coast, and Simon Kimbangu in the Congo, didn't intend to found new churches. They were part of mass movements towards

Christianity at the time all over Africa, for which the European missions were ill prepared. These movements weren't really secessions from or reactions to the mission churches, but mass conversions,[49] or African "revivals", and the followers of these revival leaders and prophets only later organized themselves into AICs. In particular, the pentecostal AICs that have arisen all over Africa in the twentieth century, both new and older ones, have attributed their emergence to the work of the Holy Spirit. Daneel expresses his view that the main cause for the AICs is religious in this way:

> The Independent Churches' real attraction for members and growth derive from their original, creative attempts to relate the good news of the gospel in a meaningful and symbolically intelligible way to the innermost needs of Africa. In doing so they are in a process of and have to a large extent already succeeded in creating truly African *havens of belonging*. (emphasis in original) [50]

Jean Comaroff reminds us, however, that these "religious" factors can only be understood with reference to the inclusive symbolic systems in which they arise.[51] Not only did the emphasis on the Spirit seem to "accord with indigenous notions of pragmatic spirit forces", but also "to redress the depersonalization and powerlessness of the urban labor experience."[52] The religious factors were indeed significant in the rise and development of many, perhaps most, AICs, but once again, we should not assume that these were the only causes, nor should we separate them from their larger context.[53] Finally, we should be aware of interpretations of the causes of AICs becoming romantic and nostalgic. Throughout the twentieth century, new Christian movements with a radically different message and orientation have arisen to challenge older ones. The "old", the "traditional", or the "rural" should not be seen as more "authentic" or even more "African" than the "new", the "modern", and the "urban".[54]

Precipitating Factors

The above five groups of causes may all be regarded as *underlying* causes. There are also, however, more immediate causes that precipitate the creation of a new religious movement. These ad hoc causes must always be distinguished from more permanent foundational factors. As Barrett points out, "If the background situation is explosive, then any one of a number of incidents may arise to trigger off the explosion."[55] Turner refers to "precipitative factors which, in a situation that is ripe for such development, push things over the edge."[56] These factors are more accidental and incidental in nature. The historical sections of this book will show many precipitating factors, including such things as a personal crisis, the 1918 influenza epidemic, sudden economic depression, discipline by a church leader or missionary, and especially the emergence of a charismatic leader with a new message, authority, and power to heal. Because of the inherently destabilizing nature of charismatic authority and new revelations, the continual proliferation of new movements is inevitable.[57] The disgracing of Bishop Samuel Crowther, first African bishop in West Africa, was undoubtedly a precipitating cause for the emergence of African churches there.[58] The influenza epidemic had a particularly stimulating effect on the emergence of the prayer healing (Aladura) movements in Nigeria, where it seemed as if the established churches had no effective remedy for this humanitarian disaster. The desire to have schools independent of missionary control gave rise to several AICs in Kenya. James Dwane, South African "Ethiopian" church founder, was accused by the missionaries of the mismanagement of money acquired during a fund-raising trip to England.[59] Although these and many other incidents may account for the emergence of AICs, they should not be considered main causes, as they presuppose the existence of other more established and foundational enabling factors.

The causes outlined in this chapter must be taken as illustrative of many various factors involved in the origins and development of the AIC movement as a whole. Writers on AICs have suggested many others. David Bosch mentions several that have been subsumed under the headings used in this chapter, some of which we have seen already: poor communication, a superficial and impoverished gospel, the relationship between Black and White, disillusionment, and traditional structures.[60] At the same time, there will always be exceptions to these causes, as in the cases of those particular AICs whose emergence can't be explained in the same way as others can, and for whom the factors outlined above may be entirely or partly inappropriate. As Barrett has pointed out, many of these circumstances have occurred in many parts of Africa, but haven't resulted in the same degree of independency as in others. The causes for the AICs should rather be seen as multiple, complex and idiosyncratic.[61]

Notes

[1] Barrett, *Schism*, 97.

[2] See Daneel, *Quest*, 68-101; Barrett, *Schism*, 83-158.

[3] F.B. Welbourn & B.A. Ogot, *A Place to Feel at Home*, London, 1966.

[4] Comaroff, 172.

[5] Hastings, *Church in Africa*, 529.

[6] Ayegboyin & Ishela, 22-3.

[7] Efraim Andersson, *Messianic Popular Movements in the Lower Congo*, Uppsala, 1958, 1.

[8] Sundkler, *Bantu Prophets*, 37, 300.

[9] B. A. Pauw, *Religion in a Tswana Chiefdom*, London, 1960, 237.

[10] Comaroff, 168.

[11] Ibid., 165-6.

[12] Ibid., 175-6, 191.

[13] Turner, *Religious Innovation*, 18.

[14] Daneel, *Quest*, 80.

[15] Pobee & Ositelu, 43.

16 Comaroff, 169.

17 Barrett, *Schism*, 154, 184.

18 Ibid., 59, 108-9.

19 Ibid., 116.

20 Ibid., 154-7.

21 Ibid., 184.

22 Ayegboyin & Ishela, 24-6.

23 Pobee & Ositelu, 3.

24 Hastings, *Church in Africa*, 493.

25 Ibid., 529.

26 Barrett, *Schism*, 83.

27 Hastings, *Church in Africa*, 498-9.

28 Ibid., 527, 532-3.

29 Barrett, *Schism*, 101.

30 Daneel, *Quest*, 92.

31 Hastings, *Church in Africa*, 527, 529.

32 Barrett, *Schism*, 117.

33 Ibid., 120-1.

34 Hastings, *Church in Africa*, 529.

35 Daneel, *Quest*, 99-100.

36 M.L. Daneel, *Old and New in Southern Shona Independent Churches, Vol. 2*, The Hague, 1974, 28.

37 Hastings, *Church in Africa*, 531.

38 Turner, *Religious Innovation*, 19.

39 Daneel, *Quest*, 100.

40 Ibid., 77-8.

41 Hastings, *Church in Africa*, 530; Daneel, *Quest*, 78.

42 Pobee & Ositelu, 34.

43 Ibid., 40-2.

44 Allan Anderson, with Samuel Otwang, *Tumelo: The Faith of African Pentecostals in South Africa*, Pretoria, 1993, 32.

45 Simon S. Maimela, "Salvation in African traditional religions", *Missionalia* 13:2, 1985, 71.

46 Daneel, *Old and New 2*.

47 Ayegboyin & Ishola, 24-5.

48 Allan Anderson, *Moya: The Holy Spirit in an African Context*, Pretoria, 1991, 31-2.

49 Hastings, *Church in Africa*, 512, 530.

50 Daneel, *Quest*, 101.

51 Comaroff, 169.

52 Ibid., 186.

53 Daneel, *Quest*, 99; Barrett, *Schism*, 95-6.

54 Rijk van Dijk, "Pentecostalism, Cultural Memory and the State: Contested Representations of Time in Postcolonial Malawi", London & New York, 1998, 159-160.

55 Barrett, *Schism*, 92.

56 Turner, *Religious Innovation*, 11.

57 Comaroff, 186.

58 Hastings, *Church in Africa*, 493-4.

59 Sundkler, *Bantu Prophets*, 40.

60 Daneel, *Quest*, 76-88.

61 Barrett, *Schism*, 96.

Part Two

HISTORY

3

PRECURSORS AND BEGINNINGS

The earliest forms of Christianity that developed in Egypt and then in other parts of North Africa are considered in this study as belonging to early Christian history, and so this will not concern us further. The Nubian church just south of Egypt, which survived until the eighteenth century, was probably the first African church independent of Latin or Greek Christianity.[1]

The Church in Ethiopia

Apart from the Nubian church, the first church initiated by Africans for Africans was probably the ancient Ethiopian Church, a distinctly African church that managed to survive the conquering Muslim armies from the north. It was founded by Egyptian Copts, it had strong Jewish characteristics, it was independent of any European church, and was presided over by the emperor—despite its theoretical submission to the patriarch at Alexandria. The story of this church provides fascinating parallels and inspiration to parts of the AIC movement to emerge in the nineteenth century, particularly for those who see Ethiopia as the model of African dignity, independence, and prestige. Aksum, ancient capital of the Ethiopian kingdom, was the "New Jerusalem" of the Ethiopian church, the place of the "Ark of the Covenant" in the church's only cathedral, and near the site of the prestigious and influential Dabro Damo monastery and other holy places. Subsequent centers of the Ethiopian kingdom further south, like Lasta and Shoa, were similarly modeled on Jerusalem, and the nation itself was called "Zion". After the Muslim conquest of Egypt, the Ethiopian church continued in isolation from the rest of Christianity and survived for over a millennium before contact was first made with Europeans in the sixteenth century. Except for a relatively short-lived courtship with the Roman Catholic Church through the mediation of Jesuit missionaries, the Ethiopian church was able to develop its own unique characteristics. These included keeping the Jewish Sabbath, male and female circumcision before baptism, Levitical regulations, distinctive musical and architectural traditions, and the central liturgical role of the "Ark of the Covenant". The very Jewish character of the Ethiopian church was reinforced by the traditional belief in the descent of the Ethiopian kings from Solomon and the Queen of Sheba, chronicled in the ancient writing, the Kebra Nagast.[2] These unique characteristics separated the Ethiopian church from the rest of Christendom, and in fact were to result later in numerous controversies and disputes.

There were also other independent African churches that arose in Ethiopia, about which we know very little. One was the movement of za-Krestos, a person who apparently claimed to be an Ethiopian Christ in Amhara in about 1604. He was executed, but his followers became a flourishing messianic movement complete with church hierarchy and rituals that included a Communion service in which was received "the body of za Krestos, our God, which he took from Amata Wangel, the Lady of us all". The movement was short-lived, severely persecuted and eventually wiped out on the orders of the emperor.[3] Ethiopia, however, was unique in Africa and its old Christian and Jewish traditions meant that the type of African religion with which Christianity interacted in the modern AIC movement was largely absent.

Before leaving Ethiopia, it must be mentioned that this country has experienced Christian prophetism not unlike that found elsewhere in Africa, and it seems to have predated the prophetic movement that swept through Africa in the early twentieth century. One of the best-known examples was Shaikh Zäkaryas (1845-1912), who converted from Islam to Christianity after receiving visions from about 1892, which at first he took to mean reforming Islam into a Trinitarian position. He used the Quran, in which he had been well educated, to vindicate these teachings and to teach the deity of Christ, at the same time repudiating Quranic teachings that denied it. His visions and supernatural feats and utterances became well known. He found increasing opposition from Muslims, culminating in his appearing before the emperor in 1906. The emperor issued an edict that because Zäkaryas had used the Quran in his defense, he was free to teach as he pleased in Muslim areas. He took the name Newayä Krestos when baptized in the Ethiopian church in 1910 (at his request, by immersion "after the manner of Christ"), with 3,000 followers. The movement of Muslim conversion to Christianity that he was the center of expanded to reach 10,000 by 1915-6, and was a clearly discernible movement within the Ethiopian church at that time.[4]

Kimpa Vita (Dona Béatrice)

A proliferation of new religious movements in the Kongo kingdom, today northern Angola, occurred from the sixteenth century onwards, where Roman Catholic missions held sway.[5] In 1632, the first known Bakongo prophet appeared, Francisco Kassola, a Catholic catechist, who had distinguished himself in the eyes of European missionaries because of his healing powers, and whom the missionaries had accompanied for some time. But when Kassola sought to Africanize Christianity and began criticizing the missionaries in his preaching, they wanted him arrested. He was reported to have declared himself the "son of God" who would bring a Golden Age to the African people, and his miracles and healing powers became legendary. He disappeared inland to escape arrest and was never heard of again. Kassola was the first recorded case of a deliberate attempt to Africanize Christianity, but as far as we know, he did not begin a prophetic movement.[6]

The earliest prophet-healing movement of more recent times ever recorded in sub-Saharan Africa was founded in 1704 by a woman in the recently colonized Kongo kingdom, subjugated by Portugal. The Kongo kingdom had been a proud and independent African nation for hundreds of years, but had been encroached upon by Portuguese colonizers and Capuchin missionaries. The nation had been defeated by the Portuguese at the humiliating Battle of Ambuila in 1665. At a time of intense religious and political expectation of the restoration of the Kongo kingdom to its former glory, the remarkable twenty-year-old prophetess Kimpa Vita (1684-1706) arose, also known by her baptized name of Dona Béatrice, born into Kongo aristocracy and well educated. She was not the first such prophet, as a little earlier a woman healer called Appolonia or Mafutta had said that the Kongolese king's residence at Mount Kibangu would burn down if he did not return to the ancient and devastated capital of Mbanza Kongo (São Salvador).

Kimpa Vita was reportedly a leader of a traditional ritual society known as Marinda, before she emerged as a Christian prophet. She had ecstatic experiences and, like many African prophets after her, experienced death and resurrection in dreams and visions, after which she is reported to have said that St. Anthony had taken possession of her. This spiritual experience was described in forms familiar in an African traditional background, except that a Catholic saint familiar to the Kongo people had taken the place of the ancestor—or was this "São Antonio" in fact the Kongolese king Antonio I who had been killed by the Portuguese at Ambuila? Kimpa Vita was commissioned to preach and teach, and she gave away her possessions, proclaiming the coming judgment of God. She led a group of followers back to Mbanza Kongo, including the old prophetess Mafutta, and they began rebuilding and repopulating the capital, the center for the movement for five years. In doing this, they allied themselves with the Kibenga, a rival of the puppet Kongo king Pedro IV. Béatrice preached against both the Catholic Church and traditional charms, saying that crucifixes and images were new charms replacing the old ones, and all were equally evil.[7] She apparently saw these as symbols of her people's oppression under the colonizing power and she provocatively burned crucifixes. She revived the traditional ceremony of people exposing themselves to rain in order to receive cleansing from impurity. She was known as a healer, in particular for barren women, and many came to her to be healed.[8] She warned of coming judgment on the Portuguese enemies and preached that Jesus Christ had been born in Mbanza Kongo, which she named Bethlehem, and was baptized in the Congo River, Nazareth. Mary and St. Francis too were Bakongo, as was St. Anthony. Christ had called African apostles and was on the side of black people— the first of many times such an idea was to be proclaimed. In her own unique way, Kimpa Vita sought the Africanization of the Christian message, two centuries before such a view was popular. She composed African hymns that were sung by her followers. Her revolutionary teachings were aimed at the restoration of the independence of the Kongo nation, by which prosperity and peace would return to her people— the lack of which was always regarded as a curse in Africa.

Her followers were called Antonians and this movement spread rapidly until it encompassed almost the whole Kongo kingdom. The Portuguese became alarmed. Kimpa Vita was finally declared seditious when she dispatched messengers all over the country to call the Bakongo people together to Mbanza Kongo to reinstate the kingdom. When she gave birth to a baby boy whose father was her male assistant Barro (called "St. John"), she was reported to have said that she had conceived the child by the Holy Spirit. She was arrested, tried, and burnt to death as a heretic in 1706 at the age of 22 together with "St. John", by command of King Pedro and at the request of the Catholic Capuchin missionaries. Mafutta and Kimpa's baby son were spared. The Antonian movement continued to thrive for three more years. The Kongo king did not recapture Mbanza Kongo until 1709, but the Antonians and Kibenga were eventually and forcefully subdued. It is thought that the Antonian movement continued after Kibenga's death for many years, as Bakongo people gathered to sing Béatrice's praises and her hymns.[9]

Kimpa Vita became a national heroine and martyr, and today is regarded as a prototype of the widespread African modern phenomenon of prophecy.[10] The only sources we have for Kimpa Vita and the Antonian Movement are those of hostile outsiders, and it may be that this was far more of a genuinely Christian movement that had drawn deeply on African tradition than these reports suggest. One of the only eyewitness reports of the events surrounding Béatrice was given by Capuchin priest Bernardo da Gallo, who interrogated Kimpa after her arrest and described her as a delirious and possessed heretic. His report is highly tendentious and its veracity is open to serious question. Nevertheless, the African church historian Adrian Hastings, a Catholic himself, observes that even this questionable evidence reveals that the Antonian movement had "a deeply Christian, and even Catholic, character".[11] In one telling incident, when da Gallo asked Béatrice whether she saw black people in her visions of heaven, she replied that there was no color in heaven. Another Capuchin who witnessed Kimpa Vita's death was deeply moved by her confession of faith before she died. Some have suggested that Dona Béatrice should be regarded as the first Christian martyr in the Kongo and a national Christian heroine.[12] It's a pity that we know so little about her movement today. Hers was not a revolt against Christianity, neither was it a deliberate syncretism, for Béatrice sought to reform what she saw as a corrupt form of Christianity and to purge it of its superstitious elements. Her emphasis was on restoring the esteem and dignity of the Bakongo people, whose honor had been lost through the encroachments of the colonizers. It was a long time before another AIC movement would arise. In 1872 a similar movement to Kimpa Vita's arose in northern Angola called Kiyoka ("Burning"), and it was also subjected to severe suppression. The significance of Kimpa Vita and her movement is that not only was it the first recorded AIC movement of comparatively recent origins, but it was also a manifestation of a phenomenon that was to be repeated frequently in Africa, particularly in the twentieth century.

Nxele, Ntsikana and Nongqawuse

There were other African prophets in the nineteenth century who might be regarded as precursors of the AIC movement, particularly in southern Africa, where the likes of Sotho prophet Mantsopa Makheta were active during a time of political and social turbulence. The pressures of religious change occurring in colonial Africa at this time were to result in many movements of resistance, and the prophetic-healing movements were to be another, later manifestation of this.[13] Probably the most famous Xhosa prophets were Nxele (1780-1820), Ntsikana (1780-1821), and the prophetess of the "Cattle Killing" Nongqawuse (1841-c.1930),[14] who all received their prophetic teachings from Christianity, with which they had had limited contact. Nxele seems to have become a Christian in about 1812, and became a zealous preacher of repentance. He prophesied that the whites had murdered God's Son (whom he called Tayi) and they had been thrown into the sea as a result. They had emerged from there to trouble the sinful Xhosa people, who must give up witchcraft, the shedding of blood, stealing, ox-racing, adultery, and polygyny before they would be delivered from the power of the whites. Without this repentance, the land would be consumed by fire and the Xhosa would be at war constantly. The ancestors would rise from the dead to assist their people against the British. Later, Nxele changed his preaching as he seemed to synthesize his Christian beliefs with the influences of Khoisan religion. He is reported to have declared himself the younger brother of Tayi (Christ) and to have espoused a revolutionary new theology in which Mdalidephu, the God of the blacks, was opposed to Thixo, God of the whites. Mdalidephu was in favor of joyful dances and lovemaking, and he was not opposed to fornication, adultery, and polygyny. Nxele was Mdalidephu's agent to destroy his enemies, the whites, and to resurrect the ancestors and their cattle, he declared sometime between 1816 and 1818. He was one of the first of several nineteenth century Xhosa prophets to advocate the killing of cattle to bring about salvation. Although from humble origins, Nxele gained the status of a national leader, and he was a key figure in the war against the British. After the defeat of the Xhosa in 1819, Nxele was arrested and imprisoned on Robben Island, from where he drowned in 1820 after a daring escape. He remains today a symbol of black resistance to colonial oppression. The later Xhosa prophet Mlanjeni (1832-53), who repeated many of Nxele's ideas and was credited with many miraculous powers, was thought to be the prophet-warrior reborn.[15]

A former follower of Nxele, Ntsikana Gaba, received a revelation that Nxele was misleading people, and because Ntsikana had never experienced colonialism, he preached a "gospel of peace and praise". Ntsikana is thought to have been converted through the LMS missionaries van der Kemp and Read, and to have been the originator of a popular Xhosa praise name for Christ, "Sifuba-sibanzi" ("the broad-breasted one"). He is also credited with forming the first "Ethiopian church" in South Africa and of composing some of the first and best-known Xhosa hymns. Although not a secession, his movement was an independent African Christian organization that sought to follow missionary Christianity, albeit selectively and rooted in African traditions. Ntsikana had a small group of followers called "the Poll-headed" (signifying cattle without horns, or pacifists) who would meet together twice daily for services. He died on his way to join a European missionary and his followers embraced missionary Christianity, although some later joined the Xhosa resistance and fought against the British. Ntsikana is regarded as one who both inspired and foreshadowed the AIC movement. He later became a symbol of Xhosa national unity in the Ntsikana Memorial Association, one of the foundational movements in the African National Congress, formed in 1912.[16]

The predictions in 1856 and 1857 of the Xhosa fifteen year-old prophetess Nongqawuse and her uncle Mhlakaza led to the slaughter of all cattle and resulted in great hardship for her people. An estimated 30,000 people died of famine, and the political and military power of the Xhosa speaking peoples was broken.[17] She seems to have been less influenced by Christianity than her predecessors were, and she cast herself in the model of a traditional diviner. The ancestors gave her revelations to slaughter all cattle in order for the dead to be resurrected, for the British to be driven into the sea, and for prosperity to come to the Xhosa people. Nongqawuse, and those who came to hear her, heard strange sounds that only she could understand and interpret with the help of Mhlakaza. She often spoke incoherently and appeared disheveled and unkempt. And yet, she too followed in the footsteps of Nxele, who Pieres said "had fused the new Christian doctrines with established Xhosa ideas to create a new religious synthesis which was to exert a powerful influence on the Cattle-Killing movement".[18] These prophets were certainly forerunners of the more widespread prophetic movements to follow, another manifestation of the tenacity and continuity of African religion.

Ethiopian Churches in South Africa

There are many interesting parallels between the early history and chronology of AICs in West Africa, particularly in Nigeria, and those in South Africa. In Uganda and Kenya too, there were similar "African" churches to those of Nigeria and South Africa, but as they arose later they will be dealt with in the chapter on East Africa. The first "Ethiopian" churches in South Africa emerged mainly as secessions from Methodist, Presbyterian, Congregational, and Anglican churches in the 1890s, followed some twenty years later by the emergence of prophet-healing or "Zionist" and "Apostolic" churches, where links with the mission churches were much more tenuous. AICs are more plentiful in South Africa than anywhere else on the continent, with at least ten million followers in 1991 comprising about half of the African Christian population there, in some 6,000 different church organizations mostly of the Zionist and Apostolic type.[19] The name "Ethiopian" is used by several AICs in South Africa today and usually signifies African-led churches which follow the "mainline" churches in liturgy, doctrine, and church organization—thus distinguishing them from the more radical innovators, the Zionists and Apostolics. Most of the Ethiopian churches, however, do not use the term "Ethiopian" as a church name, and the term is used here as descriptive of a particular "Ethiopian" ideology with biblical foundations in the promises referring to "Ethiopia" or "Cush". The decisive defeat of Italy by Ethiopia in 1896 at the battle of Adowa had profound significance for the western-educated leaders of this movement in South Africa, and represented the liberation of African peoples from colonial oppression. The Ethiopian churches are not as much movements of religious reform and innovation as are the Zionist and Apostolic churches, but they are primarily movements of indirect political protest, expressions of resistance against white hegemony in the church. They were little different from the churches from which they seceded, although some of them accepted polygyny. They rejected the political dominance of white-led mission churches, but framed their protest in familiar Protestant "orthodox" categories and therefore, did not seriously contest its social, religious and cultural components.[20] Their more lasting significance lies in the fact that they were the first to overtly challenge social structures of inequality and oppression in the church and to give a religious ideology for the dignity and self-reliance of the black person, thus foreshadowing the African nationalist and Black Consciousness movements. Clearly, these churches were concerned with more than religious freedom.[21]

AICs of the "Ethiopian" type started sporadically and, like the Nigerian churches, in a time of ecclesiastical unrest. The causes of these secessions in South Africa were very similar to those in Nigeria: the question of ecclesiastical control, often triggered by matters of discipline involving black ministers, their career prospects, and poor race relations within the European mission-founded churches. These secessions were often the result of tension between an increasingly self-aware African Christian community and a multiplying number of zealous European missionaries with colonial expansionist sympathies. In South Africa, however, there was much greater white ecclesiastical control than was the case in Nigeria, where there were considerably more black ministers and some degree of local autonomy.[22] Sundkler says that it was the "particular root cause not found elsewhere, at least to the same extent" that caused the unparalleled proliferation of churches in South Africa. That "root cause" was the "color line between White and Black", not only in society at large, but also and particularly in the church.[23]

The forming of these independent churches was also the result of the further religious change brought about by the integrating of Christianity in an African context around a new ritual leader, and that as a result, the earliest movements often had an ethnic orientation.[24] At the end of the nineteenth century there were already a great number of Protestant church organizations and European mission agencies in South Africa. Sundkler mentions forty mission societies in KwaZulu Natal alone, and says that they did not seem keen to appoint African clergy, despite encouragement to do so from their overseas mission boards.[25] The first independent African church in South Africa was formed in 1884, when the probationary Methodist minister Nehemiah Xoxo Tile set up an ethnically based Thembu National Church with the traditional Thembu chief Ngangelizwe as head, officially recognized as the church of the chiefdom by Ngangelizwe's successor Dalindyebo in 1890. In many ways, Tile's grievances were typical at this time. Tile and other African ministers had not been allowed to participate in discussions relating to the ordination of black ministers at the first Methodist conference in 1883 and the distribution of funds, and Tile himself was refused ordination after serving his probationary period. Matters came to a head when he quarreled with the white Methodist superintendent Chubb who had criticized his Thembu nationalist sympathies and support for traditional cultural practices. In fact, resistance to white authoritarian attitudes and disciplinary measures were common causes of secession at this time. Tile was even detained for his political activities.[26] His church, however, broke its ethnic affiliation when Tile died late in 1891. Tile's designated successor Jonas Goduka, not a Thembu himself, changed the name of the church to African Native Mission Church, which later merged with the inter-ethnic Ethiopian church movement.

In 1885, Tswana chief Kgantlapane helped found and appoint the ministers of a church seceding from the London Missionary Society in Taun, Botswana, the Native Independent Congregational Church. In 1889, J. Khanyane Napo, Anglican evangelist in Pretoria, founded the Africa Church. In the same year, a young German Lutheran missionary in the northern Transvaal, J.A. Winter, frustrated with the slow progress made by his Berlin Mission towards giving African (Bapedi) leaders more responsibility, helped set up the Bapedi Lutheran Church, another ethnically-based church. In 1890 Mbiyana Ngidi left the Congregationalists to form a Zulu church called the Zulu Mbiyana Congregational Church.[27]

In 1892, Methodist minister Mangena M. Mokone (1851-1934), was the first to use the term "Ethiopian" in his church name. He set up the Ethiopian Church in Johannesburg to protest against segregated conferences in the Methodist church and to claim equal rights for Africans. This was the first AIC that transcended ethnic boundaries from its inception. This appealed to the mineworkers coming from different regions into a new and strange urban environment. The name "Ethiopian" signified the fulfillment of biblical promises made to Africa, direct ideological links to the ancient church without the mediation of European Christianity.[28] Mokone was joined by several colleagues who became influential in the Ethiopian movement, among them another Methodist minister, James Dwane, Khanyane Napo, Samuel J. Brander, and Jonas Goduka, mentioned above. Dwane (1848-1915), who had quarreled with the white Methodists over the disposal of the funds he had raised in England, was chosen by the Ethiopian church leaders in 1896 to represent them in the USA to seek affiliation with the African Methodist Episcopal

Church (AME). This African-American church, which had broken with white Methodists over racism, was to play a significant role in the formation of Ethiopianism in South Africa. On his return to South Africa, Dwane persuaded the Ethiopian church leaders to join the AME, and they affiliated with Dwane as General Superintendent. In 1898, AME Bishop Henry M. Turner visited South Africa, infuriating European missionaries, but over 10,000 people affiliated with the AME as a result, and Dwane was consecrated assistant bishop. After Dwane's apparently disappointing visit to the USA in 1899 to secure better recognition and support, he led some 3,000 Xhosa followers into the Anglican Church in 1900, where they became the Order of Ethiopia. Dwane eventually became Provincial of this Order until his death in 1915, and the Order remained within the Anglican Church under Dwane's son, who was eventually recognized as a bishop.[29] The majority of Ethiopians, however, stayed in the AME, as did Mokone and other leaders, or they began new AICs. In 1904, Samuel Brander left the AME because of what he perceived as the "American" interests and financial control of its leaders, and he founded the Ethiopian Catholic Church in Zion. The name signified the new force that had entered South African church life and would eventually dominate the AIC scene thereafter. When Brander died in 1925 he was succeeded by Maegar and the church began to fragment into several groups. Khanyane Napo also became dissatisfied with the AME and re-established his African Church. Another AME minister, Henry R. Ngcayiya, helped Joseph J. Spawn to found the Ethiopian Church of South Africa in 1912, and Ngcayiya became a prominent early African National Congress leader.[30]

In KwaZulu, Samungu Shibe seceded from the American Board (Congregationalists) in 1897 to form the Zulu Congregational Church, after a decision to transfer a mission station where Shibe was leader of the congregation to white South African Congregationalists. Out of this church, several other Zulu churches seceded: the African Mission Home Church (1907), the African United Zulu Church (1916), and the Zulu of African Ethiopian Church (1918), a church which incorporated Zionist practices into its life, a tendency that was increasing among AICs. After Shibe's death in 1924, the Shaka Zulu Church and the African Free Congregational Church were formed. In 1898, the African Presbyterian Church founded by Pambami J. Mzimba seceded from the Free Church of Scotland. Mzimba was another widely traveled African minister who had raised money for his church in Scotland and had disagreed with the white mission leaders over its use. He was pastor of the congregation at the prestigious Lovedale mission, and two thirds of this congregation left the mission church with him. This AIC, however, remained an ethnically based Mfengu church, although it soon had thousands of members. Johannes Zondi founded the Cushites in 1899, and William Leshega founded the African Native Baptist Church in 1905, a significant influence on the early life of the famous Zulu prophet Isaiah Shembe. Shembe seceded from this church in 1911 to form the Nazareth Baptist Church. The great-grandson of Ntsikana, Burnet Gaba, founded the Ntsikana Memorial Church in 1911, another secession from the Presbyterians, but one that did not grow.[31]

Although the emergence of the Ethiopian churches took place some two decades before the Zionist and Apostolic churches began to appear, there were several significant Ethiopian churches that were formed later than that. A string of Zulu AICs followed the forming of the African Congregational Church in 1917 by Gardiner B. Mvuyana (1866-1925), a well-known minister and popular preacher in Johannesburg, who resigned from the American Board over a matter of discipline. This became one of the most successful of the "Ethiopian" churches, but after Mvuyana's death in 1925, several secessions occurred. Walter M. Dimba founded the African Congregational Church of Mvuyana in 1932-3. There were also other later secessions from the Methodists. The largest were those that emerged in the urban conglomerate around Johannesburg, the Bantu Methodist Church (known as the "Donkey Church" after the church symbol), founded in 1933 and the Bantu Methodist Church of South Africa, which seceded from it in the same year. Each of these churches suffered secessions within ten years. Several rather unsuccessful attempts were made to bring about cooperation and unity between the various more established African churches, even under the banner of the African National Congress. Several prominent Ethiopian church leaders were involved in the formation of the ANC.[32]

The European missions reacted with disdain, if not alarm. Eventually they began to recognize that the Ethiopian movement would not go away. One missionary leader, Jacottet, said that the European missions should take the "good in the programme of Ethiopianism" by making their churches less culturally reflective of the European continent. "Christianity must lose its European form and color", he said, and "it must become as African a religion to the Africans as it is today a European religion to the Europeans". But in order to achieve this, the church in South Africa would need to be segregated, he hastened to add.[33] Many Ethiopian churches have either adopted Zionist characteristics or have declined, and have in any case been eclipsed by the much larger Zionist and Apostolics. Jean Comaroff suggests that the decline in Ethiopianism took place because it occupied the middle ground in an increasingly polarized community, lacking both the ecclesiastical status and trappings of the mission churches and the radical alternatives of the Zionists.[34] Nevertheless, the Ethiopian type of church remains a significant part of South African Christianity today, even though it does not have the numerical growth of Zionist and Apostolic churches. It was estimated to have had about 25,000 members in total by 1904 in some seventy denominations. In 1991, possibly 8% of the African population or 2.4 million people belonged to Ethiopian churches compared to 32% or 10 million for Zionists and Apostolics.[35]

As was the case with the Zionists and Apostolics, the Ethiopian movement also spread further north to Southern and Northern Rhodesia, now Zimbabwe and Zambia, through migrant laborers from these countries. Unlike South Africa, however, the development and growth of Ethiopian and prophet-healing churches in these countries was contemporaneous. In 1910, Mupambi Chidembo returned to the Bikita district in Zimbabwe from the Transvaal, and founded the First Ethiopian Church there. Sengwayo, an evangelist with the American Board, established the African Congregational Church in the Chipinge area of Zimbabwe in 1942, after meeting the leaders of this church in South Africa. This became one of the most influential Ethiopian churches in Zimbabwe because of its deliberate Africanization policies, its anti-colonial sentiments, and its educational projects.[36] The AME, although strictly speaking not an "Ethiopian" church, became one of the largest churches in Zambia.[37]

African Churches in Nigeria

The underlying causes for the origins of the first AICs in Nigeria and those in South Africa were very similar. In West Africa, there was also the particularly aggravating dimension of the perceived "failure" of the first African Bishop Samuel Ajayi Crowther's Niger Mission. The result was that new, young white missionaries were virtually unanimous in their view that Africans were unfit for church leadership, a view that was to persist for half a century. In 1890, a "purge" involving unsubstantiated charges of "immorality" against almost all the African clergy and other workers in the Niger Mission took place. The actions of young English missionaries Brooke and Robinson in particular, forced Bishop Crowther to resign from the Finance Committee of which he was Chairman. The elderly Crowther, humiliated by these white missionaries in their twenties, died a year later and was replaced by a white bishop. Lamin Sanneh considers this to be a calculated act on the part of the expatriate missionaries, and that Crowther thereby became "the sacrificial victim".[38] At the same time, the numbers of young European missionaries to Nigeria increased significantly after 1890, and the "Settlement" of 1894 guaranteed English control of Anglican missions in West Africa for the next fifty years.[39]

In the 1890s, withdrawals began to take place from Baptist, Anglican (Church Missionary Society, CMS), and

Wesleyan Methodist churches in Nigeria, secessions that continued for twenty-five years, particularly in and around Lagos. This resulted in the formation of "African churches", which, like the Ethiopian churches in South Africa, remained close to their parent churches in doctrine and liturgy. The Native Baptist Church was the first of these churches to be established, founded in 1888 by a lay member of the Lagos Baptist Church and teacher in the prestigious Baptist Academy in Lagos, David Brown Vincent, and the first African Baptist pastor, M. Ladejo Stone, after a split in the North American mission, the Southern Baptist Convention. There was growing dissatisfaction with the increasing number of white missionaries who had colonialist mentalities, wanting to maintain their control and resisting any attempts at Africanization and independence. This was particularly aggravated by the fact that African Baptists had developed their own identity after more than fifty years of being a Christian community, and were ready for more than the merely token leadership that was being offered them.[40] Because of the American Civil War, white Baptist missionaries were withdrawn from Nigeria in 1863, and the Baptist church was left under the control of capable African leaders and an African-American missionary. When white missionaries returned in 1875 to resume control, conflict was inevitable. These expatriate missionaries, contradicting Baptist congregational church polity, were in control of the congregations and their ministers. The split in the Baptist Church was precipitated by the dismissal in 1888 of Pastor Stone by a missionary, W. J. David, who said he was free to dismiss Stone as "any of his servants".[41] Vincent and a senior colleague who supported Stone, were then dismissed from the Baptist Academy. Most members of the Lagos church seceded and the academy had to be closed for lack of staff. Although the Foreign Mission Board in the USA later reversed its support for David's actions, the conflict was beyond resolution for most African Baptists, and the Native Baptist Church (later the Ebenezer Baptist Church) was the result. David returned to the USA, but his replacement, Newton, sought to destroy the independent church by discrediting its leaders. Newton died of yellow fever in 1894, and no white missionary was available to replace him. In 1894, Vincent abandoned all western cultural baggage (including the wearing of western clothing) and he and his wife changed their names to Mojola and Adeotan Agbebi. They remained leading figures in Nigerian church life; Mojola Agbebi proclaimed the need for a non-western version of African Christianity until his death in 1917. The Baptist churches were again in the hands of African leaders and the two Lagos churches reunited in 1914, and Agbebi became its President, a triumph for the principles he had vigorously defended for so long.[42]

The Native Baptist Church established a precedent followed by many others, including the United Native African Church, formed in 1891 by William E. Cole, consisting mostly of former lay Anglicans disaffected by the CMS missionaries' treatment of Bishop Crowther. It was founded with the conviction that an African-led organization would be more effective in evangelizing the continent: "a purely Native African church be founded for the evangelization and amelioration of our race, to be governed by Africans".[43] This church remained Anglican in doctrine and because it refused to admit into membership expelled Anglicans, it did not prosper. Nevertheless, it allowed polygyny, held services in Yoruba, and introduced African music and chant. It was later renamed the First African Church.[44]

The largest and most significant African church at the time was called the African Church Organization, founded in 1901 by Jacob Kehinde Coker after a large split in a CMS church, St. Paul's Breadfruit in Lagos. The Nigerian assistant bishop James Johnson, one of the most vocal advocates of African autonomy, was dismissed from this parish during his absence, and his family and possessions dumped in the street. Two thirds of its 900 members objected and formed their own congregation, although Johnson himself failed to join them, thereby disappointing his supporters. African forms of music and worship were introduced, including drumming, and polygamists could be members but not ministers. The new church also rejected episcopal government and enshrined the rights of lay members in its constitution. They immediately built a imposing church building called the Bethel Church, from which they gained the name "Bethelites" and later the African Church, Bethel.[45]

The third major secession, this time from the Methodist Church in Lagos, occurred in 1917, when the white missionary chairman decided to expel all church leaders who were guilty of polygyny, sixty-five in all. Like the Anglicans, the European Methodist missionaries had lowered the status of their African ministers and had gradually removed African district superintendents. The expelled leaders set up a separate Methodist church called the United African Methodist Church (Eleja), the only African church to secede specifically on the issue of polygyny. By 1922 there were at least seventeen African churches in Nigeria. These churches, whilst patterned on the mission churches from which they had seceded, were more accommodating to Yoruba culture and more innovative in organization, led by extremely able people who were leaders in Yoruba society. In this way they were considered to be the first real challenge to Islam in Yorubaland.[46] In 1913, the main African churches formed an association for cooperation called the African Communion, with Agbebi as President and Coker as Secretary. After Agbebi rejoined the Baptist Church, Coker became President, but further unity proved elusive.[47] By 1921, the African churches together had some 33,000 members in Western Nigeria, second only to the Anglicans in church affiliation.[48] The African churches in Nigeria had also indirectly influenced the formation of similar churches in Ghana, such as the National Baptist Church, founded in 1891 by Christian Hayford, who had lived in Lagos. Other independent churches like the African Methodist Episcopal Zion Church (an African-American Methodist secession) introduced by J.B. Small in 1898, and the Nigritian Church of J.B. Anaman, founded in 1907, were unrelated examples of African churches in Ghana.[49] In Cameroon, Lotin Samé founded the Native Baptist Church in 1888, the same year that a similar church began in Lagos. When Baptist missionaries handed over their churches to the Basel Mission and their local autonomy was threatened, they formed their own independent church. This church was in a state of decline in the 1990s.[50]

From the foregoing sketch of events, it can be seen why the secessions in South Africa and Nigeria were to set a pattern for the next century. Secession wasn't a peculiarly African phenomenon, as AICs were simply continuing what had become commonplace in European Protestantism— especially amongst British Methodists and within most Protestant churches in the United States in the nineteenth century. By the end of this century there were already hundreds of new denominations, "faith missions", and other mission societies springing up in the West, from whence missionaries were sent to Africa. These multiplied denominations and mission societies were reproduced here, and it is hardly surprising that it should be considered a natural thing for secessions to occur, urged on by the mission policies and colonial politics of the time that were highly prejudicial to Africans. As Hastings reminds us, although the "Ethiopian" and "African" churches were indeed reactions to the tight control of European missions, they were still a very small minority by 1910 and, as Hastings points out, "still so closely controlled by a missionary model of religious life."[51] Nevertheless, the African and Ethiopian churches were part of the struggle against colonialism and were ecclesiastical forerunners of the African nationalist movements for independence. They were also seeking to make Christianity more "African", and therefore more appealing and relevant for ordinary people. But there were deeper religious and socio-cultural issues at stake, as the next century was to prove in the rise of new and more radically transforming forms of African churches, the subject of the following chapters.

Notes

1 Hastings, *Church in Africa*, 67-70.

[2] Ibid., 4, 9, 11-13, 18-21.

[3] Ibid., 160.

[4] Donald Crummey, "Shaikh Zäkaryas: an Ethiopian prophet", Addis Ababa, 1972, 55-66.

[5] M. Sinda, *Le Messianisme Congolaise et ses Incidences Politique: Kimbanguisme — Matsouanisme — Autres Mouvements*, Paris, 1972, 20.

[6] Louis Jadin, "Les Sectes Religieuses Secrètes des Antoni ens au Congo (!703-1709)", Kinshasa, 1968, 109-11.

[7] Marie-Louise Martin, *Kimbangu: An African Prophet and his Church*, Oxford, 1975, 14.

[8] Sigbert Axelson, *Culture Confrontation in the Lower Congo*, Stockholm, 1970, 141.

[9] Sinda, 58.

[10] Martin, 16-7; Daneel, *Quest*, 46-7.

[11] Hastings, *Church in Africa*, 104-8.

[12] Axelson, 136, 140; see also David M. Anderson & Douglas H. Johnson (eds.), *Revealing Prophets: Prophecy in Eastern African History*, London, 1995.

[13] Janet Hodgson, "Ntsikana — a precursor of Independency?", 1984, 19.

[14] The date of her death is unknown and speculated on. J. B. Peires, *The Dead Will Arise: Nongqawuse and the Great Xhosa Cattle-Killing Movement of 1856-7*. Johannesburg, 1989, 336.

[15] Janet Hodgson, "A study of the Xhosa prophet Nxele", 1985, 11-36; 1986, 3-23; Pieres, 2.

[16] Pieres, 33, 137; Hastings, *Church in Africa*, 218-21; Hodgson, "Ntsikana", 20-4, 26-7.

[17] H.L. Pretorius, *Ethiopia Stretches Out her Hands unto God: Aspects of Transkeian Indigenous Churches*. Pretoria, 1993, 7.

[18] Peires, 79, 91, 98-9, 134-5.

[19] Anderson, *Bazalwane*, 11-12.

[20] Comaroff, 176.

[21] Hennie Pretorius & Lizo Jafta, "'A Branch Springs Out': African Initiated Churches", Oxford & Cape Town, 1997, 215; John W. de Gruchy, *The Church Struggle in South Africa*. Grand Rapids & Cape Town, 1986, 41-5.

22 Hastings, *Church in Africa*, 493, 498.

23 Sundkler, *Bantu Prophets*, 32, 37.

24 Hodgson, "Ntsikana", 28-9.

25 Sundkler, *Bantu Prophets*, 29-30.

26 Pretorius, 14-6.

27 Sundkler, *Bantu Prophets*, 38-9, 47.

28 Pretorius & Jafta, 213.

29 There have been several secessions from the Order of Ethiopia. In 1982, there was a major rift in the order when several leaders left. See Paul Makhubu, *Who are the Independent Churches?*, Johannesburg, 1988, 10.

30 Sundkler, *Bantu Prophets*, 39-42; J.A. Millard, *Malihambe – Let the Word Spread*, Pretoria, 1999, 9-11, 20-3, 47-9, 55-7.

31 Pretorius & Jafta, 214-5; Hodgson, "Ntsikana", 29-31; B. G. M. Sundkler, *Zulu Zion and Some Swazi Zionists*, London, 1976, 164-5 (on Leshega). Shembe's movement is discussed further in chapter 5.

32 Pretorius & Jafta, 215; Sundkler, *Bantu Prophets*, 39-47, 50-3, 172.

33 Sundkler, *Bantu Prophets*, 31.

34 Comaroff, 192.

35 Pretorius & Jafta, 215; Anderson & Otwang, 14.

36 Daneel, *Quest*, 51-3.

37 W. Johnson, "The Africanization of a Mission Church: The African Methodist Episcopal Church in Zambia", New York, 1979, 95.

38 Lamin Sanneh, *West African Christianity: The Religious Impact*, London, 1983, 169.

39 Sanneh, 172; Webster, 17-21, 32-3, 40-1.

40 Hastings, *Church in Africa*, 493.

41 Webster, 55.

42 Peter B. Clarke, *West Africa and Christianity*, London, 1986, 161; Webster, 52-8.

43 Quoted in Webster, 68.

44 S.A. Dada, *J. K. Coker: Father of African Independent Churches*, Ibadan, 1986, 14.

[45] Webster, 78, 83; Sanneh, 176-7; Clarke 162-3.

[46] J.D.Y. Peel, *Aladura: A Religious Movement among the Yoruba*, Oxford, 1968, 55-6; Sanneh, 177-9; Webster, 45, 90-1.

[47] Dada, 7-8, 13-5.

[48] Webster, 95.

[49] Ayegboyin & Ishola, 45-47.

[50] Paul Gifford, *African Christianity: Its Public Role*. London, 1998, 286-7.

[51] Hastings, *Church in Africa*, 499.

4

WEST AFRICAN CHURCHES

The "African churches" in West Africa began declining in the 1920s and were completely overshadowed by the new, rapidly growing prophet-healing or "spiritual" churches—so named because of their emphasis on the Holy Spirit. Firstly, churches associated with the prophets William Wade Harris and Garrick Sokari Braide emerged, followed by churches known by the Yoruba term "Aladura" ("prayer people"). Like the Zionists and Apostolics in Southern Africa, these churches were to present a much more penetrating challenge to older European mission-founded churches than that of the "African churches", because it questioned the very heart of Christianity in Africa. In this, they were sometimes aided and abetted by new churches from the North, especially the pentecostals, whose ideas they borrowed freely yet selectively. But this was a specifically African Christian response, despite the outward trappings of rituals and customs that were innovations rather than continuations of African traditional symbols. In this regard, these new West African churches represent a reformation of African Christianity that reverberates to the present day.

The AIC movement has expanded remarkably in West Africa in the twentieth century. In 1990, AICs constituted about 19% of the total population of Nigeria, or 38% of the Christian population there, in over a thousand different churches. In Ghana, they were about 21% of the population, or 33% of Christians there; in the Ivory Coast about 7% of the total or 23% of the Christians; and in Liberia about 16% of the total population or 43% of the Christians there. Countries with Muslim majorities in the northern parts of West Africa, the Sahel and the Sahara have a much smaller number of new religious movements because of the ease with which Islam adapts to indigenous cultures.[1] But from now on, we'll be concerned mainly with those movements which have most impacted the history of Christianity in Africa in the twentieth century. These are the "churches of the Spirit", which arose almost simultaneously in many parts of the continent, contemporaneous with pentecostal movements emerging in other parts of the globe, but independent of them.

William Wade Harris

In 1913 and 1914, one of the most remarkable preachers in the history of Christianity began preaching in the Ivory Coast and from there to the Gold Coast (Ghana). William Wade Harris (1865-1929) was a Kru of the indigenous Grebo peoples of Liberia, who received a call from the angel Gabriel in 1910 while in a Liberian prison. Harris was raised in a Grebo Methodist minister's house, became a literate Methodist lay preacher who spoke perfect English, and worked respectively as a seaman, a bricklayer, an Episcopalian teacher, and a government interpreter. He lost his government job when he became involved in political activities and was imprisoned on a charge of treason. He had suggested that Liberia become a British colony rather than be ruled oppressively by Americo-Liberian settlers. He was arrested for pulling down the Liberian flag and planting the Union Flag and for leading a Grebo uprising. After he received the first of many visions, his divine mission was to be a prophet to take God's word to those who had never heard it. In order to accomplish this, he later said that the Spirit came on him as on the Day of Pentecost, and he spoke in tongues.2

Wade Harris was one of the first African Christian prophets and certainly one of the most influential, his preaching resulting in the beginning of a movement of mass conversions to Christianity that the continent had never yet experienced. After his release from prison, he began to preach from the Bible about one true God, healing from disease, and the rejection of fetishes3 and practices associated with traditional religions. Rejecting western clothing and walking barefoot, the white-bearded Harris wore a long white calico robe, a round white turban, and black bands crossed around his chest. He carried a Bible, a gourd rattle, a bowl, and a staff in the shape of a cross, striking an imposing figure not unlike a biblical prophet.4 Harris was accompanied initially by two women assistants, who were also dressed in white carrying calabash rattles. At this time, a few hundred Catholics were probably the only Christians throughout the entire Ivory Coast. The effect of Harris's ministry was electrifying, as Gordon Haliburton observes:

> The whole population of the regions through which he passed accepted him as the authentic voice of God, and as His messenger to revitalize their religion and society which, subjected as they were to new and increasing pressures, were failing them in a time of crisis.5

The method used by Harris and his companions was to approach a village singing songs accompanied by the calabash rattles. Local people would gather and Harris would preach fervently, inviting them to renounce traditional religious practices and believe in God. The thousands that did so were immediately baptized from the water in Harris's gourd dish in the name of Father, Son, and Holy Spirit, and the Bible was placed on their heads. The fact that they were given no instructions before baptism worried the Catholic missionaries, but their baptism signified that they were purified of their sins and protected from evil during their transition from the old to the new, as they received Christian teaching. Sometimes people possessed by evil spirits and traditional deities were invited to touch the prophet's staff and were sprinkled with holy water, and many ecstatic manifestations were reported during this revival. It is said that several miracles, including the traditional power of rainmaking, were associated with Harris's ministry, most of which served to demonstrate the superiority of the power of God over traditional deities and healers. Harris sometimes carried a large brass tray to which people brought their traditional fetishes, whereupon he burned them. At first, French colonial authorities considered him a "harmless maniac", but they became increasingly concerned. They imprisoned him on at least one occasion and kept him under constant surveillance.[6] He is believed to have baptized some 120,000 adult Ivorian converts in one year, often baptizing whole villages and thereby causing a minimum of disruption to traditional structures. Unlike the European missionaries, Harris tolerated polygyny, and some think he practiced it too. People traveled from distant places to hear Harris and be baptized, and as a result his message penetrated deep into the Ivorian and Ghanaian interiors where he had not been personally. He also sent out disciples to carry his message and methods far and wide. On the Ghanaian coast, Harris confronted and confounded traditional priests, many of whom were converted. It was estimated that a thousand new people came to hear him each day, until opposition from the Catholic missionaries caused him to return to the Ivory Coast.[7] The French administration and the Catholic missionaries there accused him of intimidation and fraud. Harris and three women assistants were arrested, and he was beaten and deported from the Ivory Coast towards the end of 1914. Over the next ten years, Harrist believers were systematically suppressed and village prayer houses destroyed. Harris returned to Liberia to relative obscurity until his death in 1929.

Wade Harris never intended to form a separate church and he seemed to have favored European missionaries. He directed people to existing churches, but he also encouraged converts to build their own prayer houses where there were no existing churches, led by a minister and twelve apostles chosen by the village community. Tens of thousands of his followers formed these village churches in the Ivory Coast and the Gold Coast. This was noted by a Methodist missionary some seven years later, who said that these Harrist Christians had mostly abandoned traditional beliefs and practices. Harris told his followers to wait for teachers with Bibles who would instruct them in their new faith. Many of his converts joined the Catholic Church and later, even more joined the Methodist Church after missionaries arrived at the Ivory Coast in 1924. Methodists record their beginnings in the Ivory Coast with Harris's mission there in 1914.[8] He is regarded as the father of Christianity in the Ivory Coast.

Harris's unparalleled success seems to lie in his complete identification with ordinary people, his simple lifestyle and forceful personality, and his ability to make converts without unduly creating social tensions. But he was far more than that. He both claimed and demonstrated that God had chosen an African person to be a prophet, with all the powers that accompanied this calling. His outward accoutrements were not specifically African (although quite similar to traditional Hausa garments), and the message he proclaimed was in radical discontinuity with much of traditional religion. He saw himself as a specifically Christian prophet, but found some Old Testament symbols appropriate for the people to whom he ministered. Yet Harris personified all there was about African religion that was good and reassuring for people plagued by evil forces and disease. In the eyes of his followers, he demonstrated that the God of the Bible was more powerful than the ancient divinities, ancestors, and nature spirits had been, relevant to the needs of Africans under the yoke of colonial oppression. He accepted the African spirit world as reality, but regarded the spirits as the work of Satan to be cast out. It was this message that made him so popular on the West African coast, that transcended the efforts of European missionaries and made him a pattern for many African prophets to come.[9]

The Harrist Churches

Thousands of Harris's followers soon found themselves at odds with Methodist financial policy, their prohibition of polygyny, and the foreign liturgy they introduced which was so different from the African hymn-singing and dancing practiced by Harris. They organized themselves into the Harrist Church, apparently after receiving the prophet's approval to do so.[10] Just before Harris died in 1929, he is believed to have sent back an Ivorian delegation of three men with permission to organize his followers into a new church under one of them, John Ahui. As symbols of his prophetic authority, he gave Ahui a cane cross and a Bible, and Ahui thereafter said that he had been designated Harris's successor. Like other AICs elsewhere in Africa at this time, this Harrist movement was severely persecuted by the French colonial administration, and its adherents had to meet secretly. Many coastal Ivorians, however, increasingly identified it with the nationalist struggle for liberation, and it began to grow rapidly. Ahui began preaching on foot as Harris had done and organizing churches some time after 1931 (when there was more religious toleration), but was still severely restricted by colonial authorities. Like his mentor, Ahui was credited with several miraculous incidents during this time. After about 1945, people who had been baptized by Harris began leaving mission churches to join or to establish Harrist churches. The Harrist Church in the Ivory Coast was only officially constituted in 1955, and Ahui became its "preacher bishop", later to be called "Pope". In 1964, the Harrist Church was officially recognized as one of four national religions, the others being Islam, Roman Catholicism, and Protestantism. The charismatic prophet and healer Albert Atcho became president of its Central Committee, the supreme authority, in 1967. Atcho's renown as a healer brought many more people into the church. He operated from a healing village, where people came to be healed through his prayers, herbal remedies, and his bottles of blessed water, perfume and talcum powder. Since 1972, the church has tried to modernize and through the activities of Atcho, there has been a renewed emphasis on healing and the eradication of witchcraft.[11] In 1990, the church had an estimated 176,000 members, one of the four largest churches in the Ivory Coast and the largest AIC there.[12] Ahui died in 1992 and was succeeded by Supreme Preacher Cessi Koutouan Jacob as "Spiritual Head" of the church. The church sees itself today in the tradition of Simon of Cyrene, whose encounter with Christ on his way to crucifixion "manifests God's alliance with the black continent", the "Ultimate Alliance", or "Black Easter". Harris is believed to be an incarnation of Simon of Cyrene.[13]

The movement of Ahui, although the biggest of the Harrist movements, was not the only Harrist church. Harris's style of ministry and even his clothing became a pattern for many African prophets thereafter. One was Boto Adai, a Methodist who began preaching in the Ivory Coast in 1932, and founded a church simply called the Church of Boto Adai. Adai dressed as Harris had done and claimed that only he could bring healing to his followers. He stressed the use of holy water for healing, protection, prosperity, and fertility, blessed only by himself after a public confession of sins. His church was opposed by Ahui's movement, and the "Jerusalems" (village shrines) set up by his followers were destroyed. Adai died in 1963 and was succeeded by Paul Bedi. In 1949, a group of independent Harrist churches united under Gaston N'Drin to form the Pure Harrist Party, saying that Ahui had abandoned the reading of the Bible—a cornerstone of Harris's teaching. N'Drin later submitted to the leadership of Ahui, an unusual occurrence in AICs after secession. Some Harrist movements were short-lived, whereas others became significant, combining traditional and Christian ideas. The Church of Papa Nouveau, founded by Dagri Njava (Papa Nouveau), has a "Jerusalem" called Hozalem, a 3,000-seat church building, emphasizes fertility and eliminating witchcraft, and does not use the Bible. Papa Nouveau claims to derive his power from the fact that he is the husband of the water goddess Mammy Wata. Another church that developed out of the Harrist movement is Crastchotche (originally "Christ Church") founded by the Prophet

Makoui in 1935. Makoui was imprisoned for his preaching and claimed that Harris had only come to prepare the way for himself (Makoui), the greater prophet.[14]

Most significantly, as was characteristic of many other AICs, two of these Ivorian movements were founded by women. Marie Lalou, who claimed to be the true successor to Harris, rejected the "foreign gods" of the missionaries (which had caused the return of evil spirits), and founded the Deima Church in 1942. This movement, which has instituted women as successive leaders since Lalou's death in 1951, has become the second largest AIC in the Ivory Coast. Another movement separated from Deima after its woman founder, Ble Nahi, had claimed to be Marie Lalou's true successor, changing her name to Jesus Onoi. When Ble Nahi died in 1958, however, two male prophets succeeded her. Both movements deriving from Lalou practiced the celibacy of their women leaders, healing and protection by holy water and ashes, and the rejection of fetishes, witchcraft, and the reading (or even the touching) of the Bible, a magical book. Both women founders received visions after a time of illness or extreme trouble, much in the same way that traditional healers are called to their profession.[15] There were many other schisms in the Harrist movement during this time. Most of these AICs had certain rituals in common, following the example of Harris. Harris's baptism, his clothes, his ritual accoutrements (the cross, bowl, and rattle), and the use of holy water for healing and protection are liturgical practices common to most of these groups. It appears, however, that traditional meanings were given to these symbols quite different from those intended by Harris.

Spirit Churches in Ghana

The prophet healing AICs in Ghana are now popularly known as the "Spirit churches" (in Akan, "Sunsum Sore"). Wade Harris preached in western Ghana for only a few weeks, but his influence remained, particularly in the first "Spirit church" to be formed there, the Church of William Wade Harris and his Twelve

Apostles (later the Church of the Twelve Apostles). Harris's converts, Grace Tani and Kwesi John Nackabah, founded this church in 1918 to realize Harris's instruction that twelve apostles should be appointed in each village to look after his flock. Grace Tani was a traditional priestess before she had an extraordinary encounter with Harris on a remote road, when she was converted and became one of his assistants. When Harris was deported from the Ivory Coast, Tani returned to Ghana, fell ill, and called for Nackabah to pray for her healing. Nackabah was also a former diviner until baptized by Harris and given the emblems of authority: a cup for holy water, a calabash to beat out evil spirits, a staff cross, and a Bible. Tani, now Madame Harris Grace Tani, claimed to have been Harris's wife and she remained spiritual leader of the church, with Nackabah administrative and public leader. This dual arrangement was a convenient method used by several AICs to overcome traditional male resistance to women's leadership. The new multiethnic church followed the Harrist tradition by emphasizing healing through faith in God and the use of holy water. Similarly, the Bible was placed on people's heads and gourd rattles used to drive out demons and heal people. Polygyny was permitted, and new members were first to be ritually purified through washing. An innovation was that the healing was administered in healing "gardens" (communal dwellings), a custom peculiar to these churches. The holy water was usually kept in basins under a wooden cross in the gardens. At one stage, the church considered affiliating with a British Pentecostal church, the Apostolic Church, but withdrew when their white missionary James McKeown insisted that tambourines be substituted for calabash rattles. This was seen as an attempt to deprive Africans of the power to ward off evil spirits.

Nackabah died in 1947, to be succeeded as bishop by John Hackman. After the death of Hackman in 1957 and Tani in 1958, schism occurred, largely on ethnic lines. Hackman had appointed his nephew Samuel Ansah his successor, but more senior prophets questioned his authority and Ansah died in 1958 without a clear successor. The church is now divided into several groups, the most prominent being the Nackabah People, the

William Wade Harris Twelve Apostles Church, and the Twelve Apostles Church of Ghana.[16]

Prophet Jemisemiham Jehu-Appiah (1893-1948), formerly known as Joseph W.E. Appiah, a Methodist preacher and schoolteacher, received a call from three angels in 1919 to become a king. He was filled with the Spirit and performed miracles, assisted in this work by a woman, Abena Bawa, whom he renamed Hannah Barnes. This group within Methodism became distinct, practicing prophecy, healing, and speaking in tongues. Eventually they were dismissed from the Methodist church for alleged "occult practices" in 1924. Appiah and Barnes founded the Musama Disco Christo Church (Army of the Cross of Christ), a name given by heavenly revelation. They established the holy city of Mozano ("my [God's] town"), which Appiah was given by the local chief to develop his own settlement. Appiah based his complex church organization on the traditional Fanti court and became King Jehu Akaboha I. Hannah Barnes, the Akatitibi (Queen Mother), was taken up into heaven and given instructions, including the fact that she would marry Appiah, which she did after the prophet had received a similar revelation. The movement spread and Appiah gave new heavenly names (each one unique and never repeated) to the thousands who joined, a practice that continues. Members speak a special language in greeting and wear distinctive copper rings and crosses. Akaboha I died in 1948 and was succeeded by his son Matapoly Moses Jehu-Appiah (1924-72), who was credited with a miraculous birth and became Akaboha II. In 1951 a new holy city, New Mozano, was established. This church is noted for its ban on ancestor rituals and the use of medicines. It has an elaborate system of angels whose names are to be mentioned in prayer, and demons that can appear as witches, snakes, and other reptiles. The MDCC has complex rituals, including several sacred objects, including an "Ark of the Covenant" in a holy shrine which only the Akaboha can enter once a year to offer prayers. The church has other sacred places and fast days, sacrificial animals, candles, incense, rosaries, and elaborate ceremonial gowns. Healing rituals include the use of anointing oil in preference to holy water. The office of the Akaboha, who is also called the General Head Prophet, is hereditary in the Jehu-Appiah family, and the Akaboha has both spiritual and political duties. On the death of Akaboha II in 1972, his eldest son became Akaboha III. Another son of Akaboha II, Jerisdan Jehu-Appiah, has established the MDCC in Britain.

The MDCC, the Twelve Apostles, and the African Faith Tabernacle are the largest of the "spiritual churches" in Ghana, with about 125,000 affiliates each in 1990. The African Faith Tabernacle was founded by Prophet James Kwame Nkansah in 1919, a movement influenced in doctrine and practices by the form of North American fundamentalism from which it originated.[17] The prophet Charles Kobla Wovenu, a former Presbyterian government clerk, commenced the Apostolic Revelation Society in 1939, consisting mainly of Ewe, with a holy city at Tadzewu. He left the Presbyterian church in 1945 when he was told to stop praying for healing.[18] In 1963, the Eden Revival Church (now known as the F'Eden Church) was commenced by a Presbyterian schoolteacher, Charles Yeboa-Korie (1938-), when he received visions that he was to become a healer. He used prayer with accompanying liturgical objects like Bibles, blessed water, handkerchiefs, olive oil, candles, and incense in order to bring healing from sickness and deliverance from demons to people. Later, modernization and contact with western Christianity caused the candles and incense to disappear, and Yeboa began to see his church as forming a bridge between the AICs and the "mainline" churches. In 1970, F'Eden was the first AIC to be admitted to the national Ghanaian Christian Council.[19]

The Celestial Church of Christ, founded in Dahomey (Benin) in 1947 by Samuel Oschoffa, is also a significant church in Ghana, as are several churches originating in Nigeria discussed below. The Christ Apostolic Church started in Ghana in 1938, the Cherubim and Seraphim Society was introduced to Ghana by Nigerian prophet Adegoke in 1949, and the Church of the Lord (Aladura) by another Nigerian prophet Adejobi in 1953. Several of the spiritual churches in Ghana formed an ecumenical cooperative organization together in 1962: the Pentecostal Association of Ghana, the name chosen illustrating the self-identity of the "spiritual churches" of Ghana as "pentecostal". There were more than 3,000 AICs in Ghana in 1996. Another ecumenical organization called the Council of Independent Churches in Ghana has also been formed.[20]

Aladura Churches in Nigeria

The Aladura movement and related African pentecostal churches had their roots in the Anglican church in Nigeria. The popular Anglican revivalist preacher in the Niger Delta, Garrick Sokari Braide (c.1882-1918), was formerly a Kalabari (Ijo) fisherman and trader with little formal education. He was the first of many Nigerians to be recognized as a Christian prophet and prayer-healing evangelist. His reputation as a prophet and healer grew, and he emerged from about 1912 until 1916 as a fiery preacher urging the destruction of fetishes and traditional shrines, the rejection of alcohol, and healing through prayer. Like Wade Harris, his message was simple: renounce traditional practices and believe in God. He named his hometown Bakana-Israel, and multitudes flocked there and then spread his Christian message all over the Niger Delta—and the chief beneficiaries of this mass conversion movement were the Anglicans. Braide's increasing popularity and exploits were regarded as a threat to both the colonial authority and the Anglican missionaries. Among other miraculous claims, Braide was credited with the traditional power of rainmaking. There is evidence that the area's alcohol trade decreased drastically as a result of Braide's preaching and consequently, the colonial excise revenue fell. Braide, like Harris, advocated the use of indigenous music in Christian worship with clapping and ecstatic dancing, and he encouraged the development of African leadership. Eventually, Braide was called Prophet Elijah II, and on one occasion he was reported to have said publicly that the time had come for Africans to assume responsibility for themselves, which was interpreted as an anti-colonial incitement. In 1916, Anglican Bishop James Johnson, who had confirmed Braide four years earlier, was asked by Braide's supporters to recognize his ministry. Instead, the bishop declared him a "devil-inspired" heretic and suspended any clergy supporting him. A month later, the colonial authorities, who feared further loss of revenue, had Johnson's written encouragement to arrest Braide for seditious behaviour, incitement to commit violence, and willful damage to property, in this case the traditional shrines. He spent most of the next two years in prison and died in 1918, perhaps as a result of the influenza epidemic. Although Braide remained a faithful Anglican until his death, while he was in prison in 1916, some 43,000 of his followers formed the Christ Army Church, the first "spiritual church" in Nigeria, but soon racked by internal dissension.[21] Braide died in the year that the Aladura movement began to emerge in Western Nigeria.

The largest AICs in West Africa are in Yorubaland, where the Aladura churches were at the very center of society by 1950. This movement emphasized prayer, so they were known in Nigeria as "Aladura", the "prayer people", a term that distinguished them from other Christian churches at the time. An Anglican lay leader at Ijebu-Ode, Joseph Shadare (d.1962), formed a prayer group in 1918 together with a woman schoolteacher, Sophia Odunlami, who had a vision in which she was commanded to preach healing through holy water only, and to reject medicines. This group was known as the Precious Stone (Diamond) Society, created to provide spiritual support and healing for victims of the influenza epidemic. In 1922 the society left the Anglican church (CMS) over the issues of infant baptism and the rejection of medicines, both western and traditional. It began a branch in Lagos and affiliated with a North American non-pentecostal, fundamentalist group called Faith Tabernacle, whose literature had reached Nigeria and who emphasized divine healing and adult baptism by immersion. Contact with the church in the USA was severed in 1925 after doctrinal differences over the pentecostal gifts of the Spirit (particularly speaking in tongues), the apparent failure of the Americans to support the church in Nigeria, and the American leader's alleged immorality.[22] After a revival in 1930, the group forged links with a British Pentecostal church, the Apostolic Church of Great Britain, and later it developed into the Christ Apostolic Church, described below.

In 1925, the first Aladura church started with the founding of the Eternal Sacred Order of Cherubim and Seraphim Society by an Anglican, Moses Orimolade Tunolashe, and the fifteen-year-old girl Abiodun Akinsowon, later called Captain Abiodun, also an Anglican. Orimolade's emphases caused him to be known as Baba Aladura ("praying father")—a title used by subsequent leaders of this church. Orimolade began preaching in about 1915 after partially recovering from a long illness. Crowds came to him for prayer for healing during the influenza epidemic of 1918. He was called upon to pray for Abiodun to awaken from a trance, after which she related her visions of heaven, out-of-body experiences and instructions to use special prayers and holy water for healing. The movement began as a prayer group within the Anglican church, but withdrew from it because of heavy criticism by Anglican priests. Orimolade and Abiodun associated for a time with Coker and the United Native African Church in Lagos, where they were given the name "Seraph", to which "Cherub" was later added, after a revelation that these two words should go together. The members of this prayer movement claimed a special relationship with angels, whom they represented on earth. Abiodun and Orimolade took the revival to other parts of Yorubaland on extended missionary journeys, and they challenged witchcraft openly. This brought them into considerable conflict with traditional and colonial authorities. The two leaders parted company in 1929, and Abiodun founded the Cherubim and Seraphim Society, the first of several schisms in this movement. This was followed in rapid succession by the Redemption Band of C&S, the Praying Band of the C&S under Ezekiel Davies in 1930, and the Holy Flock of Christ Church in 1932 under Major A.B. Lawrence. Orimolade died in 1933, after which Abiodun made an unsuccessful attempt to reunify the C&S movement, but by 1935 there were six independent C&S churches.

The influential daughter of a chief, prophetess Christianah Olatunrinle, known as "Mama Ondo", became Iya Alakoso ("mother superintendent") of the Western Conference of the C&S at this time, a separate conference set up to protest against the increasing secessions. She was responsible for guiding the movement into a more "pentecostal" direction until her death in 1941. Her presence in the C&S leadership was further evidence of the powerful influence of women in the Aladura movement— although she was denied the title of chairperson.[23] Another schism in 1943 took place in Ilaje, where C&S members began to condemn the traditional practice of twin killing, resulting in the Holy Apostles Community at Aiyetoro ("Happy City"). There, an internationally renowned and thriving commercial commune was developed from 1947, particularly known for its fishing and transportation industries, with community of ownership under its first Oba, Ethiopia Ojagbohun Peter. After the third Oba introduced private property to the community in 1968, members began to leave and the community gradually disintegrated. The various C&S groups came together in 1965 to form what became the National Council of Cherubim and Seraphim. By 1996, it was reported that all but four of fifty-two C&S groups had reunited in the Eternal Sacred Order of the Cherubim and Seraphim, under the Baba Aladura, Dr. G.I.M. Otubu, but divisions have since reappeared. The C&S movement continues to be very influential in Nigerian society, with schools and other community projects under its care.[24]

Another prominent Aladura church is the Church of the Lord (Aladura). Josiah Ositelu, an Anglican schoolteacher who had thousands of visions, became involved in the prophetic exposure of witchcraft. He was associated with Shadare and Babalola during the revival of 1930. Ositelu was known as a powerful healer, and broke his short affiliation with Faith Tabernacle in the same year, when the other leaders challenged his authority and practices. They objected to his concern with exposing witches, the use of "holy names" and "seals" to guarantee miracles, and his acceptance of polygyny.[25] Ositelu then founded the Church of the Lord (Aladura) (CLA) and eventually took seven wives, for which he claimed divine permission.[26] He died in 1966, to be succeeded by Apostle Adeleke Adejobi (1921-1991), who had just completed a two-year theological training course at an evangelical Bible college in Glasgow, Scotland and had established a church among West African immigrants in London in 1964. Adejobi was a man of considerable spiritual and administrative gifts and one of the most widely traveled Aladura leaders. He built the largest church building of the CLA in Lagos in 1942, planted the CLA in Freetown, Sierra Leone in 1947, and in Accra, Ghana in 1953. Adejobi's work in Ghana resulted in one of the most successful of the non-Nigerian CLA churches, and the daughter of the King of Ashanti, Princess Victoria Prempeh, became an avid supporter and eventually a minister.[27] The CLA was admitted to the World Council of Churches in 1975. Adejobi was also involved in the creation of two ecumenical associations for AICs, the Nigeria Association of Aladura Churches and the intercontinental Organization of African Instituted Churches (OAIC), created in Cairo in 1978 with offices in Nairobi. Primate Adejobi became the OAIC's first Chairman (1978-1982). The CLA was also responsible for the creation of the Aladura Theological Seminary and the "Prophets and Prophetesses Training Institute", originally established by Adejobi in 1965. On Adejobi's death in 1991, Ositelu's eldest son, Gabriel Segun Ositelu (1938-1998), a agriculturist and head of an Ibadan research institute, took his place as Primate. On his death in 1998, his brother Rufus Ositelu became Primate. The CLA seems to have evolved from a charismatic leadership pattern to a hereditary one. Aladura churches in Nigeria have sought cooperation, and when some were refused admission into the national Christian Council of Nigeria, they formed the Nigerian Association of Aladura Churches with 95 denominations and 1.2 million members in 1964, rising to as many as 1,200 member churches by 1996. The OAIC's own Nigerian section was established in 1987.[28] In 1997, Baba Aladura Dr. G.I.M. Otubu of the C&S, was elected as the third chairman of the OAIC, the second Nigerian to hold this office.

After the liberation of West Africa from colonialism in

the late 1950s, a new wave of secessions began. In the late 1960s, during the civil war in Nigeria, new AICs arose in eastern Nigeria among the Igbos, such as the True Church of God and the Spiritual Healing Church of the Lord, the latter seceding from the CLA in 1960.[29] In Western Nigeria, the Celestial Church of Christ (CCC) is also a church of later origin that may now be the most influential and largest Aladura church, although it does not share the common historical roots of other Aladura churches. The CCC was founded in Porto Novo, Benin in 1947 by a former Methodist, Samuel Oschoffa (1909-1985), who had a divine revelation to become an international evangelist after a prolonged period of prayer in a forest. Pastor Oschoffa, as he was known, soon gained a reputation as a healer and miracle worker, and was said to have raised people from the dead. The CCC's rapid growth in Nigeria took place after Oschoffa made his first annual visit to Nigeria in 1951, and the CCC was registered in Nigeria in 1958. After increasing criticism and persecution in Benin, Oschoffa finally moved to Nigeria in 1977. Alexander Abiodun Bada joined a branch of the CCC in Lagos in 1952 and was the first full-time Nigerian evangelist. He became "Pastor and Supreme Head" of the movement when Oschoffa died a few days after a motor accident in 1985. The church expanded to northern Nigeria, other parts of West Africa, and Europe and North America. CCC members wear distinctive white gowns, walk barefoot, allow polygyny, have many strict taboos, emphasize healing and spiritual trance, use traditional African music and drumming, and have prayer rituals that some consider to be a mixture of Catholic, Anglican, and Muslim practices. Prophets and prophetesses go into ecstasy and speak "angelic languages", which may be interpreted. Unlike most Aladura churches, under Oschoffa the CCC did not associate with other churches and considered other Aladura churches as forerunners of the CCC. Under Bada's leadership, however, the church moved into ecumenical associations and is now member of the Christian Association of Nigeria and of the OAIC.[30] A leadership crisis followed Bada's death in 2000.

Apart from some outward similarities, the Brotherhood of

the Cross and Star (BCS) in Eastern Nigeria is not an Aladura church, but quite different, messianic and deliberately syncretistic. This movement was founded in 1956 by Olumba Olumba Obu (1918-), a healer and miracle worker known as "O.O.O."—members paint these letters on homes and cars for protection. Although the BCS began as a Christian church of the Aladura type, Obu's followers now believe him to be the Messiah and the eighth and final incarnation of God—the seventh incarnation being Jesus. The BCS was estimated to have some 600,000 members in 1980, and has since continued to expand in West Africa, Europe and the USA. The movement claims not to be a church, emphasizes spiritual and material prosperity, and has aroused opposition from most other Nigerian churches. Obu proclaims "an apocalyptic fulfillment" to occur in 2001. It has more recently developed links with other religious bodies, including Indian gurus, Rosicrucianism, and the Unification Church.[31]

The Christ Apostolic Church

The greatest expansion of the original Aladura movement took place after a revival beginning in 1930. After a series of divine visions, former road construction driver, Joseph Ayo Babalola (1906-59), contacted Shadare of Faith Tabernacle, became a member, and began preaching at Ilesa. He was to become General Evangelist of the Christ Apostolic Church (CAC), constituted in 1941 and soon afterwards the largest Aladura church in Nigeria. Babalola heard a voice calling him to preach using prayer and the "water of life" (blessed water), which would heal all sicknesses. The ensuing revival led by Babalola and Daniel Orekoya resulted in thousands of people becoming Christians and burning their traditional fetishes. The colonial authorities became disturbed, for the revival activities were alleged to include witch-hunting and opposition to hospitals and medicine, and therefore endangered public health. Some of the leaders of the revival, including Babalola, were arrested and jailed. This pentecostal revival movement felt the need to have some outside assistance to enable them to purchase land and be allowed to preach. They invited British Pentecostals to Nigeria, and missionaries from the Apostolic Church of Great Britain arrived in 1932, supported by the Nigerian church. The association was broken in 1939 over the British missionaries' attempt to control the church and their opposition to the use of "water of life". The African leaders also found the missionaries' use of medicine and quinine objectionable. Both in Ghana and in Nigeria, after these disagreements had taken place, the European Pentecostal missionaries remained and formed separate church organizations that still exist, the Apostolic Church being a significant church in both countries.

The first President of the Christ Apostolic Church (since 1940) became ruler (Olubadan) of Ibadan, Sir Isaac Babalola Akinyele (1882-1964), one of the first converts in Ibadan and a strong financial supporter of the church. Akinyele became a member of Shadare's Faith Tabernacle in 1925. Babalola died in 1959 and Akinyele in 1964, but the CAC continued to grow. By 1990 it had over one million affiliates, making it one of the largest churches in Nigeria, and the church had spread to several other countries in Africa, Europe, and North America. There were also inevitable schisms, one of the most significant being the Christ Gospel Apostolic Church, founded by the prophet Peter Olatunji, a prominent CAC leader, in 1948. The CAC tends to distance itself from other Aladura churches and has been regarded more favorably by government and "mainline" church leaders than other Aladura churches, because of its more definite Christology and emphasis on the Bible, its educated leadership, and its considerable involvement in education.[32] Unlike most other Aladura churches, CAC members and ministers do not wear white gowns, and monogamy is practiced. However, the church shares the customs of other Aladura churches of prayer, fasting, water and oil for healing purposes, sacred hills and mountains, and the rejection of medicines, alcohol, and tobacco.[33] The CAC is significantly different from other Aladura churches and is widely respected. It considers itself, and is probably more correctly regarded, an African Pentecostal church.[34] Sanneh considers this to be "among the élite of the charismatic Churches" because of its ability to combine the Pentecostal spiritual gifts common to all Aladura churches with considerable administrative skills and experience.[35]

West African Churches in Europe

We have already noted Nigerian Aladura churches planted in Britain. Although large churches from other African countries (like the Kimbanguists) have established themselves in Europe, especially in Belgium and France, most of the African churches in Europe are from West Africa, and in particular from Nigeria and Ghana. These churches continue to proliferate. For example, in Amsterdam alone there were at least twenty AIC congregations in 1998.[36] Many of the AIC congregations in Europe are independent of their African origins, and a new form of "international" AIC is being formed all over Europe. Most of these are of a Pentecostal and Charismatic type, and their leaders see themselves as African missionaries to Europe—indeed a telling, if ironic reversal of roles.[37] In more recent years, these churches have also spread to North America. The largest congregation in Britain in 1999 was a Pentecostal church established by a Nigerian.[38]

African Caribbean churches were established in Britain when immigrant laborers from the Caribbean, especially Jamaica, arrived there soon after the Second World War. These churches are almost entirely "classical" Pentecostal with origins in North America, and are not the focus of this study.[39] The AICs in Britain have been there since 1964, but those in other parts of Europe are more recent. The West Africans who joined these churches, unlike the African Caribbean churches, were mostly students, professionals, and (more recently) refugees and asylum seekers. In 1964, the CLA was the first Aladura church to arrive in Britain, followed by the C&S, the CCC, the CAC, and the Aladura International Church, forming once again places to "feel at home" in an alien and often unwelcoming environment. The MDCC was the first Ghanaian "spiritual" AIC to establish itself in Britain. Like the African Caribbean churches before them, the creation of AICs throughout Europe was often encouraged by a feeling of estrangement and loneliness, and sometimes, through indifferent and racist attitudes in European churches. But perhaps more importantly, the intense and holistic spirituality of the AICs, their particular contextualization of the Christian message, and their revivalist tendencies were often absent from these churches and left African believers with a sense of emptiness. The AICs in Europe have attempted to fill this void.

The Aladura International Church was established by a Nigerian Anglican priest, Olu Abiola, who had gone to Britain to study, and was the first AIC actually founded in Britain. He has since become one of the best-known Aladura church leaders in Britain and has established churches in France, Italy, and Germany.[40] The African churches in Britain are increasing remarkably. Including the churches of African Caribbean origin, in 1995 there were estimated to be between 200 and 300 black-led denominations in some 3,000 congregations in Britain.[41]

The Aladura movement cannot be regarded primarily as a reaction to western Christianity, although this factor was by no means absent. This was a Pentecostal revival movement of massive proportions, sometimes influenced by western Pentecostalism, but usually only on the invitation of the African church leaders. This mass conversion movement took place mostly amongst urban people, and was marked by a rejection of traditional religion and medicines. During the 1950s, Aladura churches spread to Ghana, Liberia, and Sierra Leone, through the efforts of traveling Nigerian preachers, especially Apostles Oduwole and Adejobi of the Church of the Lord (Aladura), and new Ghanaian churches in the traditions of Aladura seceded. From Africa the Aladura churches spread to Europe. The Aladura movement fundamentally changed the face of West African Christianity, and therefore can be regarded as an African reformation movement. Like the Aladura churches did to the African churches before them, so the Aladura churches themselves were to be overtaken and impacted by the new wave of Pentecostalism that swept over Africa in general, and West Africa in particular, in the last quarter of the twentieth century.[42]

Notes

1 New Islamic movements have also arisen there, like the Mahdist movements and the Children of the Israelites in Nigeria and the Sudan, which have combined both Muslim and Christian elements. Clarke, 1995; Ian Linden, "Between Two Religions of the Book: The Children of the Israelites (c. 1846- c.1920)", London, 1982, 79-98.

2 Gordon M. Haliburton, *The Prophet Harris: A Study of an African Prophet and his Mass Movement in the Ivory Coast and the Gold Coast 1913-1915.* London, 1971, 30-32, 35.

3 The word "fetish" is used in this chapter as West African Christians use it, to denote traditional charms, images, and amulets, etc. used to ward off evil or to do someone else harm. It does not have any pejorative sense or imply any value judgement.

4 Haliburton, 1.

5 Ibid., 38.

6 Ibid., 49, 51, 57; Sheila S. Walker, "The Message as the Medium: The Harrist Churches of the Ivory Coast and Ghana", New York, 1979, 11-4.

7 Haliburton, 79, 88-9.

8 Sheila S. Walker, *The Religious Revolution in the Ivory Coast: The Prophet Harris and the Harrist Church,* Chapel Hill, N. C., 1983, 63.

9 Haliburton, 2-3, 47.

10 Walker, "Message", 19-20.

11 Walker, *Religious Revolution,* 82-3; Barrett & Padwick, 85; Barrett, *Schism,* 177; Walker, "Message", 22, 25-6.

12 Patrick Johnstone, *Operation World,* Carlisle, 1993, 184.

13 World Council of Churches, "Consultation with African Instituted Churches", Geneva, 1996, 9-10.

[14] Walker, "Message", 36-46.

[15] Ibid., 46-50; Shiela S. Walker, "Women in the Harrist Movement", Norwood, 1979, 93-6.

[16] G. C. Baëta, *Prophetism in Ghana: A Study of some "Spiritual" Churches*, London, 1962, 9-27.

[17] Kofi A. Opoku, "Changes within Christianity: the case of the Musama Disco Christo Church", London & New York, 1980, 309-20; Baëta, 28-67; Ayegboyin & Ishola, 114-23; Johnstone, 241-2.

[18] Baëta, 79.

[19] David M. Beckman, *Eden Revival: Spiritual Churches in Ghana*, St Louis, 1975, 48-58.

[20] World Council, 16.

[21] Harold W. Turner, *History of an African Independent Church (1) The Church of the Lord (Aladura)*, Oxford, 1967, 6; id., *Religious Innovation*, 122, 138-44; Sanneh, 180-4; G. O. M. Tasie, "Christian Awakening in West Africa 1914-18: a study in the significance of native agency", London & New York, 1980, 299-306; id., "The Prophetic Calling: Garrick Sokari Braide of Bakana", London, 1982, 99-115.

[22] Turner, *History (1)*, 11-2; Ayegboyin & Ishola, 71-2.

[23] Peel, 59-60; Sanneh, 190-4; Akin. Omoyajowo, *The Cherubim and Seraphim Church in Relation to Church, Society and State*, Ibadan, 1975, 11-22; Terence T. Booth, "We True Christians", Birmingham, 1984, 57; Helen Callaway, "Women in Yoruba tradition and in the Cherubim and Seraphim Society", London & New York, 1980, 331.

[24] Elizabeth Isichei, *A History of Christianity in Africa: From Antiquity to the Present*, London, 1995, 282-3; S.O.A. Authority, *"Aiyetoro": The Happy City*, Lagos, 1966; Omoyajowo, 86-91; Stanley R. Barrett, "All Things in Common: The Holy Apostles of Western Nigeria (1947 onwards)", London, 1982, 149-62; World Council, 10-1.

[25] Turner, *History (1)*, 22-5.

[26] Ibid., 49-50.

[27] Turner, *Religious Innovation*, 125.

[28] Sam Babs Mala, "African instituted churches in Nigeria", Elkhart, 1991, 26-9; World Council, 15.

29 Gabriel I. S. Amadi, "Continuities and Adaptations in the Aladura Movement: the example of Prophet Wobo and his clientele in South-Eastern Nigeria", Lewiston, NY, 1987, 75.

30 Afeosemime U. Adogame, *Celestial Church of Christ,* Frankfurt am Main, 1999; Isichei, *History,* 284; Clarke, *West Africa,* 201; Ayegboyin & Ishola, 97-105; Olu Obafemi, *Pastor S.B.J. Oshoffa: God's 20th Century Gift to Africa,* Lagos, 1986; World Council of Churches, 8-9.

31 Isichei, *History,* 292.

32 Sanneh, 184-6, 194-7; Peel, 91-113; Turner, *History (I),* 31-4; Ayokunnu Ogunranti, "Pastor and Politician: Isaac Akinyele, Olubadan of Ibadan (1862-1955 [sic])", London, 1982, 131-9; Johnstone, 241, 421.

33 Ayegboyin & Ishola, 74-9.

34 Christopher O. Oshun, "Christ Apostolic Church of Nigeria: A Pentecostal Consideration of its Historical, Theological and Organizational Developments, 1918-1878", Exeter, 1981.

35 Sanneh, 194.

36 Pobee & Ositelu, 52.

37 ter Haar, Gerrie, *Halfway to Paradise: African Christians in Europe,* Cardiff, 1998, 3.

38 The Kingsway International Christian Centre in London, described in chapter 8.

39 The two largest "Black-led" churches in Britain are both Trinitarian, "classical" Pentecostal: the New Testament Church of God and the Church of God of Prophecy. One of the most comprehensive studies to date on African Caribbean churches in Britain is Roswith Gerloff, *A Plea for British Black Theologies: The Black church movement in Britain in its transatlantic cultural and theological connection with special reference to the Pentecostal Oneness (Apostolic) and Sabbatarian movements.* Frankfurt, 1992.

40 T. Jack Thompson, "African Independent Churches in Britain: an introductory survey", Aarhus, 225; ter Haar, 90.

41 ter Haar, 92.

42 These churches are discussed in Chapter 8.

5

SOUTHERN AFRICAN CHURCHES

No country in Africa has as many church denominations as South Africa, perhaps as many as six thousand, and most of these are AICs of the "prophet-healing" or "spiritual" type, usually called "Zionist" and "Apostolic" churches.[1] At the end of the twentieth century, the AICs comprised probably half of the African Christian population of South Africa (an estimated 47% in 1991), at least 10 million people, compared to 21% only 30 years earlier. In comparison, the older "mission churches" have declined from 70% of the African Christian population in 1960, to 33% in 1991.[2] Various factors could be at work in this development. The rapid increase in urbanization among black South Africans after 1960 may be one. The insecurities inherent in rapid urbanization provide strong incentives for people separated from their roots to seek new, culturally and socially meaningful religious expressions, especially in a society where there is no access to the instruments of social and political power. The increasing disillusionment experienced by black people in South Africa's political matrix after 1948 resulted in a rejection of

European values and religious expressions such as those found in "mainline" churches. Jean Comaroff depicts the emergence of Zionist churches as "a more radical expression of cultural resistance" for those dispossessed by colonialism than those offered by the more orthodox Protestant churches. She sees the symbols of Zionist ritual as an enduring form of resistance to white hegemony, "returning to the displaced a tangible identity and the power to impose coherence upon a disarticulated world". Comaroff's study suggests that the forms of socio-political protest exhibited by this "cultural resistance" are implicit rather than explicit, but are nevertheless all-pervasive.[3]

As elsewhere in Africa, the AICs in Southern Africa are of a tremendously wide variety. Attempts to categorize them are not very helpful, particularly as these churches are dynamic and under a constant process of change. As the so-called "Ethiopian" churches of South Africa have already been described, most of the churches in this chapter are the much more prolific AICs with a strong pentecostal emphasis on the role of the power of the Spirit, manifested particularly in healing, prophecy, and deliverance from evil forces. We will mostly refer to them as "Zionist and Apostolic" churches, although these churches include the Zionist (or Zion) churches, the Apostolic churches (also called "prayer churches"), and large churches that do not use either designation, like the *amaNazaretha* and the International Pentecost Church.

Zionist and Apostolic Churches

For the most part, the beginnings of African Zionist and Apostolic churches in Southern Africa were not exclusively African. The history actually begins in Zion City, near Chicago, USA, a Christian "theocracy" created in 1896 by the former Australian Congregationalist healer, John Alexander Dowie. He was "First Apostle and Prophet of the Restoration" in a movement called the Christian Catholic Apostolic Church in Zion, later Christian Catholic Church in Zion,[4] which emphasized divine healing and triune baptism of adult believers by immersion. This church was established in Johannesburg by a former Baptist pastor, Johannes Buchler, in 1895. Pieter L. le Roux, a Dutch Reformed missionary for ten years, differed with his church over his belief in divine healing, having decided that using medicines and infant baptism were unbiblical.[5] He joined Dowie's Zion movement in 1903, together with three African evangelists (Daniel Nkonyane, Muneli Ngobesi, and Fred Lutuli), and with some 400 African lay preachers and converts in Wakkerstroom in the eastern Transvaal, (now Mpumalanga). Dowie sent Daniel Bryant, to South Africa as Overseer in 1904. Bryant baptized 141 black and white Zion believers together in the river near le Roux's mission church. In Zion City, Dowie's newspaper *Leaves of Healing*, exulted that the prophecy "Ethiopia shall haste to stretch out her hands unto God" was "being fulfilled in and through Zion". The paper made a revealing reference to those "nations, classes, or individuals" who had "wrongfully exercised their power in the oppression of this great family of the human race", and said that Dowie had "boldly championed their cause". This group of "Zionists" grew within a year to 5,000, and the great majority of these were Zulus.[6] During these early years, there were reports of gifts of healing, prophecies, visions, and speaking in tongues in this movement. Included in these early revelations were instructions to wear white robes, sashes, crosses and staffs, practices with obscure origins, but later a cause of division with white Pentecostals.[7]

In 1908, a team of missionaries from the North American Pentecostal movement, led by Thomas Hezmalhalch and John G. Lake, the latter formerly an elder in Dowie's Zion (like le Roux), arrived in Johannesburg and used the Zion church building there for services. The evangelist Lake was to emerge as the leading figure, particularly because of his divine healing emphasis. Le Roux joined Lake's Apostolic Faith Mission (AFM) and by 1915, after Lake's return to the USA, had become its president. His African fellow-workers, however, remained Zionists, whilst they embraced the new doctrine of the Holy Spirit, with speaking in tongues and prophecy emphasized by the Pentecostals. In those early days, the words "Apostolic Faith" were universally used to refer to the new Pentecostal movement. Several parallels between the African Zionists of today and these early Pentecostals include triune baptism by immersion, an emphasis on divine healing accompanied by a rejection of medicine and doctors, and taboos against alcohol and tobacco. Sundkler emphasizes the continuity between the Zionists and the Pentecostals, for which reason, Zionist and Apostolic churches may be considered an African form of Pentecostalism.[8]

The Zion church in Johannesburg became the AFM's first headquarters, and many of the AFM's first members were formerly members of this Zion church. Although the first Pentecostal services in Johannesburg were held in an African church and were racially integrated, the white members soon decided to segregate. The African Pentecostal church at the time was called the Zion Apostolic Church, continuing to cooperate with the white Pentecostals, but the whites passed racist church laws and kept all significant leadership positions for themselves. This lack of trust in and commitment to black leadership in white South African Pentecostalism undoubtedly contributed to the many schisms that took place from this time onwards. Estrangement between African and white Pentecostals occurred gradually, and it seems as if the Africans were characteristically tolerant of the many affronts to their dignity. This racism remained in the AFM, now South Africa's largest "classical" Pentecostal denomination, until well after the democratic government was elected in 1994, and although agreement for the structural unity of the AFM was reached in 1996, the deep-seated divisions in this church continue to make real unity elusive.[9]

The seeds of division did not take long to germinate. One of the Zulu Zion leaders, Daniel Nkonyane, had seceded from the AFM, possibly as early as 1910, forming the Christian Catholic Apostolic Holy Spirit Church in Zion, having already obtained and paid for a "three hundred acre" building site in northern Natal (perhaps even before Bryant's arrival in 1904) which became a prototype for many African "Zion Cities" to come.[10] Principal leaders of Zionist and Apostolic churches were seen as Moses figures who bring their people out of slavery into the promised land, the new "City of Zion". The Exodus event was a liberation from the old life of trouble, sickness, oppression, evil spirits, sorcery, and poverty. The new Israel incarnate in Africa was moving out of Egypt towards the new Jerusalem, the Zion of God, where all these troubles are forgotten. The people of God are the members of this new African church, which has been able to discover its Promised Land for itself. Zion, the new Jerusalem, is the holy place—not in some far off foreign land at some distant time in the past, but present here and now in Africa.

In 1917, Elias Mahlangu, probably another of the original Zion workers, founded the Zion Apostolic Church of South Africa. From Mahlangu's church, Edward Motaung (known as Edward Lion), seceded in 1920 to form the Zion Apostolic Faith Mission (ZAFM)—the chosen name showing a desire to maintain identification with the AFM. Engenas Lekganyane's Zion Christian Church (ZCC) seceded from the ZAFM in 1925—now the largest church in South Africa and one of the largest in Africa.[11] Paul Mabiletsa, another founding Zion leader, commenced the Apostolic Church in Zion in 1920 (one of the larger Zionist churches whose leadership has remained in the Mabiletsa family), and J.C. Phillips, a Malawian, commenced the Holy Catholic Apostolic Church in Zion.[12] Not only did African Zionists retain most of the practices of the Pentecostals, but they also tended to favor both names "Apostolic" and "Zion". Most AIC denominations in South Africa today have favored one or both of these terms in their church names. Speaking in tongues and prophesying were encouraged by the Pentecostals and were practiced by Zionists and Apostolics. Differences that began to emerge were mainly external, as le Roux and other white Pentecostals objected to the use of external symbols like staffs and the wearing of uniforms and robes.[13] But Pentecostalism's African-American roots made the transplanting of its central tenets more easily assimilated by Africans.[14]

In theology, there are no significant differences between African Zion and Apostolic churches on the one hand and the more western-influenced Pentecostal churches on the other, but in liturgy and in other practical ways the differences are quite considerable. A Zionist becomes a Christian through baptism by triune immersion in water, which usually must take place in running water, that is in a river often called "Jordan". There is an emphasis on divine healing, although the methods of obtaining this healing differ. Whereas most Pentecostals practice laying on hands or prayer for the sick, this will usually be accompanied in Zion and Apostolic churches—and, as we have seen in many other AICs—by the use of symbolic objects such as blessed water, ropes, staffs, papers, ash, and so on. Prophecy and speaking in tongues are also practiced in most Zion and Apostolic churches. There are strong regulations for members, and many churches do not allow alcohol, tobacco, medicines, or eating pork—also taboos for early western Pentecostals. The attitude to traditional religious practices in Zion and Apostolic churches is generally ambivalent, particularly when it comes to ancestors, and some of these churches allow polygyny. For the outsider, the biggest distinguishing feature is the almost universal use of uniform clothing, which are usually white robes with colored belts and sashes and other markings, or in the case of the ZCC, khaki uniforms for male members and green and gold colors for more senior men and women. These churches do not have many church buildings and often meet in the open air.

The Zion Christian Church

The ZCC, by no means a typical Zionist church but by far the largest, was founded by Engenas Lekganyane (c.1880-1948), born in the Mamabolo area of what is now the Northern Province of South Africa. He was an evangelist in the Free Church of Scotland when he met le Roux and the AFM in Johannesburg soon after it started in 1908.[15] He was working in the area at the time, perhaps as a migrant worker, and had suffered from a serious eye disorder for many years. He had a vision in which a voice had told him that when he went to Johannesburg, he would find healing if he joined a church baptizing by triune immersion. Lekganyane may have joined the AFM—he received "Spirit baptism" (the distinctive teaching of the Pentecostals) and at first belonged to a Zionist congregation near his home. ZCC tradition says that in about 1910, the official year for the commencement of the church, Lekganyane was praying on a mountain when a whirlwind blew off his hat and filled it with leaves. He took this as a revelation that God would give him strength to found a large church. Lekganyane followed the Mahlangu brothers, Elias and Joseph, on arriving in Johannesburg in 1912. It seems that Elias Mahlangu baptized Lekganyane, resulting in his healing. Mahlangu did not break with the white Pentecostals until about 1917, to found the Zion Apostolic Church of South Africa (ZAC).[16]

In 1916, Lekganyane was ordained, and he emerged as leader of his own ZAC congregation in his home village Thabakgone. In 1918, he became leader of the work in the Northern Province, and won many converts. At this stage, he continued in the traditions of the western Protestant and Pentecostal missions with which he had been associated. The Pentecostals had emphasized the idea of direct and personal revelation by the Spirit, and Lekganyane began to operate as a prophet. It seems that he continued with Mahlangu for about three years after the break with the AFM in 1917, but that differences soon developed. Mahlangu began to promote customs amongst ZAC members that Lekganyane objected to, such as wearing white robes, growing beards, and taking off shoes before services. These practices are found in many Zionist and Apostolic churches today, but are not allowed in the ZCC.

Prophecy in Pentecostal circles and in African tradition included predicting the future, and Lekganyane was no stranger to this form. In 1917, he prophesied the defeat of Germany by Britain and when this happened a year later, his prestige as prophet and "man of God" grew. Clearly, Engenas was primarily seen as a unique prophet with extraordinary gifts of revelation and healing. His final break with the ZAC came in 1920, when he went to Lesotho and joined Edward (Lion) Motaung's Zion Apostolic Faith Mission (ZAFM), where he was ordained bishop for the Transvaal. Once again, differences emerged between Lekganyane and the leader, mainly on administrative matters, and Lion was soon thereafter to get into serious trouble with the Protectorate administration.[17] Although probably not the main factor in this secession, Lekganyane's marriage to a second wife was one reason for the break with Motaung, who opposed polygyny.[18] At about the end of 1924, Lekganyane returned to Thabakgone to found his own church, the Zion Christian Church.

The ZCC grew rapidly. When he first applied in 1925 for government recognition, Lekganyane claimed 926 adherents in fifteen congregations in the northern provinces— but this application was not approved. Recent events were not on Lekganyane's side. Government authorities were highly suspicious of independent African churches after the Bulhoek massacre of 1921, in which 163 Israelites, followers of the prophet Enoch Mgijima, were killed in a clash with police. The government-appointed Native Churches Commission of 1925 declared that "the Church Separatist movement symbolizes the general ambition of the Bantu for liberation" and that the Israelites were "a branch of a fanatical politico-religious body from America"—probably a reference to the Zionists.[19] Obviously, the ZCC was tarred with the same brush. In 1930, Lekganyane was involved in a dispute with his local chief over the mistreatment of a ZCC woman by her husband, and was forced to leave his home village. He bought a farm in Boyne, also near Pietersburg, for which church members raised the purchase price. This farm became the church headquarters named Moria, to which Zionists flock today. In keeping with John Alexander Dowie's Zion City near Chicago, Daniel Nkonyane's Zion City in KwaZulu Natal and Edward Motaung's Zion City in Lesotho, Lekganyane established a mecca for pilgrimage, a center of ritual power.

During this period, Engenas had supreme charismatic authority in the church. In 1930 he instructed that the practice of leaders in outlying branches praying for the sick themselves by laying on hands be discontinued. The headquarters in Moria was being established, and it appears that Engenas was seeking to centralize his control over the rapidly developing organization.[20] In 1935 the ZCC membership was about 2,000, but by 1942 when the church was at last officially registered, there were fifty-five congregations and 27,487 members, having spread to Zimbabwe, Botswana, and the Northern Cape Province. A year later, government sources estimated the ZCC membership at over 40,000.

Lekganyane emphasized divine healing, first by laying on hands, but as the church developed this became impractical and he began to "bless" various objects like strips of cloth, strings, papers, needles, walking sticks, and water to be used for healing and protective purposes. These symbolic ritual practices emerged in the latter part of Lekganyane's ministry, to be continued by his successors, and may be a reason for the present distance between the ZCC and "Classical" Pentecostal churches. Several remarkable miraculous incidents were attributed to Lekganyane in his later years, including healings, particularly of barren women, the blessing of harvests, and rain-making—a traditional sign of power for which Lekganyane was well known. Today, the most common healing method in the ZCC, as in many other AICs, is liberal sprinkling with "blessed water", a protective and cleansing ritual. Blessed water has many uses: to purify people or objects after they have become contaminated (such as after a funeral), to welcome visitors, for protection against sorcery and misfortune, for obtaining employment, for abundant harvests, for cooking and washing, and for the "gate test" whereby prophets can determine the presence of evil before a person enters the church enclosure. The ZCC also uses special tea made for healing purposes, labeled the "tea of life" and manufactured at Moria. Walking sticks blessed by the bishop, as well as ropes and strings or strips of cloth worn around the body are believed to have protective powers. Similarly, members tie copper wires across their gates or in their houses to protect against sorcery and lightning. Another method of healing in the ZCC is where a prophet prescribes that a patient be pricked on the hands, legs, or in the nostrils in order to get rid of what is traditionally believed to be the source of sickness and pain, impure blood. Salt is used to clean the stomach and excess bile through vomiting. The use of a small piece of wood, a sheet of paper waved rapidly over the patient's body, sand from a certain river or dam, and the use of other objects named by the prophets are all common healing customs in the ZCC. Behind all these practices is the fundamental conviction that a prerequisite for protection is the prior confession of sins, without which the "medicine" is useless.[21]

Engenas Lekganyane died in 1948 after a long illness, and a leadership struggle ensued between his two sons Edward and Joseph. It wasn't clear who Engenas had appointed as successor, and the brothers formed two separate churches in 1949. The followers of Joseph, the minority faction, now "St. Engenas Zion Christian Church", use a silver dove on a green flash as their badge. The majority of Engenas' people followed Edward in the "Zion Christian Church", with the now familiar five-pointed silver star on a green flash as their badge. The two headquarters are on adjacent farms, and in beliefs and practices there is very little difference between the two.[22] Edward Legkanyane (1925-1967) was working in Johannesburg when his father died and it seems that he was initially reluctant to take on the church bishopric. But under his leadership the ZCC continued to grow so that by 1954 the membership was already some 80,000, probably the biggest AIC in southern Africa at this time. In 1963 Edward enrolled in the three-year course for evangelists at the Dutch Reformed Church's theological college near his Moria headquarters. It seems that he sought to renew the ZCC into a more biblical direction, and he is said to have strongly rejected any attribution of "messianism" to his church by critics.[23] Edward Lekganyane was a considerably effective leader. Two days after his premature death from a heart attack in October 1967, the black newspaper *World* said that he had been "one of the most powerful leaders who have dominated the religious scene in this generation".[24]

Edward's son Barnabas Ramarumo, the present bishop (b.1954), succeeded him, but was only thirteen when his father died. Although the General Council of the ZCC confirmed him as new leader, the church was to be governed in the interim by a superintendent until 1975, after his twenty-first birthday. After secondary school education, he took a Bible correspondence course at the All-Africa School of Theology of veteran North American Pentecostal missionary, Fred Burke. This Pentecostal Bible training is reflected in many of Lekganyane's sermons printed by the ZCC in their official magazine, *The ZCC Messenger*.

The ZCC and Apartheid

The apartheid government that emerged in 1948 adopted a policy of "non-interference" in the affairs of African churches, which in effect meant encouraging the development of churches that were totally "independent" of what were sometimes seen as troublesome mission churches. The development of AICs was seen as in complete harmony with the apartheid ideology, which opposed any sort of social mixing, including integrated churches. Since being registered with the South African government in 1942, the ZCC enjoyed the favor of the ruling regime. Edward Lekganyane invited the government to the Easter conference in the wake of the Sharpeville shootings, during apartheid's worst years. This was to establish a precedent for the relationship between the ZCC and the state thereafter. The ZCC bishop, however, was careful not to align himself with the regime's ideology, but kept the relationship pragmatic. The first high-level government visit occurred in 1965, when "Minister of Bantu Affairs" de Wet Nel visited the Easter conference. There, Edward Lekganyane thanked the government for their "kindness" and "goodwill", but probably did not intend this to mean more than polite acknowledgement of the official recognition accorded the ZCC and famine relief given during a particularly severe drought in the region. This speech, however, included a note of servility: "I thank the Whites for leading us out of darkness", and "Our church has no room for people who subvert the security of the state and break the laws of the land". But in a significant gesture, Lekganyane presented Nel with a carved wooden scepter. He referred to Moses leading the Israelites to freedom and said, "We present this scepter to you for you and your government [to] lead the Bantu to orderly freedom".[25] The ambiguity in this speech was characteristic of the attitude of the Lekganyanes to political issues and suggested that all was not well in the relationship with the regime.

Like his father, Barnabas also initiated invitations to the regime, beginning with the visit of "Bantu Affairs" Minister Piet Koornhof to Moria in 1980. In the much-publicized event at the 75th anniversary celebration at Easter 1985, President P.W. Botha was given the "freedom of Moria". After this event, ZCC members in Soweto were subject to a spate of violent attacks. The visit reinforced the suspicion that the ZCC was a supporter, or at least a willing and unresisting prisoner, of the status quo. The international media declared that the invitation "appeared to be a statement of allegiance by an oppressed people to their oppressor".[26] Some observers said that the regime had exploited the innocence of the ZCC to demonstrate their alleged "support" among the African population.[27] Matthew Schoffeleers described the "political acquiescence" of what he calls the "healing churches", drawing particular attention to the ZCC. The invitation of Botha to the conference amounted to "massive cooperation, and even collaboration" between the ZCC and the South African regime.[28] The occasion, however, was noteworthy for what Barnabas Lekganyane did *not* say rather than what he said. After a perfunctory speech by Botha, Lekganyane preached on love and peace in the ZCC and the reasons for their growth, and did not address Botha or the political context directly. More significantly, a year later, *The ZCC Messenger* reported a speech by Lekganyane in which he spoke out against apartheid. He said, "The Zion Christian Church and I, as a leader, detest apartheid together with all its discriminatory laws. We also abhor killings and allowing people to starve especially black people [sic]."[29]

The ZCC has emerged from the fear of a powerful and oppressive regime to attempt to play a role in the radical changes that have taken place since 1990. One ZCC writer said, "All the ZCC bishops through all the generations of the church have consistently preached racial harmony and reconciliation".[30] Each of the three most influential political leaders in South Africa at the time (Nelson Mandela, de Klerk, and Buthelezi) were separately invited to the Easter Festival in 1992 at Moria. All three accepted the invitation and were obviously keen to take the opportunity to solicit the enormous ZCC vote. This was a pragmatic effort on the part of the bishop to play a constructive role in the negotiations currently being conducted, and thereby to help promote peace during a time of violent nation-wide strife. Barnabas this time was less hesitant about addressing political issues, much easier to do in the climate prevailing in 1992. The bishop's sermon, directed at the three leaders, lashed out at "warmongering" and inflammatory political speeches, and made a plea for peace. He avoided any impression of taking sides. Schoffeleers suggests that AICs in South Africa have gone through "a process of progressive depoliticisation". ZCC leaders generally took a "neutral" stance and forbade their members active participation in structured political activities. In this way, "political acquiescence" as a "Church's avowed policy to avoid political activism of a critical nature" is an appropriate description of the ZCC leadership.[31]

During research in the satellite township of Soshanguve (near Pretoria) in 1991-1995, 168 ZCC members were interviewed. There was certainly evidence of "depoliticisation" among some members, but more noticeable was the degree of political awareness emerging among them after decades of press censorship, propaganda, institutionalized violence, and banned political organizations. Some ZCC members said that Christians should not take part in politics, but should pray for the political situation. A ZCC minister said that members were expected to abstain from political activities, because if they should be injured or arrested during such activities (then still a distinct possibility), it would not be the business of the church to attend to them. It appeared that urban ZCC members expressed their political convictions more by their participation in trade unions and civic associations than in structured political parties. Nevertheless, the majority of ZCC members were members of African nationalist organizations, especially the African National Congress, of which a significant 42% were supporters. This statistic in 1991, only a year after the ban on the ANC was lifted, suggests that "political acquiescence" could not be taken for granted in the ZCC by this time. As the ZCC was one of the more conservative AICs, it may be concluded that most other AICs were even more supportive of liberation movements and reflected the general aspirations of ordinary people.[32]

The AmaNazaretha

The largest AIC amongst the Zulu, the Nazareth Baptist Church, better known as the "amaNazaretha" or "Isonto LamaNazaretha" and "Shembe Church",[33] was founded by Mdliwamafa Mloyisa (Isaiah) Shembe (c.1869-1935), who experienced several visions and audible voices. These revelations told him to leave his four wives and children and to use no medicine, and showed him people in white gowns who would follow him. He began his Christian life as a Methodist, but was baptized in about 1900 in William Leshega's African Native Baptist Church (an early African secession from the white Baptists), by which time he was already a renowned healer. He was ordained an evangelist and he began to baptize in the sea near Durban, a practice of many coastal AICs today. In about 1911, he seceded from this church over his beliefs about putting off shoes in worship, leaving the hair uncut, not eating pork, night Communion services with foot-washing, and the seventh day Sabbath. He founded the amaNazaretha, and biblical references to Nazarites were applied to his followers, who were to obey these laws. In 1916 he established a "high place", Ekuphakameni, outside Durban, and a holy mountain, Nhlangakazi, sites for annual festivals in July and January respectively. Shembe wielded great influence in Zulu society. When he died in 1935, a sacred mausoleum was built over his grave at Ekuphakameni, now the headquarters of the church, and his son Johannes Galilee Shembe inherited the leadership.[34] On Galilee's death in 1976, a fierce and acrimonious schism resulted, with court cases, violent clashes, and even killings between the two factions. A small part of the church followed Galilee's son Londa Shembe, who was murdered in 1989 in the midst of the KwaZulu Natal violence, leaving no clear successor. The majority of members followed Isaiah's other son Amos Khula Shembe. As an indication of the prestige attained by the Shembe family, President Nelson Mandela attended Amos's funeral in 1995. His son Mbusi Vimbeni Shembe, who seems to have retained the loyalty of the vast majority of the church, succeeded him.[35]

The amaNazaretha show great veneration for their founder, which has been interpreted to mean that he is seen as an African Christ, a mediator between his people and God, standing at the gate of Heaven to admit only his followers.[36] AmaNazaretha greet their leader with the shout, "He is holy!". Shembe is believed to have "risen from the dead", he appears to people in revelations, is believed to reveal God to the Zulus, and in his name prayer is directed.[37] The criticisms of this movement have centered on the person of Isaiah Shembe and reflect prevalent assumptions made by earlier western theologians about the AICs. Sundkler, who later reversed this assessment, said that Shembe's followers regarded him as "a semi-divine being... the Black Christ", and that the Nazarite hymnbook was "a mine of information" about the "Black Christ ideology" of this church. Shembe had "usurped" the place of Christ "in the creed and life of the believers" and had become "the Christ of the Zulus", and in the process, the very image of God had been fundamentally changed.[38] Such a movement as the amaNazaretha was an example of what has become one of Sundkler's most notorious passages: "the syncretistic sect becomes the bridge over which Africans are brought back to heathenism".[39] Similarly, Oosthuizen placed the amaNazaretha in a "post-Christian" category and an "easy bridge back to nativism".[40]

Evidence from the amaNazaretha themselves, however, is

ambiguous. In the views of at least some of his followers, Shembe has very extraordinary, perhaps even divine powers. One member has a dream in which Shembe appears, which is interpreted as a vision of God. Another refers to Shembe as the "Man of Heaven" who speaks of his pre-existence and his four previous incarnations as a prophet to different nations. He is also the one who stands at a gate in heaven and admits only his followers—but significantly, in one account Shembe only gives admission to the amaNazaretha "village" in heaven, and white people are admitted to their own denominational towns. The mission church was for whites only, reflecting the rigid apartheid structures of South African society at that time.[41] But most frequently, other, lesser mortal descriptions are given by amaNazaretha. Instead of being a divine "Messiah" or "Black Christ", Isaiah Shembe is a human "servant of the Lord", "the man sent by God", who is obedient to the bidding of God.

AmaNazaretha wear white robes and remove shoes, men are circumcised (a custom not practiced in Zulu society), polygyny is allowed, and members may not shake hands with outsiders, eat pork, or take alcohol or medicines. Isaiah Shembe composed over two hundred hymns which are sung by church members, some of which are accompanied by sacred dancing in African dress, and some of which are believed to have been written after his resurrection. Baptism by immersion, communion at night, and foot washing are practiced as sacraments, and the Sabbath is observed as well as the *hlonipha* (respectful avoidance) rules of the Zulu. The amaNazaretha have greatly influenced other Zulu AICs (especially Zionists) in rituals, and they represent a unique blend of Christianity with the best of Zulu culture.

Other South African AICs

The St. John Apostolic Faith Mission, known by its members simply as "St. John" was founded by former AFM worker Christina Nku in 1933. Members of this church prefer to regard themselves as "Apostolic" rather than "Zionist".[42] It is one of the largest and most prominent independent churches in the northern provinces of South Africa.[43] One of the most notable things about St. John is that it was founded by a woman— Christina Nku, known to her followers as Ma (Mother) Nku.[44] She was born in 1894 to a Dutch Reformed family, and as a young girl began to have the first of many revelations. At the age of twenty, she was seriously ill and had visions of heaven, in which God told her that she would not die, and she was to abstain from eating pork. Ten years later, after she had married Lazarus Nku, she had another time of illness when she had a vision of a large church with twelve doors and was told to follow the baptism of John and Jesus. She knew she had been called to build the church of her vision. She and her husband were baptized in the AFM in 1924, and became acquainted with le Roux, but it seems that she did not remain there long. She said that le Roux had objected to "some of her more elaborate displays of prophetic rapture". It is not clear whether this was the reason why Ma Nku left the AFM, or whether it was because she felt called to establish her own church, which she did in 1933. She had another vision in which she was shown the exact spot where she was to build the twelve-door church on white-owned land near Evaton, south of Johannesburg. She began to go to this site to pray, until eventually the area was set aside for black freehold housing and she could buy the site, a rare event at that time. Ma Nku was known as a person who spent many days in prayer, but above all, she became famous as a healer, and gathered thousands of people into her church. The name of her church, like that of the ZAFM of Edward Lion, showed her continuity with the AFM and the Pentecostal movement. But her practices, particularly her healing rituals, brought increasing distance between St. John and the white-led Pentecostals. She prayed over water in thousands of bottles and buckets, which received healing power to be used by the faithful. The church soon became popularly known as the *Chibini* Church ("Water Church").[45]

In the growth and development of St. John, Ma Nku was assisted by her husband, Bishop Lazarus Nku and Elias Ketsing, who Ma Nku had met in 1918 while he was a preacher in the

AFM. This was the time, according to her own account, when she was filled with the Spirit and spoke in tongues.[46] Ketsing died in 1948 and Lazarus Nku a year later, and Ma Nku began to rely increasingly on her son Johannes, whom she made a bishop and eventually gave the senior male position of Archbishop. The church in Evaton, known as the "Temple", was built sometime in the 1950s, for many years the largest AIC building in the enormous urban conglomerate around Johannesburg. Ma Nku took the title "Founder and Life General President" of the church but her grip on the church began to wane as she approached eighty years of age. The church was to elect the Archbishop in 1970, and Bishop John Nku (his mother's choice) and Bishop Petros John Masango were the two candidates. Masango won the election and Ma Nku thereupon announced that Masango would only occupy the office temporarily, and she would appoint another Archbishop the following year.[47] Masango announced that a conference would be held at the new headquarters of the church in his home area at Katlehong on the East Rand, and not, as was usual, at the "Temple" at Evaton. This was soon followed by the resignation of Johannes Nku, which elicited sharp criticism from his mother. Ma Nku announced that Masango would be expelled from the church, to which the bishop replied that he refused to obey an unconstitutional order, but would honour Ma Nku as the founder of the church. The differences between Ma Nku and Masango resulted in protracted litigation in the Supreme Court, the final ruling in March 1971 declaring Masango lawfully elected Archbishop of the church. Traditional patriarchism had prevailed.

St. John had some 50,000 members in the mid-seventies.[48] Masango remained Archbishop of the church until his death in 1984, by which time the church membership was over 100,000 throughout South Africa. Masango broke all ties with the Nku family and established himself as "founder" of the church, with his own special place for baptisms dedicated at Katlehong in 1983. After Masango's death there was a bitter struggle for control of the church between Masango's chosen successor Ben Nkosi, elected Archbishop in 1985, and Bishop Maraga, even resulting in armed conflict between the two factions.[49] Maraga's faction appeared to be in the majority by 1986. Christina Nku died in 1988. By 1992 it was not clear who the leader of St. John was, although Masango's son was continuing the leadership of the church with the help of advisors.[50]

The second church considered here, the International Pentecost Church (IPC),[51] was founded in Meadowlands, Soweto in 1964 by Frederick S. Modise, a former ZCC minister. It is today one of the largest AICs in the northern provinces, and the largest schism from the ZCC since the 1948 division between the Lekganyane brothers. At the time of writing, the IPC is in a time of transition, following the death of its founder in late 1998. It's not a "Pentecostal" church in the strict sense of the word (despite its name), and it's quite different from other AICs. In the first place, Modise declared that Saturday was the Sabbath Day, and the main activities of the church take place from Friday night throughout Saturday. The church has westernized the AIC movement, at least in the outward appearances of its members. Men dress in distinctive gray suits with maroon shirts, married women wear a maroon skirt and a gray blouse with a white *duku* (headscarf), white gloves and shoes, and girls wear maroon skirts with white gowns, gloves, and shoes. In the second place, Modise abandoned speaking in tongues, prophecy, and other manifestations of the Spirit associated with the Pentecostal and Zionist churches, and he was one of their most vocal critics. But nevertheless, there is a pronounced emphasis on the Spirit who is believed to have come upon Frederick Modise in a singular way, and on the gift of healing which operated through him. Modise's emergence from the ZCC is revealed in some continuity with this organization, despite several contrary characteristics. The system of church conferences at a sacred place, leadership pattern, polygyny, and the integration of African cultural values, baptism, the use of secret rules, and even the badge of the church, a *six*-point star (one more point) are all reminders of the ZCC.

The IPC is founded on Modise's healing powers and strong personality. Modise was one of the leading ZCC ministers in the Soweto area, a carpenter, and a wealthy undertaker. He had a leadership clash with Edward Legkanyane, who thought that the Soweto ZCC members were becoming too independent over their choice of choir uniforms. Modise left the ZCC, became seriously ill, and lost everything he had. He went to diviners and other healers, and then to medical doctors, but failed to find healing. After a year in Baragwanath hospital in Soweto, one day in September 1962, he believed that the voice of God told him to get up from the bed and proclaim healing, and that he would found a large church. He is reported to have healed seven people in the hospital and it was evident to him that God was now with him. He moved his headquarters from Meadowlands to Oskraal (a Tswana village near Pretoria) in 1970, where a large auditorium was built called "Jerusalem". Members from the church, particularly in those early years, testify to healing received through the hands of Modise, and the church grew rapidly. The IPC, like the ZCC, actively pursued good relationships with the National Party government in South Africa. In 1991, President de Klerk attended the opening of the new and impressive headquarters called "Silo" (Tswana term for the biblical Shiloh), west of Johannesburg.

The IPC appears to place great emphasis on the person and powers of the founder. Although God (in Sotho-Tswana languages, *Modimo*) is regarded as the *general* name for God—much like *Elohim* in the Old Testament—Modise had a "revelation" of the true name of God ("fire" or *mollo*) to which he claims exclusive knowledge. Members are not allowed to utter this name, except in the secret prayer that Modise has taught them to recite. This particular theology was frequent in Modise's preaching. His own entrance into the 10,000-seat auditorium at Silo was heralded by the lighting of a lamp, symbolic of this enigmatic knowledge of God. This appeared to give Modise a special revelation of God which is unlike that of any other Christian church, and which in fact placed him in a position of unequalled privilege among humankind. God is relegated to the periphery and becomes the mysterious, transcendent, somewhat remote being that he seems to be in traditional religion. Modise, however, as the human "Representative" (Tswana: *Moemedi*) of God takes over the functions of the ancestors in traditional religion, and some IPC members regard Modise as *Modimo* (God). Further studies may reveal how this has developed after his death in 1998, or whether the IPC has moved in a more biblical direction.[52]

The AICs in South Africa have formed ecumenical co-operative associations, some of which have floundered for various reasons, but others still exist. The African Independent Churches' Association, the oldest ecumenical AIC association, was launched in 1965 and by 1972, a year before its dissolution, it had 400 member churches. Internal wrangling, leadership disputes, and financial difficulties ended this achievement of unity. The Council of African Independent Churches emerged from its ashes and like its predecessor, is affiliated with the South African Council of Churches. Other umbrella organizations include the African Spiritual Churches Association, the Federal Council of Indigenous Churches, and the Christ the Rock Indigenous Churches Association. None of these councils includes the largest churches like the ZCC or the amaNazaretha. The fact that all attempts to bring a truly representative body of AICs together have largely failed says something about the highly fissiparous nature of the South African churches.[53]

In Swaziland, very close to the birthplace of South African Zionism, Zionists have been particularly proliferous. In 1939, King Sobhuza II himself was involved in various abortive attempts to create a national Swazi church, an amalgamation of all AICs in the kingdom, and he presided at regular Zionist church gatherings and arbitrated in church conflicts during the 1950s.[54] AICs in other parts of Southern Africa were also greatly influenced by developments in South Africa, from whence Ethiopian and Zionist ideas quickly spread to Lesotho, Botswana, Zimbabwe, Zambia, and Malawi,[55] mainly through migrant workers. Different types of AICs arose simultaneously in these countries, some of which were the same churches established in South Africa. But almost always, the mere geographical distance and communication difficulties coupled with personal leadership ambitions, eventually resulted in churches independent of the

South African churches.

Zionists in Zimbabwe

AICs in Zimbabwe were projected to constitute over 36% of the entire population in 2000, compared to only 24% for Catholics, Protestants, and Anglicans combined, a significant statistic.[56] They have been involved in Zimbabwean society for the past eighty years. They too have formed an ecumenical association called *Fambidzano* (African Independent Church Conference), which was set up in 1972 with the help of the most prolific author on AICs, Inus Daneel. In 1987 *Fambidzano* had some fifty member churches and a successful theological training by extension program.[57]

Zionist and Apostolic churches, arriving in Zimbabwe from about 1921 onwards, soon eclipsed Ethiopian AICs in size and influence. Both the Ethiopian and the Zionist churches were formed by migrant laborers returning from South Africa. The main "Ethiopian" churches in Zimbabwe were the First Ethiopian Church founded in 1910 by Mupambi Chidembo, followed by the African Congregational Church and in 1953, the African Reformed Church.[58] The Zionists were influenced by white Pentecostal missionaries, particularly from the AFM (which began here in 1915), but this influence was not as great as it was in South Africa.[59] The first Zionist church was the Christian Apostolic Church in Zion, planted in Matabeleland by migrants from Mabiletsa's church in South Africa. David Masuka joined the Zion Apostolic Church of South Africa (ZAC) of Elias Mahlangu in 1921, when he was working in Pietersburg, and he returned to be minister for the church in Zimbabwe in 1923.[60]

The ZCC is the most significant Zionist church in Zimbabwe and, like its South African counterpart, is distinguished from other Zionists by khaki uniforms. The *ndaza* (sacred cord) Zionists wear white or multicolored robes tied with cords. The ZAC of Masuka was one of the first of these among the Mashona.

Like many other Zionist churches, the ZAC experienced schism after schism from 1930 onwards, starting with the Sabbath Zion Church, the Zion Protestant Church, the Zion Apostolic City (to mention but three), and several other schisms retaining the name "Zion Apostolic Church". In contrast, the ZAFM under the flexible and highly respected Andreas Shoko, one of the first Zionist leaders, managed to avoid any further serious schisms after Mutendi left the church with Lekganyane to form the ZCC.[61]

The ZCC in Zimbabwe existed separately from the South African church under the leadership of Samuel Mutendi (c.1898-1976). A Dutch Reformed Church member, Mutendi had the first of a series of dreams in 1919 revealing that he would start an African church, and he received the power of the Spirit. The ZCC is careful to point out that this revelation was before he met the ZAFM in Pretoria. Engenas Lekganyane baptized him in Pretoria in 1923 and the Spirit again entered him. He was commissioned as the ZAFM's missionary to Zimbabwe and he returned home, contacted Masuka of the ZAC, who accompanied him on his first preaching tours. At first, Mutendi traveled on foot from village to village, baptizing new converts, who would often accompany him on his tours, singing, dancing, and testifying. In 1925, Lekganyane called Mutendi and other Zionist leaders to Pretoria, where the ZCC was organized. Mutendi was the only Zimbabwean leader who joined the new church, and Lekganyane ordained him as minister. Mutendi modeled the new Zimbabwean church on the ZCC in South Africa, and remained loyal to Lekganyane until his death in 1948. Thereafter, the two ZCC churches had less contact. Although Edward Lekganyane managed to visit Mutendi in 1953, this was the last time they met and Mutendi felt no particular allegiance to the younger Edward. The ZCC in Zimbabwe thus became fully autonomous. The same process of gradual independence after the death of the South African founder happened to the ZAFM and the ZAC in Zimbabwe.

Mutendi was credited with several miraculous powers, including healing, exorcism, bringing fertility to barren women, rainmaking, and raising the dead. The ZCC had thirteen schisms between 1929 and 1961, but none succeeded in drawing away large numbers.[62] The most serious schism occurred after Mutendi's death in 1976. A succession struggle between his sons Ruben (the oldest) and Nehemiah resulted from uncertainty as to which of them Mutendi had appointed. Both sons claimed that they had been chosen, confirmed by dreams in which their father had appeared to them. The result was almost a carbon copy of the events in the South African ZCC three decades earlier. Two separate ZCC churches were formed, Ruben with the smaller but rapidly growing faction of 40-50,000 members in 1987, and Nehemiah, who had received the support of most of the senior ministers, with over 200,000 members.[63]

African Apostles in Zimbabwe

The largest AIC and the second or third largest denomination in Zimbabwe, is the African Apostolic Church of Johane Marange[64] (AACJM), known as *Vapostori,* estimated at almost one million affiliates in Zimbabwe in 1999,[65] with thousands more in countries further north. The Vapostori has more affinity with Pentecostalism than most other AICs in Zimbabwe. Some early Pentecostal (AFM) preachers in Zimbabwe wore white robes, carried staffs, shaved their heads, and grew beards, and taught Old Testament laws—characteristics of both the South African non-ZCC Zionists and of the African Apostles in Zimbabwe that came afterwards. AFM leaders had early contact with Marange, Masowe, and other African Apostolic leaders.[66] Johane (John) Marange (1912-63), grandson of a chief, received frequent dreams and visions from the time he was six years old. In 1932 an audible voice told him he was "John the Baptist, an Apostle" called to preach internationally and convert people, baptize them, and to tell them to keep the Old Testament laws and the seventh-day Sabbath. He spoke in tongues, was given further ecstatic manifestations of the Spirit, and he founded the AACJM on the basis of these revelations. In July 1932 the first mass baptism of 150 people in the Marange chiefdom took place. Marange in thirty years preached as far as Mozambique, Zambia, Malawi, and central Congo, exorcising evil spirits and baptizing thousands of people, commanding them to renounce traditional ritual practices and witchcraft. Abero (Abel) Marange, Johane's son and successor, held a *Pendi* (or "Pentecost" festival) in the southern Congo in 1964 attended by 10,000 people, but this was only one part of a deeply divided AACJM region.[67] The AACJM has few rivals among AICs for missionary zeal, spreading to many parts of central and southern Africa, as far as Uganda and even Ghana. Although members may make annual pilgrimages to the Marange chiefdom for the main festival of the AACJM in July, the centripetal nature of an African Zion is not emphasized as it is in Zionist churches.[68]

A unique feature of this church is that it employs the widespread setting up of hundreds of *Pendi* (Pentecost) centers. At each local *Pendi,* annual festivals are held in which the church leaders minister and give the sacraments to several congregations gathered together from that district. The AACJM also has a canonical addition to the Bible containing the visions and personal experiences of Marange, called *The New Revelation of the Apostles.* Apart from the characteristic open-air mass services, shaved heads, beards, staffs, and white robes that all Marange apostles wear, the AACJM also practices night vigils known as *mapungwe,* a practice that has become a feature of many types of grassroots Christianity in Zimbabwe. In the *pungwe,* the AACJM practises rituals that involve walking on fire and picking up burning embers with bare hands, symbolizing the power of the Spirit at the end of the world. Sometimes, Marange is praised and sung to as "the king of heaven", but he is not regarded as superseding Christ.[69] When Marange died in 1963, a schism occurred between his sons and his cousin, his eldest son Abero succeeding him as Priest, the name given to the paramount leader of this church. Johane's cousin, Prophet Simon Mushati, one of the first Vapostori who had assisted Johane on *Pendi* rounds, began a new church called the African Apostolic Church, St. Simon and St. Johane.[70]

At the same time that Marange established his church, another enigmatic Shona prophet, Johane (John) Masowe ("wilderness" or "open place"), formerly Shoniwa (c.1915-73), started the Apostolic Sabbath Church of God, known in Shona as *Vahosanna*, after the frequent calling out of the word by members in church gatherings. He had been a preacher in the AFM in 1930, but separated himself from this church soon afterwards. He fell sick and dreamt that he had died and risen again as the "Messenger of God", a "John the Baptist" figure like Marange. He was convinced that he had been sent from heaven to preach to African people. He began to preach that people must leave witchcraft and adultery, destroy all religious books (including the Bible, a restriction that was later lifted), and shun all inventions of the whites. His followers should not carry identification documents, plough their lands, or work for the whites. The biblical prophets would descend from heaven and drive the whites out of the country.[71] He was restricted to his home district and was imprisoned for failing to obey the restriction order. His followers organized themselves into a closed religious community that moved from Zimbabwe in the early 1940s to South Africa, eventually settling in Port Elizabeth in 1947. There they lived in a deprived community of about a thousand in the slum area of Korsten. The community engaged in various crafts and industries, including basket making, and they were known as the Korsten Basket-makers. When their company went into liquidation, they began to use the name African Gospel Church, the name of an African Pentecostal church in South Africa.[72] They were declared illegal residents in South Africa under the draconian laws regarding residence and 1,880 people were repatriated in 1962 to Zimbabwe. Masowe told his people that they were Jews who must return to Israel and in 1963, some of the Vahosanna began a migration from Zimbabwe, reaching Lusaka in Zambia. Masowe continued to travel and make converts throughout Zambia and in Kenya, Tanzania, Mozambique, and the Congo. Only Masowe himself could perform baptisms, but his illness in 1964 left him a recluse in Tanzania for the rest of his life. In 1972 the name of the church was again changed to "Gospel of God Church". Increasing importance was given to a group of nuns, the "wives" of Masowe or the "Sisters", who would be part of the headquarters, remain celibate, function as ritual singers, and move with the people of God as a guarantee of God's presence and power among them. They constituted the "ark of the covenant" and the "new Jerusalem". By 1975 there were over a hundred Sisters; most were in Lusaka, but moving to Nairobi. Masowe died in Zambia after a long illness in 1973, planning the next stage of the journey to Kenya, and he was buried at his home in Zimbabwe. Many of the Masowe Apostles and the Sisters have been in Nairobi since 1972. There were claims of half a million Masowe Apostles in 1975 scattered from South Africa to Kenya.[73]

There are many other AICs in Zimbabwe, none perhaps as controversial as the City of Jehovah (*Guta raJehova*) movement, also called the "Mai Chaza Church", and founded in 1955 by Mai (Mother) Chaza. She was a Methodist who became ill and was divorced from her husband in 1953. She claimed to have been resurrected from the dead, and in revelations on mountains she was called to live a celibate life and preach healing, especially to barren women. Her fame as a healer spread, and people came to her for healing from all over Zimbabwe and other countries in Southern Africa. She referred to herself as the "Messenger" of God, but her followers gave her the messianic titles "Savior" and "Lamb", and saw her as an African reappearance of Christ. Healing centers were established in various parts of Zimbabwe, called "Cities of Jehovah". Members of this church, both men and women, wear khaki tunics and shorts with red belts, a radical break with custom for African women, and monogamy is enjoined. A book of revelation called the *Guta raJehova Bible*, in which Mai Chaza's words and deeds are recorded, has replaced the New Testament and she is depicted as a member of the Trinity. Mai Chaza died in 1960 and after a minor secession, her spirit was believed to have entered a Malawian man, Mapaulos, who became known as Vamatenga ("someone from heaven"). Like Mai Chaza, Vamatenga was believed to be an incarnation of God, but he did not have the same influence as Mai Chaza. The movement was estimated to have some 60,000 members by

2000.[74]

Exotic movements like these notwithstanding, the fact is that a religious revolution, an African reformation, has been going on in Southern Africa for many years, and Christianity has been irrevocably changed in this process. It no longer makes sense to speak of AICs and Pentecostal churches in this region as "sects" and European mission-founded churches as "mainline". The reverse might now be more appropriate here. Nowhere is this fundamental change as demonstrably illustrated as in Southern Africa.

Notes

1 Sipho Tshelane, "The Witness of the African Indigenous Churches in South Africa", *International Review of Mission* 83: 328, January 1994 (177), suggests that in 1976 there were over ten thousand AICs in South Africa.

2 Allan Anderson, "The Lekganyanes and Prophecy in the Zion Christian Church". *Journal of Religion in Africa*, 29:2, August 1999; Anderson, *Zion and Pentecost*, 33; Anderson & Otwang, 7-8; Pretorius & Jafta, 211-2; West, 2.

3 Comaroff, 166, 254, 261.

4 The word "Apostolic" was dropped to distinguish it from the new Pentecostal movement, at first called the "Apostolic Faith".

5 Sundkler, *Zulu Zion*, 16-28, 66.

6 *Leaves of Healing* 15:25, 8 October 1904, 853; Anderson, *Bazalwane*, 20.

7 Sundkler, *Zulu Zion*, 46-52.

8 Sundkler, *Zulu Zion*, 51; Anderson, *Bazalwane*, 4; Hollenweger, 151; Cox, 246.

9 Sundkler, *Bantu Prophets*, 48; Anderson, *Bazalwane*, 22, 32-5; id., *Zion and Pentecost*, 96-110.

[10] Sundkler, *Zulu Zion*, 55-6, n54; Pretorius & Jafta, 218. *Leaves of Healing*, 8 October 1904, 855 refers to Nkonyane's "home and church located on several acres of ground" and that Nkonyane had raised "among the Zulus... the most of five hundred and ninety dollars, to pay for seventy acres of land and to erect upon it another house of worship". The "three hundred acres" in the Utrecht district of Natal is referred to in Nkonyane's report in *Leaves of Healing*, 30 December 1905, 320.

[11] Daneel, *Old and New 1*, 300; Sundkler, *Zulu Zion*, 65-6.

[12] Sundkler, *Bantu Prophets*, 49; Makhubu, 11.

[13] Sundkler, *Zulu Zion*, 50-1.

[14] Anderson, *Bazalwane*, 27-8.

[15] E.K. Lukhaimane, "The Zion Christian Church of Ignatius (Engenas) Lekganyane, 1924 to 1948: an African experiment with Christianity", Pietersburg, 1980, 9; Christof Hanekom, *Krisis en Cultus*, Pretoria, 1975, 39; Anderson, "The Legkanyanes".

[16] Lukhaimane, 14-7.

[17] G. H. Haliburton, "Edward Lion of Lesotho", *Mahlomi, Journal of Southern African Historical Studies* I, 1976, pp. 64-70.   It is not known whether Lekganyane knew of the allegations of immorality against Edward Lion at this time, or whether they played any role in this schism.

[18] Lukhaimane, 18, 20.

[19] Joan Millard, "The Bulhoek Tragedy", *Missionalia* 25:3, November 1997, 418, 426; Pretorius & Jafta, 218-9.

[20] Lukhaimane, 62-5.

[21] Anderson & Otwang, 78-80.

[22] Lukhaimane, 41, 62, 65-7, 72-6.

[23] See, for an example of this charge, Marie-Louise Martin, *The Biblical Concept of Messianism and Messianism in Southern Africa*, Morija, 1964, 131.

[24] Quoted in Hanekom, 44.

[25] Reported in *baNtu* 12 (6), June 1965, 239.

[26] *The Guardian*, London, 21 April 1987.

[27] Makhubu, 15.

[28] Matthew Schoffeleers, "Ritual Healing and Political Acquiescence: The Case of the Zionist Churches in Southern Africa", *Africa* 60 (1), 1991, 3.

29 *The ZCC Messenger 5*, 1986.

30 *The ZCC Messenger* 22, 1992, 6.

31 Schoffeleers, 3, 5.

32 Anderson & Otwang, 59, 64; for a full treatment of the ZCC, see Anderson, "The Lekganyanes".

33 "AmaNazaretha" is Zulu for "the Nazarenes" (sometimes referred to as "the Nazarites"), and "Isonto lamaNazaretha" is "the Church of the Nazarenes/ Nazarites".

34 Hexham & Oosthuizen, 22-6, 33-4; Sundkler, *Bantu Prophets*, 110-1.

35 Carmel Rickard, "The strange death of the messiah's kindly grandson", *Weekly Mail*, Johannesburg, 14 April 1989, 13; Musa Ndwandwe, "Zulu traditions and Christian beliefs in the Shembe Church", *Challenge* 34, Johannesburg, 1996, 24-6.

36 Sundkler, *Bantu Prophets*, 114; G.C. Oosthuizen, *Post Christianity in Africa*, London, 1968; id., *The Theology of a South African Messiah*, London, 1967.

37 Sundkler, *Bantu Prophets*, 159, 283-4, 328-30.

38 Ibid, 114, 281-8.

39 Ibid., 297. On Sundkler's retraction, see especially *Zulu Zion*, 190-205.

40 Oosthuizen, *Post Christianity*, xi.

41 Hexham & Oosthuizen, 133, 168-9,190-2.

42 Anderson, *Zion and Pentecost*, 45-6, 72-4.

43 West, 65.

44 Sundkler gives an outline of her career. *Zulu Zion*, 79-82.

45 Hans-Jürgen Becken, "Die Wasserkirche — St John's Apostolic Faith Mission", in *Neue Zeitschrift für Missionswissenschaft*, 42(2), 1986, 91-2. Becken explains that the word in Zulu signifies an extent of water, and refers to the importance of water in the rituals of the church.

46 Ibid, 92.

47 West, 66.

48 Sundkler, *Zulu Zion*, 82.

49 Becken, 91, 97-8, 101.

[50] Ma Nku's daughter, Dr Lydia August, told me in January 1997 (she died later that year) that the church was now reunited. There are several splits from St. John in existence today, one of which is called St. Christinah Apostolic Faith Mission after the founder.

[51] Also called the International Pentecost Holiness Church, almost no written information was available on this church until *Bazalwane* (Anderson, 109-14) was published. The information in this section was gleaned through personal research and an interview with Frederick Modise in May 1992.

[52] Allan Anderson, "Frederick Modise and the International Pentecost Church: an African messiah?". *Missionalia* 20:3, November 1992 (186-200).

[53] West, 142-70; Pretorius & Jafta, 220.

[54] Sundkler, *Zulu Zion,* 223-238.

[55] For simplicity's sake, the post-independence names for these countries will be used here and elsewhere in this book, even though these names were not used during this colonial era. Northern Rhodesia and Nyasaland became Zambia and Malawi in 1964, Bechuanaland and Basutoland became Botswana and Lesotho in 1966, and (Southern) Rhodesia became Zimbabwe in 1980. Swaziland did not change its name after independence in 1968.

[56] Titus L. Presler, *Transformed Night: Mission and Culture in Zimbabwe's Vigil Movement,* Pretoria, 1999, 289.

[57] M.L. Daneel, *Fambidzano: Ecumenical Movement of Zimbabwean Independent Churches,* Gweru, 1989; id., *Quest,* 211-3; Pobee & Ositelu, 57.

[58] Daneel, *Old & New 1,* 369-70.

[59] David Maxwell, "Rethinking Christian Independency: The Southern African Pentecostal Movement ca. 1908-1960" (1997), traces the links between the AFM and AICs in Zimbabwe and is dealt with in a forthcoming book. on the history of Zimbabwean Pentecostalism.

[60] Daneel, *Old & New 1,* 286, 288-9.

[61] Ibid., 302-10.

[62] Ibid., 289-301, 310.

[63] Daneel, *Old & New 3,* 268-98.

[64] "Marange" is sometimes spelt "Maranke".

[65] Presler, 161, 290. The Roman Catholics have about 30,000 more affiliates than the AACJM, but the Zimbabwe Assemblies of God Africa (ZAOGA), established in 1967, an independent Pentecostal church, was reckoned to be the largest denomination by 1990. See David Maxwell, *Christians and Chiefs in Zimbabwe: A Social History of the Hwesa People c.1870s-1990s*, Edinburgh, 1999, 192.

[66] Maxwell, "Rethinking", 30-1.

[67] Benetta Jules-Rosette, "Prophecy and Leadership in the Maranke Church", 125.

[68] Bond, G. et. al. (eds.), *African Christianity: Patterns of Religious Continuity*, New York, 1979 (109-36).

[69] Presler, 157, 163-79.

[70] Daneel, *Old & New I*, 315-39.

[71] Clive M. Dillon-Malone, *The Korsten Basketmakers: A study of the Masowe Apostles, an indigenous African religious movement*, Manchester, 1978, 12-3; Clive Kileff & Margaret Kileff, "The Masowe Vapostori of Seki: Utopianism and Tradition in an African Church", Norwood, 1979, 153; Maxwell, "Rethinking", 30.

[72] Masowe is alleged to have promised his followers that they would never die, and that he was the Son of God. For this reason, Sundkler calls him a "Messiah" (Sundkler, *Bantu Prophets*, 325; Kileff & Kileff, 153).

[73] Dillon-Malone, 28-44. Many Masowe Apostles were deported from Kenya following disturbances in the community and tension with Kenyans in the 1990s.

[74] Presler, 290; Marie-Louise Martin, "The Mai Chaza Church in Rhodesia", Nairobi, 1971, 109-21; Daneel, *Quest*, 252.

6

CENTRAL AFRICAN CHURCHES

Central Africa is a vast area, and in this chapter we will be concentrating on the countries immediately to the north of the Zambezi River, particularly the Congo (Kinshasa) and Zambia. Those who live here are predominantly Bantu speaking peoples, one of the greatest families of languages in Africa. The largest concentration of AICs in this region is in the Congo River Basin, where the most numerous of all AIC movements began, starting with one of Africa's greatest prophets, Simon Kimbangu.

Simon Kimbangu and Kimbanguism

The largest AIC in Africa, with an estimated seven million members in 1996,[1] is the "Church of Jesus Christ on Earth by the Prophet Simon Kimbangu" (EJCSK),[2] or the Kimbanguist Church. Simon Kimbangu (c.1887-1951), a Kongo baptized in the Baptist Missionary Society (BMS) in 1915, was born in the village of Nkamba in western Congo. During the influenza epidemic of 1918 he had a dream in which a voice called him to special service. The BMS, however, wouldn't make him an evangelist because they said he couldn't read well enough. For a while he was a lay preacher, but he went to find work in Leopoldville (Kinshasa) for a short while. He returned to Nkamba and on April 6, 1921, taken as the founding date of the church, he was reported to have performed the miraculous healing of a paralyzed woman, a blind man, a deaf man, and a crippled girl, the first of many reported miracles. His fame spread and thousands flocked to Nkamba (later to be called "Nkamba-Jerusalem") to be healed and to experience this revival for themselves. Ever increasing reports of miracles at the hand of Kimbangu included the raising to life of a child three days dead. It was believed that a new African Pentecost had come. Kimbangu was the chosen instrument of the Holy Spirit that had been poured out, not in some distant foreign land, but right in the heart of Africa. Kimbangu preached against fetishes and proclaimed trust in God, moral chastity, monogamy, loving one's enemies, and obedience to government authority. Within a few weeks, prophets appeared throughout the region, and Kimbangu declared most of them to be "false prophets" possessed by a "demon". Protestant churches began to fill and although missionaries were skeptical about Kimbangu and the other prophets, a BMS missionary enthused that this was "the most remarkable movement which the country has ever seen".[3]

In spite of Kimbangu's peaceful message, the local Belgian colonial administrator Morel, after a visit to Nkamba, reported that it was "necessary to oppose Kimbangu since he has a tendency towards pan-Africanism".[4] Agriculture and industry had ground to a halt as a result of crowds flocking to Nkamba, Catholic churches were becoming deserted, and the movement was regarded as anti-colonial. Morel was ordered to arrest Kimbangu in June and Nkamba was plundered by soldiers. Many of Kimbangu's supporters (including Baptist deacons) were imprisoned, but the prophet himself managed to escape. Less than two months after the beginning of the revival, Kimbangu was forced to go underground. The movement continued to grow, and in August 1921 a state of emergency in the region with military occupation was declared. Morel reported the arrest of a hundred prophets in the area. Stories abounded about Kimbangu's miraculous escapes from arrest until he, following Christ's example, gave himself up voluntarily to the police in September. On October 3, 1921, after a trial before a three-man military tribunal without the opportunity of defense, Kimbangu was found guilty of sedition and hostility towards whites, and sentenced to 120 lashes and the death penalty. Catholic missionaries had apparently agreed with the death sentence, but pleas for mercy made by the Baptists through their missionary Jennings to the Belgian king resulted in Kimbangu's sentence being commuted to life imprisonment, after he had received the 120 lashes in Leopoldville. He was taken to prison in Elizabethville (Lubumbashi), 2,000 kilometers from his home, to be put in solitary confinement. He was never released, his family was never allowed to visit him (nor was any Protestant minister), and he died in prison thirty years later, on October 12, 1951. Catholic sources said that he became a Catholic before his death, but it is unlikely that this "conversion" was voluntary, if at all it occurred. Kimbangu was seen as an African nationalist martyr, and rumors were rife that he had risen from the dead and had appeared to give specific instructions to his followers in detention.[5]

Kimbangu had not started a church and had a public ministry of only five months. In spite of his imprisonment and eventual death, his followers, forced underground, continued to increase. Kimbangu was now a national hero and his wife, Muile Marie, became the leader of the underground Kimbanguist movement until her death in 1959. The colonial authorities, supported by European missions, persecuted Kimbanguists everywhere. They were imprisoned, exiled and restricted— about 150,000 Kimbanguists were deported during the period 1921-57. Deportations actually helped the movement spread across the entire Congo and become a multiethnic national movement. The Kimbanguists held a demonstration in Leopoldville in 1955 against their persecution, and the following year appealed to the

United Nations. They did not organize themselves into a denomination until 1956, and the EJCSK was only formally constituted in 1961. In 1957, a deputation of leading Kimbanguists went to the Belgian governor-general with a petition asking for the persecution to stop, and the way was paved for formal recognition.[6] The church formed a catechism in 1957, which followed Protestant catechisms for the most part, in which Kimbangu was declared to be the "envoy of our Lord Jesus Christ" and to have "died and rose again and is with us in the spirit".[7] In December 1959, six months before independence, the EJCSK was given official recognition. The three sons of Kimbangu became the leaders of the church, with the youngest son Joseph Diangienda (1918-93) head of the church as "Legal Representative", and his elder brother Salomon Dialungana Kiangani (b.1917) keeper of the holy city, Nkamba-Jerusalem. The church tried to show itself to be more respectable and rid itself of all Ngunzism (explained below) and other radical influences. Among its strict ethical codes it forbade polygamy, violence, alcohol, tobacco, cannabis, and the eating of pork. Shoes are removed in places of worship and women are expected to wear head coverings, although women are also able to become pastors and perform the sacraments. After independence the church grew rapidly, but failed in its attempt to unite all the disparate Kimbanguists into a single national church. In 1960 Simon Kimbangu's remains were reinterred at Nkamba-Jerusalem and a mausoleum was built in his honor, now a place of pilgrimage. The pool at Nkamba, called Bethesda, where Kimbangu used to send the sick to bathe, is regarded as holy water and used in rituals all over central Africa, sprinkled and drunk for healing, purification, and protection. The prison estate in Lubumbashi, where Kimbangu spent the last thirty years of his life, has been purchased by the EJCSK as a holy place. The church has spread to neighboring countries and in the aftermath of the "Lumpa rising" of 1964, the church was banned in Zambia.[8]

Kimbangu himself was seen by his followers as an African example of the essence of Christianity, or what Daneel calls a "concretization of the biblical message".[9] His surrender to the authorities in 1921 was his Gethsemane, and his innocent suffering was following in the steps of Christ. As Jesus healed the sick and raised the dead, so did Kimbangu. People see in Kimbangu an African expression of Jesus Christ, "a re-enactment of the life and suffering of Christ".[10] EJCSK leaders will point out that Kimbangu was no more than an apostle and an ambassador, and was not considered to be Christ. Sometimes Kimbanguists "pray" to Simon Kimbangu or sing to him, as a messenger of God who has brought a message from Christ and bears the people's prayers before him. They also believe that he will return to earth and sit in judgment with Christ. He appears in dreams and visions to his followers and in at least one of the older Kimbanguist documents, Kimbangu was said to have been "from the beginning with God". He is regarded as the first African to have received the Holy Spirit in fullness and some observers say he is referred to as the visible Holy Spirit given to Africa.[11] With regard to rituals, EJCSK members, unlike most other AICs, do not wear special clothes and do not use water in baptism. Baptism is administered to people who have decided for themselves whether they want to be Christians, and they are then baptized "by the Spirit" by laying on hands, the only form of baptism recognized by Kimbanguists. A multitude of 350,000 Kimbanguists held their first Communion service at Nkamba on April 6, 1971, fifty years after Kimbangu began his public ministry and, it was said, in obedience to his post-resurrection command. The bread was made from potatoes and eggs, and the wine from honey and water. Two months before this occasion, Joseph Diangienda "sealed" thousands of members in the Lower Congo with a "special blessing", the sign of the cross. The Eucharist is now celebrated three times a year by the EJCSK, at Christmas and on April 6 (the founding date of the church) and October 12 (the date of Kimbangu's death). Pilgrimages to Nkamba are encouraged, where pilgrims dip themselves three times in the spring, and take water and soil from Nkamba to their homes.

Several secessions from the EJCSK occurred during the 1960s, but President Mobutu's severe repression and tougher laws regarding the registration of churches discouraged these. In 1966 an EJCSK building seating 3,000 was erected in Kinshasa and later a temple was built at Nkamba. By 1968 there were 93,600 children in EJCSK schools, and clinics, agricultural settlements, brickyards, and many other successful enterprises were established. In 1969 the EJCSK was admitted to the World Council of Churches and was soon afterwards declared by President Mobuto to be one of three recognized churches in the Congo, the largest after the Catholics.[12] Many began to see the EJCSK as a collaborator with an oppressive regime, and the growth of the church may have declined in the 1980s. Nevertheless, Diangienda established the EJCSK to be by far the largest AIC in Africa. He died in 1993, and was succeeded as the head of the church by his elder brother Dialungana, in what appears to be a period of transition.[13]

Ngunzi Movements

At the same time that Kimbanguism was developing, an alternative Kimbanguist movement known as Ngunzism (from the Kikongo *ngunza,* "prophet") began to appear. This movement, like some of the Harrist movements in West Africa, went much further than Kimbangu had intended, seeing Kimbangu as a political figure, a black Messiah who would dramatically return from prison and destroy the colonialists with a holy war. Some said he would restore the ancient Kongo Empire. André Matswa founded the Amical Balali movement for the liberation of the French Congo (Brazzaville) in 1926. His movement known as Amicalism was at first a movement for political liberation. Matswa was imprisoned in 1930, where he remained until his death in 1942. He, like Kimbangu before him, was transformed by his followers into a religious figure, a savior and messiah who would come back to free his people from oppression and restore the old Kongo Empire. According to Martin, who herself became a Kimbanguist, the Bible was neglected by Ngunzists, magical elements were introduced, and for some, Kimbangu had become the "God of the blacks". Many legends about miracles surrounding Kimbangu after his arrest were propagated. Borrowing elements from the Salvation Army, which had arrived in the Congo in 1934, several Ngunzist groups were formed, including the independent Congolese Salvation Army. The "S" on Salvation Army uniforms was believed to refer to Simon, and their white commander was seen as a reappearance of Kimbangu.[14]

Simon-Pierre Mpadi, who trained as a Salvation Army officer, founded the "Mission of the Blacks" in 1939, the best-known of the Ngunzi movements. The colonial authorities saw all these groups as belonging to one Kimbanguist movement and they sought to destroy them—even though the Kimbanguists and Kimbangu himself had repudiated the views of Ngunzism. Mpadi's movement was even more powerful, known as Mpadism or the Khaki movement, after the khaki uniforms worn by his followers. Mpadi became the second and "greater" prophet of this Congolese church, and he built on the traditions surrounding Kimbangu and Matswa. He tried to unite various Ngunzist groups and succeeded in bringing Amicalism into his movement after Matswa's death. Mpadi himself was arrested in 1949 and imprisoned in the same prison as Kimbangu, and during that time his followers formed one of the most influential churches in the Congo. A decree on Christmas Eve 1959 by the colonial administration gave recognition to the existence of religious "sects". On his release from prison in 1960, when a general amnesty was given to African prophets in preparation for independence, Mpadi refused to join the Kimbanguists when invited to do so. He reorganized his "Mission of the Blacks" as the "Church of the Blacks and Africa". He said that Kimbangu's sons had been to the whites' schools and had been educated in the witchcraft of the whites, and that the Catholic clergy had killed off the prophetic succession. He declared that Kimbangu had appointed him, Mpadi, head of the Kimbanguist church. In contrast to the EJCSK, Mpadi's church made polygyny compulsory and encouraged dancing, drumming, and displays of ecstasy. Mpadi was a messiah-like figure who wore a red gown with a crown and a scepter and claimed to have been resurrected fourteen times.[15]

Relationships between the prophetic churches and the government in the Congo (Kinshasa) were strained. In 1971 President Mobutu forced the consolidation of most of the churches in the country by declaring an approved list of only six churches, one of which was the EJCSK. Even harsher laws were imposed in 1979, severely curtailing the activities of any unregistered religious groups. Several significant AICs had to seek and obtain registration by affiliating with the Église du Christ au Congo (Church of Christ in the Congo), the recognized Protestant ecumenical council.[16] The Ngunzist movement differs from the EJCSK in several ways. Unlike the latter, this is a heterogeneous movement largely in the western Congo Basin, consisting mostly of small, unorganized groups loyal to a local prophet. Christian hymns, prayers, and the Bible are of secondary importance, and the main emphasis is on "organized quaking" and the beating of drums, accompanied by collective ecstasy, shrieking, and trance, which manifestations are believed to be possession by the Holy Spirit. Although many of these ecstatic manifestations were found in the ministry of Kimbangu, the EJCSK later discouraged any excessive emotionalism. Traditional African rituals and customs including polygyny are usually promoted in the Ngunzist movement.

A recent addition to the religious movements emanating from Kimbanguism, perhaps a modern Ngunzi movement, is the "Bundu dia Kongo" ("Kongo Church"), founded in 1986 by "Ne Muanda Nsemi" ("the creative Spirit"), originally a chemist, Badiengisa Zakalia. Ne Muanda Nsemi, who began having revelations in 1969, declared himself solidly in the tradition of the great Kongo prophets (*ngunza)* Kimpa Vita, Simon Kimbangu, Matswa, and Mpadi. He had come to complete their work, namely, the restoration of Kongo religion and culture and ultimately, of the Kongo Kingdom itself. In order to achieve this he has written a sacred book, *Makongo,* published in 1992, and he espouses a Kongo Trinity and a sacred city, the ancient capital Mbanza Kongo in northern Angola. Like Mpadi, Nsemi says that the EJCSK has concealed the true message of Kimbangu. This ethnically based movement was said to have 50,000 members by 1994.[17] Religious groups like this begin as movements of cultural and religious renaissance, others as political and anti-white protest movements, but most have made use of the mystique associated with the name of one of Africa's greatest prophets, Simon Kimbangu.

Other Central African Churches

In 1900, John Chilembwe founded one of the first AICs in Central Africa, the Providence Industrial Mission near Blantyre, Malawi, although this church was not an AIC in the strict sense of the word as it had the involvement of African-American Baptist missionaries until 1906. Chilembwe's slogan of "Africa for the Africans" and the uprising of 1915 concerning compulsory drafting into the war by the colonial authorities resulted in his death. Thereafter, there was severe repression by the British colonial government on AIC movements, although Chilembwe's church was revived in 1926 and has became a respected church in Malawi.[18] There are many other AICs in Central Africa, including the "Mutumwa" ("Apostle") and the "Nchimi" ("Diviner, Healer") churches in Zambia, significant spiritual healing movements that began in the witch-finding movement in north-east Zambia in the 1930s. The churches' healers diagnose witchcraft as the most common cause of sickness, which in the case of the Mutumwa churches is to be removed by the power of the Holy Spirit through prayer and exorcism, and in the case of Nchimi churches, by the additional use of traditional herbal medicines. These churches were registered as churches in Zambia in the 1970s.[19]

A significant early AIC in Zambia and Malawi was the Watch Tower Society, called in the local languages "Kitawala" and based on Jehovah Witnesses' publications, but independent of that movement. This church was possibly associated with the movement founded in 1908 by Elliot Kamwana Chirwa, a Tonga from Malawi, and it may have been connected with Chilembwe's uprising in 1915. Kamwana returned to Malawi from South Africa as a Watch Tower preacher in 1908 (having met preachers from the movement there), and he baptized 9,000 people in six months, saying that Christ would come in 1914 and chase away the whites. He was arrested and exiled to South Africa and the Seychelles for twenty years, to reappear in Malawi but no longer as a Watch Tower preacher. His movement spread to Zambia in about 1913. Prolonged conflict thereafter with both the colonial and the post-colonial governments resulted from their refusal to register as voters, join UNIP, or honor national symbols. Some of the Watch Tower preachers, of which the best-known was Tomo Nyirenda (also from Malawi), became notorious witch-eradicators. Nyirenda became known as "Mwana Lesa" ("son of God"), and was hanged in 1926 for drowning 22 suspected witches during baptisms by immersion. The Watch Tower movement in Zambia had an ideology that was fundamentally anti-colonial, teaching that the white colonizers had unjustly deprived the Africans of their wealth and freedom, treating them as slaves. It was also a protest against traditional authority, and it appealed particularly to migrant workers in Zambia's Copperbelt, but also to peasant agriculturists. Most of the African Watch Tower movement affiliated from about 1936 with the Jehovah's Witnesses, from whom they had received their initial inspiration. White missionaries from South Africa were sent to oversee the movement, and they have become one of the largest religious groups in Zambia, with the highest percentage of Jehovah Witnesses in any country in the world.[20]

An important secession from the Watch Tower movement was the Last Church of God and his Christ, founded by Jordan Msumba in Malawi in 1924. Msumba had accompanied Kamwana to South Africa, but had been expelled from the Watch Tower church the previous year because of his polygyny. His new church sought to combine Christian and African traditional practices and it spread across the border to Tanzania.[21] The Zionist movement also came to Malawi from South Africa and Zimbabwe, first in 1923, when the Christian Catholic Apostolic Church in Zion was introduced, followed by a number of other Zionist and Apostolic churches. AICs have proliferated in Malawi since independence, and there are now estimated to be over three hundred in this country.[22]

In northern Angola, several Kimbanguist movements started after the prophet's arrest in 1921. The first significant AIC began there under the prophet and former Baptist teacher and choirmaster Simâo Toco (1918-84), the Church of our Lord Jesus Christ in the World, also known as the "Red Star" after the church's symbol. This movement started in 1949 in the western Congo in a decisive Pentecost of its own, with trembling and speaking in tongues. Toco was arrested by Belgian officials and handed over to the Portuguese government at the Angolan border in 1950, together with 82 Angolan followers. The movement was severely repressed, but had 10,000 adherents by 1965 and had become multiethnic, thanks to the Portuguese practice of exiling Tocoists to distant provinces. Toco himself was exiled to various parts of Angola and eventually in 1963 to the islands of the Azores, where he worked as a lighthouse keeper until 1974. During the Angolan civil war, Toco, who now lived in Luanda, was in a precarious position because of his origins in an area that supported an anti-government party. A leadership struggle in the church followed Toco's death in 1984, and the government did not include the Tocoist Church in its list of twelve recognized churches. The dispute was resolved in 1988 when Luzaisso Antonio Lutango was elected leader of the church and the government lifted its suspension of the church's activities. There were many remarkable similarities between the careers of Simâo Toco and Simon Kimbangu, besides their first names. Like Kimbanguism, the church requires monogamy and forbids pork and alcohol. Tocoist members must wear white in worship, and are thought to regard Toco as the second member of the Trinity.[23]

Gabon also has significant new religious movements, particularly syncretistic ones among the Fang people. One of the largest is Bwiti (or the Church of the Initiates), a group of several religious movements named after a traditional initiation society.

Members meet all night with traditional music and dance, have an elaborate mythology, and use traditional narcotic drugs to acquire religious power and encourage communication with the ancestors. Bwiti is essentially a revitalization of ancient Fang ancestor rites, a movement commencing at the beginning of the 20th Century. But it had incorporated some Christian (Catholic) elements by 1945 and is constantly changing. The movement was said to have 10-60,000 members by 1967 in Gabon and Equatorial Guinea, some 20% of the Fang people, but Bwiti cannot be regarded as an AIC, as it does not intend primarily to be a Christian church.[24]

Alice Lenshina and the Lumpa Church

The 1950s were years of political unrest and social upheaval for the peoples of Central Africa. In 1953, a Bemba woman from the Chinsali district in the Northern Province of Zambia, Alice Mulenga, later known as Alice Lenshina (1920-78),[25] declared that after a serious illness in which she had died, she had returned from heaven with a special message. She was also told to relate her visions to the local Presbyterian missionaries and to continue her catechetical training for membership in the church. For a while she prayed for the sick in her home village Kasomo while remaining in the Presbyterian Church, and large crowds went there. She seems at first to have been favored by the missionaries, but when she started baptizing converts herself there was conflict. In 1955 she founded the "Lumpa" church, from a Bemba word meaning "excelling all others, most important". Lenshina's ethical teachings followed the strict Calvinistic fundamentalism of the Presbyterian missionaries. She preached against witchcraft and rejected traditional rituals, adultery, divorce, polygyny, tobacco, and alcohol. But Lenshina also shunned the sacrament of Holy Communion, which she regarded as an ancestor rite, and only she was allowed to baptize converts. She exercised complete control over the new church and its preachers, who were women as well as men. Each Lumpa congregation had preachers and "judges" who were appointed by Lenshina personally. Lenshina composed some 400 hymns using Bemba traditional music, and this appealed much more to Africans than the stiff hymn translations of the Presbyterians, who with the Catholics were the dominant European missions in the area. The church grew so quickly that a thousand people a week were visiting Kasomo in 1955-6, and the church spread throughout the rural Northern and Eastern Provinces of Zambia and into urban areas as far away as Zimbabwe and the Congo. Entire Bemba villages became Lumpa, as the movement separated itself from the world, starting its own separate communities where there were none. A great Lumpa cathedral, one of the largest church buildings in central Africa, was opened in 1958 at Kasomo with a pillar on which it was believed that Christ would alight at his coming. The church had become comparatively wealthy, having a chain of rural shops and a fleet of trucks and cars, and a hierarchical organization with Lenshina at its pinnacle. Members from outlying districts at regular intervals were expected to visit Kasomo, which was renamed Sioni (Zion), where they were conscripted as laborers for various building and agricultural projects.

By 1959, there were perhaps 150,000 Lumpa members, larger than any other church in north-eastern Zambia. But their growth began to decline, particularly with the emergence of the African nationalist movement, the United National Independence Party. UNIP was formed in that year and led by Kenneth Kaunda, who himself was from Chinsali and the Presbyterian mission. Consequently, this part of Zambia had been UNIP's main rural stronghold and furthermore, at a more personal level, Kaunda and Lenshina had attended the same school, and Kaunda's own brother was a Lumpa leader. Lenshina prohibited Lumpa members from joining the struggle for independence, and this was particularly a sore point for UNIP. Because of her policy of withdrawal from the world outside and the barricading of Lumpa villages, clashes with the authorities were inevitable. Members were prohibited from appearing at secular courts and after 1964, from sending their children to schools. The authority of both the UNIP transitional government and the traditional leaders, who tended to support UNIP, was rejected.

Lenshina returned to Sioni in 1962 after more than a year away visiting various Lumpa churches, and she discovered that her support had decreased substantially through the activities of UNIP. She immediately forbade her members from joining the party and staged a public burning of UNIP party cards. Violent clashes between Lumpa members and UNIP supporters ensued during the national elections that year. Lenshina announced that the end of the world had come and all her followers were to withdraw from their villages and live in their own settlements in preparation for the end. During this time, Kaunda had several extended meetings with Lenshina at Kasomo in an attempt at reconciliation. UNIP won the first election by universal suffrage in 1964. When Kaunda handed the Lumpa church an ultimatum to abandon their settlements, virtual civil war broke out from July to October 1964. Over a thousand people, mostly Lumpa members, were killed.[26] The Lumpa were defeated, their settlements demolished, and the church banned. Lenshina and many of her followers were imprisoned two weeks before the independence of Zambia, but some Lumpa members disappeared into the thick Zambian bush and continued to clash with government forces for some months afterwards. The "Lumpa rising" was also both a severe setback and a considerable embarrassment for the new UNIP government. Imprisoned Lumpa members were later returned to their original chiefdoms, where it was expected that they be reintegrated fully into society. This involved them being required to participate in ancestor rituals, to publicly acknowledge the chief's authority, and to apply for membership in one of the established churches and in UNIP. Those Lumpa members, perhaps 15,000, who refused to adhere to the ban on their practices and the strict conditions for their integration, fled to the southern Congo to a settlement near Mokambo. There, a steadily increasing Lumpa community existed of several thousand refugees for thirty years, thought to consist of 30,000 by 1990. The state of emergency that had been declared in Zambia during the conflict remained, and Kaunda himself was reported to have used the Lumpa incident as an example of what would happen to those who threatened the unity of the state. Lenshina herself was kept in prison and restriction without trial, despite a general amnesty for Lumpa members announced in 1968, in which only about 3,000 returned from the Congo. Lenshina escaped from restriction for a week in 1967, but she was recaptured with 48 followers near the Angolan border and put back in prison.[27] After her release from prison in 1975 she was placed under house arrest in Lusaka. She was alleged to have renounced her loyalty to the Lumpa Church and rejoined a mission church before she died in 1978, but this is now thought to have been highly unlikely. Perhaps this report, like the similar one concerning Kimbangu twenty-seven years earlier, was a deliberate ploy to recover power and prestige by those who felt the loss most keenly, the "established" churches. After the defeat of the UNIP government in 1991, other Lumpa followers returned to Zambia. But they were prevented from returning to Kasomo, where Lenshina's body lies in a tomb in the middle of her ruined cathedral, now a place of pilgrimage. In October 1998, the Lumpa Church, now known as the New Jerusalem Church and represented by Lenshina's daughter Jennifer Bwalya Bubile, sued Kenneth Kaunda and UNIP for the death of 60,000 Lumpa members and other crimes against the movement.[28]

The Lumpa Church was undoubtedly another African reformist church, but was more radical than most AICs were in its total rejection of the outside world, whether traditional, colonial or post-independence. It criticized both the existing Presbyterian and Catholic missions for failing to adhere to what it saw as Christian principles, and it rejected UNIP's appeal for political loyalty. It mounted a sustained attack on African religion as well, going further than the European missions had done. Its separated settlements and eschatological outlook were further reminders of its radical reforming and millennial character, not unlike that of the Anabaptists in post-Reformation Europe.[29]

All of these movements in Central Africa sought to make Christianity more African and relevant to African people, and in order to accomplish this their preachers and prophets suffered harassment, imprisonment, extreme hardship, and even death, but their message lives on.

Notes

1 World Council, 14.

2 Abbreviation of the French, "Église de Jésus Christ sur la terre par le prophète Simon Kimbangu".

3 Martin, *Kimbangu*, 45-51; MacGaffey, 33-8; Ayegboyin & Ishola, 126-30.

4 Martin, *Kimbangu*, 57.

5 Martin, *Kimbangu*, 61-4; MacGaffey, 38-43.

6 Martin, *Kimbangu*, 105.

7 Hastings, *History*, 129-30.

8 Wim M. J. van Binsbergen, *Religious Change in Zambia: Exploratory studies*. London & Boston, 1981, 267.

9 Daneel, *Quest*, 64.

10 Martin, *Kimbangu*, 47.

11 Ayegboyin & Ishola, 133-4, 136. It is unlikely that the EJCSK will adhere to these more "unorthodox" beliefs today, since becoming a member of the WCC.

12 Martin, *Kimbangu*, 107, 110, 128, 158.

13 Martin, *Kimbangu*, 111, 143-8, 159, 179-80; MacGaffey, 62-6; World Council, 14; Ayegboyin & Ishola, 139.

14 Martin, *Kimbangu*, 73, 89.

15 Nathaniel Ndiokwere, *Prophecy and Revolution: The Role of Prophets in Independent African Churches and in Biblical Tradition*, London, 1981, 52-3; MacGaffey, 41, 58, 60.

16 MacGaffey, 41-3.

17 Ernest Wamba-dia Wamba, "Bundu dia Kongo: A Congolese Fundamentalist Religious movement", Oxford, 1999, 213-28.

18 C. M. Pauw, "Independency and Religious Change in Malawi: A New Challenge for the Church", *Missionalia* 21:2, 1993, 138-9; Hastings, *Church in Africa*, 486-9.

19 Clive Dillon-Malone, "The 'Mutumwa' Churches of Zambia", *Journal of Religion in Africa* XIV: 3, 1983, 204-22; id., "Indigenous medico-religious movements in Zambia: a study of Nchimi and Mutumwa 'churches'", *African Social Research* 36, 1983, 455-74.

20 J. V. Taylor & D. A. Lehmann, *Christians of the Copperbelt: The Growth of the Church in Northern Rhodesia*. London, 1961, 24, 238; van Binsbergen, 267, 283-4; Hastings, *Church in Africa*, 504-5; Gifford, *African Christianity*, 186-7; J.M. Assimeng, "Sectarian Allegiance & Political Authority: the Watch Tower Society in Zambia, 1907-35", *The Journal of Modern African Studies* 8:1, 1970, 97-112; C.J. Martin, "Millenarianism in Africa", *Critique of Anthropology* 15 (4), 1980, 85-93.

21 Owen J. M. Kalinga, "Jordan Msumba, Ben Ngemela and the Last Church of God and his Christ 1924-1935", *Journal of Religion in Africa* 13:3, 1982, 207-18; Ranger, Terence O. "Christian Independency in Tanzania", Nairobi, 1971, 125-9.

22 C. M. Pauw, 139, 143.

23 Isichei, 204; Hastings, *History*, 32; Carlos Estermann, "O tocoísmo como fenómeno religioso", *Garcia de Orta* 13:3, 1965, 325-42; F. James Grenfell, "Simâo Toco: an Angolan prophet", *Journal of Religion in Africa* 28:2, 210-26.

24 Isichei, 205; Barrett, *Schism*, 288; James W. Fernandez, "The Idea and Symbol of the Saviour in a Gabon Syncretistic Cult", *International Review of Mission* 211: 53, 1964, 281-9; Stanislaw Swiderski, *La Religion Bouiti*, Tome I: Histoire, Ottawa, 1985.

25 "Lenshina" is thought to be derived from Regina, "Queen", and she is sometimes referred to as "Lenshina Mulenga".

26 The figure in various reports for the number killed varies between 700 and 1,500, but may be much higher. In 1998, Lumpa representatives claimed 60,000 were killed during the conflict.

27 Hugo F. Hinfelaar, "Lumpa and Reconciliation", *AFER* 26(5), 1984, 292; id., "Women's Revolt: The Lumpa Church of Lenshina Mulenga in the 1950s", *Journal of Religion in Africa* 21:2, 1991, 99-129; George C. Bond, "A Prophecy that Failed: The Lumpa Church of Uyombe, Zambia", New York, 1979, 142-3, 153-5; Taylor & Lehmann, 248; van Binsbergen, 266-7; Hastings, *History*, 125, 157.

28 Gifford, *African Christianity*, 184; *Times of Zambia*, "Lumpas drag Kaunda to court", Lusaka, 21 October 1998.

29 Bond, 151-3.

7

EAST AFRICAN CHURCHES

AICs are found in Tanzania and Uganda, but are much more numerous in Kenya, where there were more than three hundred in 1999. The first president of an independent Kenya, Jomo Kenyatta, was himself an AIC pioneer in his early adulthood. Although a recognized distinction is made between "African" and "spiritual" churches in this chapter, these distinctions are becoming increasingly difficult to delineate, as most AICs in East Africa place an emphasis on the Holy Spirit. All have been impacted by various revival movements in the region, especially the African "Holy Spirit" movement that began around the time of the First World War, and the later East African Revival movement. The Holy Spirit movement operated outside of, and usually with the opposition of European missions and the colonial administration. The influence of this movement on the East African Revival, which enjoyed much more support from established mission churches, may not have been given sufficient consideration or acknowledgement.

The "official" East African Revival in the Anglican church prevented the use of spiritual gifts such as speaking in tongues, prophecy, and healing, which often brought it into conflict with those Africans who desired more tangible evidence of God's presence and power.

AICs in Tanzania and Uganda

In the Rungwe area of south-western Tanzania, movements from neighboring Malawi like the Watch Tower church, the African National Church, and the Last Church of God have had some success. The Church of the Holy Spirit, influenced by the East African revival, became for a time the largest AIC in Tanzania. Lutheran evangelist Felix Kabunga started this church in 1953, but half of its members returned to the Lutheran fold in 1962 and few now remain. A major ethnic secession from the Evangelical Lutheran Church in Tanzania in 1995, after a violent dispute over a new diocese declared in the Meru area, resulted in the formation of the African Missionary Evangelical Church, claiming 70,000 Meru members. By this time there were at least seventy AIC groups in Tanzania, but as elsewhere in Africa, the most remarkable increase was happening among Pentecostal churches.[1]

AICs in Buganda predated those of Kenya, but none of these early churches developed into very large movements. In 1914, Joswa Kate Mugema (1850-1942), a prominent chief in Uganda, founded the Society of the One Almighty God, better known as the "Bamalaki" ("Malakites") or KOAB.[2] Mugema, who became an Anglican lay reader in 1893, rejected the use of medicines and medical doctors early in his Christian life. He and five others, including Malaki Musajjakawa seceded from the CMS over this issue and built their own church. This was at first a strong movement. Malaki baptized over 10,000 people in 1914, and the church had 91,000 members in Buganda by 1921. The CMS opposed it but didn't have the support of the colonial governor to suppress the movement, although the governor referred to KOAB's leaders as "silly, misguided, obstinate old men". KOAB began to observe a Saturday sabbath in 1915, banned the eating of pork, and permitted traditional beer and polygyny. For refusing to cooperate with government vaccination programs, Mugema was dismissed from his chiefdom in 1919. Rioting erupted in 1929 after an attempt was made to force the Bamalaki to accept health regulations. Mugema and Malaki were deported until their death, Malaki on a hunger strike in 1929 and Mugema from an illness in his old age. James Biriko became leader and the movement declined, almost to disappear in the 1950s. Some Bamalaki, who became known as "Bayudaya" ("Jews") declared themselves Jews and observed all the Mosaic laws.[3]

The story of Reuben Mukasa Spartas, formerly a Muganda Anglican in the military forces, is an intriguing one of an AIC leader who sought to maintain the dignity of an independent African church with all the legitimacy that the oldest church in the world could afford. Spartas was an ardent African nationalist who contacted Marcus Garvey's "Back to Africa" movement in North America and their African Orthodox Church (AOC). Patriarch Alexander McQuire of the AOC in America consecrated Daniel Alexander as Archbishop of South Africa in 1927. When Spartas contacted Alexander, he was made a lay reader in the AOC. He announced his resignation from the Anglican Church in 1929 in one of his most memorable speeches, declaring that this would be "a church established for all right-thinking Africans, men who wish to be free in their own house, not always being thought of as boys". Archbishop Alexander visited Uganda in 1931-2 and ordained Spartas and his brother-in-law Obadiah Basajjakitalo as priests, Spartas becoming Vicar General. Soon after this, when Spartas was visited by a Greek Orthodox priest from Tanganyika (Tanzania) who told him that his ordination was invalid, he severed the connection with the AOC in South Africa, and in 1934 the AOC became the African Greek Orthodox Church. The church claimed to have 5,000 members, thirty centers and twenty-three church schools by 1936.

In 1946 the Greek Orthodox Church formally recognized the AGOC in Uganda through the Patriarchate of Alexandria, as a result of Spartas's visit there, and by this time the church claimed over 10,000 members. However, Spartas's request to be consecrated bishop was rejected, and he was appointed vicar-general. Spartas gathered other AICs in Kenya claiming to be "Orthodox" into the AGOC. Spartas was imprisoned from 1949-53 for involvement in the Buganda riots, and he continued to work for Ugandan independence after his release, now a nationalist hero.

Spartas' troubles were not over, for a Greek patriarch was appointed for East Africa in 1966. Spartas objected and seceded to form the African Orthodox Autonomous Church South of the Sahara. Once again, Archbishop Alexander, who visited Kampala in 1968 and was now 85, came to his rescue and consecrated Spartas as bishop. In 1975, with the apparent collusion of the Greek Orthodox Church, President Idi Amin banned Spartas's church and seized and handed over its property to the Greek-related Uganda Orthodox Church. A protracted lawsuit continued into the late eighties. Although Spartas was an ardent African nationalist, he steered his movement in and out of submission to the Greek Orthodox Church, believing that this was a more legitimate church than the other European missions in Africa had been. But as a true AIC pioneer, he refused to countenance anything that he perceived as foreign dominance. His ardent resistance to all forms of paternalism, whether from Europe, North America, or elsewhere in Africa, makes his story paradoxical, but Reuben Spartas remains one of the most influential figures in the history of the AICs in East Africa.[4]

The history of post-independent Uganda has been one of the most violent in Africa, especially during the bloody regimes of Idi Amin and Milton Obote. This violence also has had a religious dimension, with prophetic movements at the center. One of the most notorious of these was that of Alice Auma (b. 1956), a Catholic member better known as Lakwena. Alice was first possessed by "spirits" or "angels" in 1985, the chief spirit of which was a former Italian man who had drowned in the Nile, referred to as "Lakwena", Acholi for "messenger". Alice and her followers regarded him as a manifestation of the "Holy Spirit", as he spoke to her the words of God in 74 different languages, and the movement she founded was regarded by its followers as a Christian movement. Alice sought military support for her activities which, she declared, were aimed at preventing bloodshed and converting the Acholi people of northern Uganda from violence to God-fearing ways. She was not the first religious leader to be attached to a military force, as Ugandan military factions often sought the protection of diviners. This 25-year-old prophetess and healer was believed to have extraordinary powers that were greatly feared throughout the region. Her soldiers, Acholi-speaking young men and boys, were sprinkled with water and anointed with oil. The elaborate initiation rituals were replete with Christian symbols like baptism, holy communion, and the burning of magic charms, but to these traditional Acholi rituals were added, as well as the introduction of new ones. Initiates had to abstain from using charms, from consulting other healers or mediums, from engaging in ancestor rituals or sexual intercourse, and from consuming pork, alcohol, and tobacco. Alice laid her hands on those initiated into her movement, cleansing them of past misdeeds, particularly significant for the many ex-soldiers who joined her. In 1987, Alice led her 7-10,000 strong Holy Spirit Movement 800 kilometers southwards, in an attempt to overthrow the government of President Yoweri Museveni, a southerner. As they marched, they sang hymns and shouted "Christ has died, Christ is risen, Christ will come again". Alice had reportedly prophesied that stones thrown at the enemy would explode like grenades, nut oil smeared on their bodies would deflect bullets, and they would each have fifteen wives after the victory.[5]

Their army was routed, and Alice and a few of her supporters fled to Kenya, where they were imprisoned as illegal immigrants. The discredited prophetess was still living there in a refugee camp in 2000, as her demands of the Museveni government for her to return were impossible to meet. Possibly

10,000 people were killed during this campaign of terror. She declared that those who died in the war (on both sides) had been sinners. When journalists interviewed her in a Kenyan prison in 1988, she said, "I am not a warrior, simply the one who has been chosen by Lakwena to save Uganda. The Holy Spirit is everything, I am nothing".[6] Alice's father Severino Lukoya, Joseph Kony, and other prophets took up the offensive thereafter in what was first called "Lakwena Part Two". Lukoya was captured in 1989 and is now the leader of a Christian church. Kony went on to lead the infamous Lord's Resistance Army, still in 2000 waging a campaign of terror that included child abduction, but without the popular support enjoyed by Lakwena.[7] In early 2000, a sect called the Restoration of the Ten Commandments of God came to world attention, with the gruesome discovery of the bodies of over a thousand of its followers. This movement was thought to be led by former Catholics in south-west Uganda, Joseph Kibwetere and Credonia Mwerinde, and included priests among its victims.[8]

African Churches in Kenya

The churches described in this section are more or less "African" or "Ethiopian" churches, sticking fairly closely to the mission churches they came from, seceding mainly for political reasons, and claiming their initial membership from mission churches. They began among the Agikuyu in central Kenya as popular movements of protest against the colonial seizure of land and in particular, missionary attacks on female circumcision, a central political issue. The African Independent Pentecostal Church of Africa (AIPC) and the African Orthodox Church (AOC) began in a climate of increasing demands by the Agikuyu for political independence, expressed by the Kikuyu Central Association, and in a corresponding struggle for schools independent of European missions. By 1929, the Kikuyu Independent Schools Association (KISA) under Johana Kunyiha and the Kikuyu Karing'a Educational Association (KKEA), which had the support of Kenyatta, had been formed to provide such independent education. And yet, after the model of mission education, the independent schools also sought to provide a Christian foundation, and for this they needed ordained clergy. The request of KISA to the Anglicans in 1933 to allow two young men to receive theological training was met with such stringent conditions that KISA and KKEA were forced to look elsewhere. KISA invited Archbishop Daniel Alexander in South Africa to come and supervise the training of their clergy, at KISA's expense. Alexander had told KISA that the AOC was "perpetually autonomous and controlled by Negroes entirely" and that it was "a church of Africans governed by the Africans and for the Africans".9

Alexander arrived in Kenya in November 1935 and remained there until July 1937, during which time he opened a theological seminary with eight students, seven of whom were sponsored by KISA, and one by KKEA. Before his return to South Africa, he ordained three deacons and two subdeacons. The newly ordained clergy did not agree among themselves about the organization of their new church. Some, supported by KKEA and including the deacon Arthur Gatung'u Gathuna, wanted to remain in the AOC. Others, supported by KISA, formed a separate church altogether, the African Independent Pentecostal Church, which adopted the name "Pentecostal" not because it emphasized the experience of the Spirit, but because it had clergy appointed by the Spirit and was controlled by the Spirit and not by foreigners. And so, in September 1937, the AIPC emerged from KISA and the AOC out of KKEA.10 As most AICs were regarded with suspicion by the British colonial administration, both churches were banned in 1952-3 during the Mau Mau uprising and the independent schools were closed. But after independence in 1963, thousands of nominal Presbyterians openly joined the AIPC, which soon had 100,000 members and was led by Bishop Philip Kiande, one of the original four ordained in 1937. By 1989 this church, now with the expanded name of African Independent Pentecostal Church of Africa (AIPCA), may have been the largest

AIC in Kenya and one of the four largest on the continent, with 1,250,000 adherents.[11] Shortly after independence a smaller sister church, the National Independent Church of Africa, strong among the Embu and Meru peoples, obtained separate registration with the Kenya government.

The AOC, under the leadership of Gathuna, sought affiliation with Reuben Spartas of Uganda in 1939. Like Spartas, this church was involved in various disputes with foreign Orthodox groups with which it sought affiliation. By 1946 the AOC had 20,000 members and had joined Spartas in affiliating with the Greek Orthodox Church in Alexandria—although the East Africans did not see this as a surrender of autonomy. Gathuna was detained in 1953 on allegations of Mau Mau membership, and he was only released in 1961. The AOC was severely hampered during the seven years of its banning, and began to reorganize itself in 1960. Gathuna resumed the leadership and the church was registered with the Kenyan government in 1965 as the African Orthodox Church of Kenya, although it retained links with the Greek Orthodox Church in Alexandria. By 1972 there were an estimated 250,000 members in this church. Gathuna was consecrated bishop in 1974, but conflict with the Greek archbishop in Nairobi soon emerged over the issue of Gathuna's soliciting funds without the authorization of the archbishop. The patriarch in Alexandria deposed Gathuna in 1978, but Gathuna seceded to form the True Orthodox Christian Church with 35,000 followers. After his death in 1987, Gathuna's group was led by Bishop Nipon and there were now two factions in the AOC of Kenya.[12]

During the 1940s, the African Brotherhood Church (ABC), and the African Christian Church and Schools (ACCS) were founded. The ABC, predominantly a Kamba church, was founded in 1942 in Nairobi by Simeon Mulandi (1914-1975), a former Salvation Army officer who had received visions about founding a new church. The ABC was a reaction to the missionary attitudes of that time and most of its first members were dissatisfied members of the Africa Inland Mission, an evangelical missionary organization. Mulandi said that missionary Christianity meant that "you always had to be apologizing for being an African". Like so many Kenyan AICs, this church was presumed to be nationalistic and anti-colonial from the beginning and was accused of being a front for the Mau Mau. It developed independent schools and a theological college in 1950, was one of only four AICs admitted to the AACC in 1966, and had over 100,000 members in 1998. Mulandi himself was dismissed from the church in 1950 for sexual misconduct, and his capable administrative assistant Nathan Ngala became head of the church, later to be called Bishop. Ngala invited Canadian Baptists to send missionary partners in 1978, to work mainly in education.

The ACCS was founded in 1949 as the result of a schism in the Africa Inland Mission over the question of the ownership of church property. Unlike most of these churches, the ACCS was cooperative with the colonial government and one of the first AICs to apply and be admitted to the ecumenical Christian Council of Kenya in 1954. In 1970 this church received the first eight Canadian Baptist missionaries it had invited to Kenya for an initial ten-year assignment that continues today.[13]

In 1958, in the wake of the East African Revival, the Anglican Church in western Kenya found itself with a major schism. A new Luo church called the Church of Christ in Africa with Mathew Ajuoga (b.1925) as Chairman (and later Bishop) was registered with the government, with at least seven Anglican priests, 130 congregations, and 16,000 followers at its foundation. Ajuoga was ordained an Anglican priest in 1954. While training for the ministry, he had formally protested to the CMS about missionary paternalism and discrimination against African clergy. The cause of the schism was the tension between the followers of the Revival movement (the "JoRemo", "people of the blood") supported by Luyia assistant bishop Festo Olang', and the Luo followers of Ajuoga (the "JoHera", "people of love"), who regarded themselves as less schismatic and more Anglican than the JoRemo were. Ajuoga, at the time acting Rural Dean, wrote a fifteen page letter to Bishop Beecher in Mombasa in 1956, deploring the division plaguing the Anglican church in Nyanza in western Kenya and what he saw as the doctrinal errors of the "Wahamaji", another term used to describe the JoRemo.[14] He saw his JoHera movement as the true revival movement in the Anglican church. However, the JoHera were forbidden from assembling, the seven priests who refused to comply were suspended, and the massive exodus from the Anglican church began. In some areas, fighting ensued between the two factions and 26 church buildings were destroyed or ruined. After a direct appeal to the Archbishop of Canterbury in March 1958 for recognition and ordination, Ajuoga was told to submit to Beecher. Ajuoga politely replied that his church council would not allow this to happen "unless the Bishop of Mombasa himself shows real change of mind and spirit in Christian love". The CCA had appealed to the archbishop because of Beecher's attempts to "fiercely destroy" their church.[15] The application of the CCA for membership in the WCC was twice rejected in 1960 and 1967, and Ajuoga subsequently led his church into the fundamentalist International Council of Christian Churches. In 1960, a further schism in the CCA resulted in the Holy Trinity Church in Africa under Bishop Meshak Owira, one of the original seceding Anglican priests. The CCA has expanded to Uganda and Tanzania and is now a multiethnic church with over 200,000 adherents in 1990, one of the largest AICs in Kenya.[16] In 1995, the church opened its own theological college, St. Mathews Masogo Bible College. Bishop Ajuoga has also been a very active participant in the OAIC, as we will see below.

Among the first AICs to emerge in Kenya were the churches that began among Luo Anglicans around Lake Victoria in the province of Nyanza, an area administered at the time by the CMS diocese of Uganda. One of the earliest and more unusual of the African churches was the Nomiya Luo Mission, founded by a former Catholic Johana Owalo in 1914, and emerging as a deliberate and consciously syncretistic movement combining elements of Unitarian Christianity, Islam, Judaism, and Luo traditional religion in reaction against both Catholic and

Protestant forms of Christianity, but using the Anglican Book of Common Prayer in worship. The angel Gabriel appeared to Owalo in 1907 and told him to preach that people should worship God only, not Jesus or Mary. In a vision of heaven, he was told to circumcise his male followers (contrary to Luo custom), teach people to obey the laws of Moses and keep the seventh-day Sabbath, and baptize them in rivers. Owalo died suddenly in 1920 and the church was plagued with division over who should succeed him as leader. Eventually Petro Ouma became bishop, to be followed after his death by Benjamin Oundo. By 1944 the movement had spread to Luo living in Tanganyika, and had over 50,000 members in Kenya by 1966.

Kenyan Spirit Churches

In 1960, the Holy Spirit descended on several Nomiya Luo people who began speaking in tongues, prophesying, revealing sins, and jumping in ecstasy. A former Catholic, John Juma Pesa began preaching and healing, claiming to be the successor to Owalo, and in 1967 the supporters of this Holy Spirit movement were expelled from the church. They formed a new church called the Nomiya Luo Roho ("Spirit") Church under Bishop Zablon Ndiege, Archbishop from 1978. This church has suffered several schisms, including Pesa starting the Holy Ghost Coptic Church, and Cornell Bunde beginning the Nomiya Luo Roho Gospellers Church. The Nomiya Roho Sabbath Church started in 1974 out of a desire to return to the Sabbath observance that had been abandoned by the Nomiya Luo Roho Church.[17]

The Roho ("Spirit") movement commenced in 1912, firstly as a popular charismatic movement among young people within the Anglican church, only interrupted by the conscription of young men that followed the outbreak of the First World War, including its main leader Ibrahim Osodo.[18] Roho's best-known founders are Alfayo Odongo Mango (1884-1934) and his nephew Lawi Obonyo (c.1911-34). Mango became a Christian sometime before 1912, attended an Anglican school, was baptized in the

Spirit in 1916, and received a special calling in a vision. The CMS Archdeacon Owen later reported that Mango was the "inspirer and mainstay" of "a movement characterized by much hysteria and visions", although Mango seems not to have practiced his spiritual gifts for long, until 1933 when he was involved with Lawi.[19] Mango prophesied the end of colonialism and agitated for the restoration of lost lands, but he also preached against certain Luo customs. His land claims for the Nilotic Luo brought him into increasing conflict with the Bantu-speaking Wanga (Luyia) who had their own claims, aggravated by Owen's apparent bias towards the Luyia. Nevertheless, Owen appointed Mango a deacon in 1927 and sent him to Mombasa to do a two-year theology course the following year. After his return to Musanda, a village under Luyia control, he was threatened with deportation from his home if he did not acknowledge that he was a tenant of the Luyia. This he formally agreed to in early 1933. Lawi began a prophetic ministry at about this time, when several remarkable healings and other miracles were reported. Owen and two other European missionaries attended one of Lawi's revival meetings in October 1933, in which they publicly denounced him as a "deceiver" and ordered the meeting to disperse. In Owen's opinion, Lawi was involved in "the most extravagant forms of hysteria and emotionalism". Mango was ordered "to restrain Lawi's unauthorized activities".[20] Instead, Mango became involved in the Roho revival movement, installed new rites of baptism and Communion, and his home in Musanda became a center to which people came and from where missionaries, women and men, fanned out. After Owen's confrontational attitude, Mango and Lawi no longer trusted him and refused to see him. Mango began to prophesy the end of colonial rule and made other predictions about future development in Kenya. Mango, who felt that his death was imminent, appointed Elijah Oloo as "king" and organized the administration of the Roho movement for after his death, with Lawi as archbishop and Baranaba Walwoho as bishop. The Roho were accused of "acts of violence" against non-Roho Luo, were banned from attending the local Anglican church, and Owen reported on January 17, 1934 that

Mango through his actions had "broken away from the Anglican church". Five days later, Mango, Lawi, and seven of their followers were murdered by a Wanga mob of several hundred, as Mango's house in Musanda was set alight.[21]

The JoRoho thereafter began a vigorous missionary expansion movement called Dini ya Roho ("Religion of the Spirit"), emphasizing the power of the Spirit and dressing in white robes with red crosses. The Roho churches say that Mango's sacrificial death atoned for their sins and opened heaven to Africans. Mango is prayed to as "our Savior", and he has inaugurated a new era of the reign of the Holy Spirit in Africa. These churches enjoin monogamy on their leaders, and are known for their processions through the streets of towns and villages. After the 1934 massacre the church was given a new language by the Holy Spirit (a transliterated form of Dholuo), which members used to communicate among themselves, and which is still used occasionally in worship. The Roho church under Baranaba Walwoho split in 1941 to form two churches, the Ruwe Holy Ghost Church of East Africa under Walwoho (Ruwe JoRoho), and the Musanda Holy Ghost Church of East Africa under Andrea Okoyo, first known as the Roho Msalaba ("Spirit Cross") Church. Together with another Luo Roho church, the Ruwe and Musanda churches were registered with the Kenyan government in 1957 as the Holy Ghost Church of Kenya. In 1960 the churches again separated, and they now have separate organizations with an estimated total of 50-75,000 members in 1991. The Roho movement spread to Tanzania in 1947.[22]

A Holy Spirit movement among the Abaluyia emerged after a pentecostal revival in a Friends (Quaker) mission in 1927, encouraged by North American missionary Arthur Chilson—although the Abaluyia were probably later influenced by similar movements among the neighboring Luo, and they also called their movement Dini ya Roho.[23] The local church leaders and American mission authorities of the Friends Africa Mission discouraged the revival and banned public confession of sins and spiritual gifts like prophecy and speaking in tongues. Chilson didn't return to Kenya after his furlough in 1928 and the revivalists, who had been expelled from the Friends mission in 1929, eventually organized themselves under their leader Jakobo Buluku. Buluku died in 1938 as a result of a violent confrontation between his followers and non-charismatic Friends. The movement began to organize, and a split on the issue of Sabbath observance in 1940 resulted in the Holy Spirit Church of East Africa (HSCEA), eventually led by Archbishop Japheth Zare. The largest church to emerge was called the African Church of the Holy Spirit (ACHS), led by Kefa Ayub Mavuru as "High Priest" since 1952, officially registered in 1957, and joining the National Christian Council of Kenya in 1960. Schisms from the ACHS resulted in the Church of Quakers in Africa in 1962 (called the African Church of the Red Cross from 1965), which was itself taken over by the Lyahuka Church of East Africa, another schism from the ACHS in 1971. Another small church, the Gospel Holy Spirit Church of East Africa, emerged out of the ACHS in 1964. All these Roho churches, like the Friends, don't have sacraments of water baptism and Communion, but teach the "baptism in the Holy Spirit of adult persons upon repentance". Rituals for purification from evil precede all church services and must occur before meals and before entering and leaving houses. In common with other spiritual and prophetic churches, these Roho churches reject the use of medicines, wear white robes with a red cross, turbans, and beards, and remove shoes in services. The churches emphasize the freedom and power of the Spirit in their church meetings with ecstatic phenomena, especially prophecy, speaking in tongues, the interpretation of dreams, and healing. The churches have also spread, mainly through migration, to Tanzania and Uganda. In 1975, the ACHS and the African Israel Nineveh Church were the first two AICs in Kenya and jointly the second in Africa to become members of the WCC.[24]

The African Israel Church Nineveh (AICN), now usually known as the African Israel Nineveh Church, founded in 1942 by the Pentecostal Luyia evangelist Daudi Zakayo Kivuli (1896-1974), is a prominent prophet-healing church in western Kenya.

Kivuli associated with the Pentecostal Assemblies of Canada from 1925, and was made a supervisor of schools for this mission. After an ecstatic Spirit baptism experience in 1932, he embarked on an evangelistic and healing ministry officially authorized by the Canadian missionary Keller in 1939, and he was well known among both the Luyia and the Luo. When he was elected liaison leader for the church in 1940, some other African leaders didn't support him. Apparently with the blessing of Keller, Kivuli founded his own church organization called at first "Huru Salvation Nineveh" and soon after, "African Israel Church Nineveh". Kivuli took the title "High Priest" and his home became the headquarters of the church called Nineveh and the place to which people flocked. The church was registered with the government in 1957. The AICN has many practices similar to those of many other pentecostal type AICs in other parts of the continent. Members wear long flowing white robes and turbans, practice constant singing and dancing, emphasize Spirit possession, observe Old Testament dietary and purification taboos, and have a holy place (Nineveh) where the present archbishop, a grandson of Kivuli, resides. The AICN, like other Roho churches, is known for its joyful and colorful processions and open air meetings in which flags, drums, staffs, and trumpets are used in singing to traditional African tunes. Friday, the day of Christ's crucifixion, is declared to be a day of worship specifically for repentance, together with Sunday, the day of resurrection, and the church places great emphasis on the open confession of sins and daily dawn prayers. Polygamists are accepted as church members, but monogamy is enjoined on all leaders and unmarried members. Alcohol, tobacco, pork, fish without scales, and sexual intercourse on Fridays are all proscribed. This church did not isolate itself as some other Pentecostal churches had done, but after its first application was rejected in 1957, it joined the National Council of Churches of Kenya by 1975 and as we have seen, was admitted to the WCC in 1975.

When Kivuli died in 1974, his wife Rabecca Jumba Kivuli (1902-88) succeeded him as leader and remained "High Priestess" of the AICN until her retirement in 1983. A large number of secessions have occurred in the AICN, nearly all using the word Israel in their name, and looking back to Kivuli as their founder.[25] Kivuli's grandson John Mweresa Kivuli II (b.1960) became High Priest in 1983, but from 1991 he has been known as archbishop and has embarked on a process of "modernization". Kivuli II, who completed a theological degree, explained that his change in title was because the AICN had grown in theological understanding, and saw all believers as priests and Christ as the only High Priest. Although Luyia and Luo people dominate the membership, the AICN has become an interethnic national movement of many thousands.[26]

The Arathi ("Prophets"), also known as "Watu wa Mungu" ("People of God"), or as now better known, Akurinu,[27] is a prophet-healing movement among the Gikuyu of central Kenya that selectively rejects western dress, medicine and education, and uses the Bible together with some elements of Gikuyu tradition. This movement started in a pentecostal revival that began in 1922, when manifestations of the Spirit, including speaking in tongues, prophecy, visions, and other ecstatic phenomena were present, and where there was an emphasis on prayer and the confession of sins. Joseph Ng'ang'a received a divine call in 1926 in a dream after illness, when his new name "Joseph" was revealed and he was baptized by the Spirit. After a four-year seclusion in a cave for prayer, Bible reading and fasting, he began preaching the downfall of European colonialism. Ng'ang'a rejected both traditional Gikuyu religious practices and western food, medicine, and dress, all of which he said were against the Bible. He emphasized the presence of the Holy Spirit and rejected water baptism. His followers wore long white robes and expected a new golden age for the Gikuyu. When the Spirit came on them they roared and shook violently, a practice that continues today. Several other Gikuyu prophets appeared at this time, including Musa Thuo Chege, who said that God was going to punish the

Europeans for their oppression. As the movement spread throughout the Gikuyu region, the colonial authorities became increasingly nervous of what they saw as a religious expression of the African nationalist independence movement. The Akurinu were expelled from some districts and their meetings banned, and Ng'ang'a and five other leaders were arrested. The movement began using traditional weapons to defend themselves and in 1934, while they were praying, Ng'ang'a and two others were killed by a contingent of nineteen policemen. The repression of the movement increased, and many Akurinu were arrested and imprisoned. Others fled to other parts of Kenya where the movement spread further, setting up communities and living together wherever they went. Many joined the movement in prison as a result of the witness of Akurinu there.

A follower of Musa Thuo, Joshua Ng'ang'a Kimani established Akurinu communities in the Rift Valley from 1941 to 1944, when he returned to Thuo and began writing down the doctrines and practices of the movement in an attempt to unify it. Some of these rules were too stringent for many in the movement, especially those that separated the Akurinu communities from the outside world and the opposition to polygyny. Schisms began to appear in 1949, when Samuel Thuku founded the God's Word Holy Ghost Church and the following year, Johana Waweru commenced the African Mission of the Holy Ghost Church. Hezron Tumbo started the Holy Ghost Church of Kenya in 1958, which changed its name to the Holy Ghost Church of East Africa in 1972. The group under Thuo also seceded from Kimani and became the Kenya Foundation of the Prophets Church in 1960, a more liberal and politically active group. A split in this church in 1968 led to the African Holy Ghost Christian Church led by Daniel Nduti which sought to return to many of Kimani's principles. There are now more than thirty Arathi churches in Kenya, nearly all of whom use "Holy Ghost" in their church title. Like the Roho churches, they do not baptize with water but practice a "baptism of the Holy Spirit" by a threefold shaking hands and laying on hands. The significance of these churches is that, despite the similarities with the Roho movement in western Kenya, the Akurinu movement was formed with little or no contact with western missions or spiritual churches elsewhere. It has consciously attempted to form a radically African type of Christianity, where the pattern of the mission churches plays no significant role, and this may make the Akurinu churches unique.[28]

A somewhat different and unique case is the largest secession from the Roman Catholic Church anywhere in Africa, the Legion of Mary or Maria Legio, with estimates of membership in the 1990s ranging between 250,000 and two million. This movement was founded by Catholic Luos in western Kenya in 1963, the year of Kenya's independence, and it has had many changes of name. The first leaders were lay people, Simeon Mtakatifu ("Holy") Ondeto (1920-91) and Gaudensia Aoko, a young woman whose two children had both died on the same day, after which she had begun to denounce witchcraft and sorcery. Ondeto established a headquarters on a holy mountain of Got Kwer, to be called the "New Jerusalem" and the "Holy City", and Aoko began mass baptisms. Within a year, the church had 100,000 members. It retained much Catholic liturgy including the Latin language, a celibate leadership, an order of nuns, and titles like Pope and Cardinal. But the Maria Legio also had many characteristics much like other spiritual churches: healing rituals, deliverance from witchcraft, prophecies and spirit possession, prohibiting pork, tobacco, alcohol, and dancing, and allowing polygyny. Aoko left the Maria Legio in 1965 to found her own movement after Ondeto began restricting the role of women in general, and her own role as charismatic founder of the movement in particular. Although she later returned, she was soon again head of her own Legio Maria movement. Another woman called "Mama Maria", is believed to be the black incarnation of the Virgin Mary who had "returned to heaven" in 1966 and was believed to be the "spiritual mother" of Ondeto.[29] The church initially spread only among Luos but has become increasingly multiethnic, reaching many parts of Kenya, Tanzania, and other surrounding East African countries. A former vice-president of Kenya, Oginga Odinga, was connected with Legio Maria. In Tanzania, a schism from this church six months after its founding there resulted in the African Catholic Church. Ondeto, who was buried at Got Kwer in 1991, became Baba Messias ("Father Messiah"), and is regarded by some Legios as Christ reincarnated in Africa, and the "living God". Pope Timothy Blasio Ahitler (1941-98) became leader until his death in 1998, when a new Pope, Lawrence Pius Jairo Chiage, was appointed.[30]

Organization of African Instituted Churches

Nairobi, Kenya, with its extensive ecumenical and continental contacts, is the fitting home of the most ecumenically representative association formed by AICs in the continent. The Organization of African Independent Churches (OAIC) was founded in 1978 in Cairo, Egypt. The link with Egypt was significant, for AICs saw Egypt and Ethiopia as the birthplaces of the oldest independent churches in Africa, the Coptic Church and the Ethiopian Orthodox Church, established alternatives to western Christianity. Many previous attempts to bring together AICs in ecumenical associations had ended in failure. Applications to ecumenical associations like the AACC and the WCC had been rejected. By 1985 the AACC had accepted only fifteen AICs into membership and the WCC had admitted only seven, out of literally hundreds of applications to both organizations from across Africa. Reuben Spartas of Uganda and Arthur Gathuna of Kenya were pioneers in establishing links with the Coptic church, first visiting Cairo in 1943. A certain Bishop Markos was sent from Alexandria to Durban in 1949 to establish a new Coptic diocese but it failed to receive support and was aborted a year later. AICs in several African countries began to form national councils and by 1986, some ninety-five such councils had been formed, a remarkable achievement—although forty-one of these councils were in the two countries of South Africa and Nigeria. The first to be established in Kenya, in 1961, was through the efforts of James Ochwatta of the AOC, the Kenya African United Churches. This was short-lived, however, and in 1963 Ochwatta helped form the East African United Churches, which included all the large AICs in Kenya and was supported by politicians like Kenyatta and Odinga. Zakayo Kivuli of the AICN was "Grand Metropolitan", Lucas Nuhu of the HSCEA Chairman and Ochwatta General Secretary. This council unsuccessfully tried to register with the Kenyan government and to join the AACC and the WCC. It was deregistered in 1968, but one of its successor bodies registered as Ethiopian Orthodox Holy Spirit Churches with Nuhu as Chairman, renaming itself several times, eventually becoming the International Holy Spirit and United Independent Churches in 1984.[31]

In 1976, Pope Shenouda III, Coptic Patriarch of Alexandria, consecrated M.S. Mikhail as Bishop of African Affairs, based in Nairobi and named Bishop Antonious Markos. Bishop Markos (not the same as the Markos mentioned earlier) began an extensive tour of AICs all over Africa and met political and "mainline" church leaders. Two years later, Pope Shenouda invited twenty significant AIC leaders for the inauguration of the OAIC in Cairo, with the basic aims of facilitating teaching, training, and theological education. The executive elected then included (among others) Joseph Diangienda of the Congo as a member, Nigeria's Primate Adejobi as Chairman and Bishop Markos as Organizing Secretary. The second conference was held in 1982 in Nairobi with representatives from 17 African nations and 31 AICs, when a constitution was approved and Bishop Mathew Ajuoga of Kenya was elected Chairman, a post he held for fifteen years.

In 1985 the name of the OAIC was changed to the Organization of African *Instituted* Churches at the request of the Kenyan government, when registration was effected. Bishop Markos resigned as OAIC Executive Secretary in 1990 after increasing tension with AIC leaders, and in 1995 the OAIC reorganized itself into eight regions. The OAIC was officially unaligned with either the ecumenical or the evangelical movements from 1982. Because evangelicals continued to view AICs as "not really Christian", the OAIC became increasingly identified with the ecumenical movement, and since 1995 it has been an associate member of the AACC and a recognized ecumenical partner of the WCC. The first issue of an official OAIC magazine, *Baragumu: The African Independent Churches Voice*, was launched in 1996. The third conference of the OAIC was held in 1997, when Nigerian Baba Aladura Dr. G.I.M Otubu was elected Chairman and the General Secretary was Kenyan Archbishop Njeru Wambugu of the National Independent Church of Africa. A significant shift in policy was that member churches became members of the OAIC through their regional councils, and could no longer join by applying directly to the international office.[32] The Good News Theological College in Accra, Ghana and the Khanya Institute in Johannesburg, South Africa (among others) are also theological colleges for AICs. The OAIC office in Nairobi continues to be actively involved in projects for theological education by extension, and development. In 1998 the OAIC began to dialogue with the World Alliance of Reformed Churches to promote mutual understanding. One of the questions facing the OAIC and its member churches at the end of the millennium was how to progress with assistance from the North without losing precious independence and identity to some new form of dependency called "partnership". The question becomes all the more cogent as many African countries spiral into greater economic crises and debt.

Notes

1 Terence O. Ranger, "Christian Independency in Tanzania", Nairobi, 1971, 125-9; Barrett, *Schism,* 30, 290; Richard B. Saah, "African Independent Church studies", *Church History in East Africa* 7:3, 1991, 46; C.K. Omari, "The Making of an Independent Church: The Case of the African Missionary Evangelical Church among the Meru of Tanzania", Oxford, 1999, 196-212.

2 "Bamalaki" means "those of Malaki", charismatic leader of the movement. "KOAB" is the abbreviation of the church's full name in Luganda, *Katonda Omu Ayinza Byona.*

3 F. B. Welbourn, *East African Rebels: A Study of Some Independent Churches,* London, 1961, 31-53.

4 Welbourne, 77-102; Barrett & Padwick, 15, 62, 69-70.

5 Tim Allen, "Understanding Alice: Uganda's Holy Spirit Movement in Context". *Africa* 61 (3), 1991, 375-9; Heike Behrend, *Alice Lakwena & the Holy Spirits: War in Northern Uganda 1986-1995.* Oxford, 1999, 43-5, 67, 78-98, 131-7.

6 Marie-Jeanne Serbin & Catherine Simon, "Alice, la grande prophetesse Ougandaise", *Africa International,* 203, March 1988, 46 (translation from French).

7 Allen, 370-5; Serbin & Simon, 45-7; Behrend, 191-7; Anna Borzello, "Kidnapped to Kill", *The Guardian Weekend,* 11 October,1997, 33-9; Ronald Kassimir, "The Politics of Popular Catholicism in Uganda", Oxford, 1999, 250-3.

8 Massimo Introvigne "Tragedy in Uganda: the Restoration of the Ten Commandments of God, a Post-Catholic Movement", April 2000, http://www.cesnur.org/testi/uganda_002.htm

9 Francis K. Githieya, *The Freedom of the Spirit: African Indigenous Churches in Kenya,* Atlanta, 1997, 97.

10 Ibid., 98-103.

11 Barrett & Padwick, 39. If this figure is correct, then the church membership is probably only exceeded by the EJCSK in the Congo, the ZCC in South Africa, and the CAC in Nigeria.

12 Welbourn, 113-61; Githieya, 96-116; Barrett, 10-4, Barrett & Padwick, 15-6, 76.

[13] David Sandgren, "Kamba Christianity: From Africa Inland Mission to African Brotherhood Church", Oxford, 1999, 169-95; Barrett & Padwick, 18, 70; Hastings, *History,* 79, 252; Welbourn, 155.

[14] Letter dated June 1, 1956 by Mathew Ajuoga to the Bishop of Mombasa, Harold Turner Collection, University of Birmingham. "Wahamaji" is Swahili for "migrants", and was used by Ajuoga to describe those who, in spirit, had migrated from the main body of the church — which is ironic, since it was the JoHera who actually left.

[15] Letters dated 27 March 1958 and 24 October 1958 by Mathew Ajuoga to the Archbishop of Canterbury, Harold Turner Collection, Birmingham.

[16] Hastings, *History,* 127-8; Welbourn & Ogot, 56; Barrett, 11-3, 254-61; Barrett & Padwick, 21.

[17] Cynthia Hoehler-Fatton, *Women of Fire and Spirit: History, Faith and Gender in Roho Religion in Western Kenya*, Oxford, 1996, 74-5; Debbie Clark, "History of Nomiya Luo Roho church", Birmingham, 1984.

[18] Hoehler-Fatton, 12-8.

[19] Ibid., 23.

[20] Ibid., 44, 46.

[21] Ibid., 3-6, 58-64.

[22] Barrett, *Schism*, 10; Hoehler-Fatton, xx, 96-7, 120-2.

[23] The Luyia Spirit churches were probably not influenced by the Luo Spirit churches until 1936, when a delegation from Musanda attended the funeral of Daniel Sande of the Bukoyani people (Ane Marie Bak Rasmussen, *Modern African Spirituality: The Independent Spirit Churches in East Africa, 1902-1976,* London & New York, 1996, 34).

[24] Rasmussen, 11-63; Hoehler-Fatton, 74, 96; World Council, 5, 11-2.

[25] Among these are Bethsaida Roho Israel, Roho Israel Church of God, Israel Assemblies of Kenya, Sinai Church of East Africa, God of Israel Zion Church, Kenya Israel Evangelistic Church of East Africa (Western Diocese), Israel Church in Africa, and Christian Israel Church.

[26] Welbourn & Ogot, 73-89; Barrett & Padwick, 18, 63; John M. Kivuli II, "The Modernization of an African Independent church", Nairobi, 1994, 58-63; Peter Wilson Kudoyi, "African Israel Nineveh Church: A Theological and Socio-Historical Analysis", Nairobi, 1991.

27 The name may be related to a popular slogan meaning "who is the redeemer?". Philomena Njeri, "The Akurinu Churches: A Study of the History and Some of the Basic Beliefs of the Holy Ghost Church of East Africa", Nairobi, 1984, 23; Solomon Waigwa & Simon Mugwe, "Origins and Theology of the African Holy Ghost Christian Church", Harold Turner Collection, Birmingham, 1995.

28 Njeri, 57-97; Githieya, 123-45; Jomo Kenyatta, *Facing Mount Kenya: The Tribal Life of the Gikuyu*, London, 1961, 278; Solomon Waigwa & Simon Mugwe, "Origins and Theology of the African Holy Ghost Christian Church (commonly known as the Akurinu Church)", Nairobi, 1995.

29 Lawrence O. Murunga, "I'm Jesus, says Kenyan", *Drum (East)*, Nairobi, 1986, 14-6.

30 Nancy Schwartz, "Christianity and the Construction of Global History: The Example of Legio Maria", Columbia, 1994, 140; Hastings, *History*, 177-8; Juliana Omale, "Legio Maria: What's the Future after the Founder's Death?", *African Christian*, Nairobi, 1991, 4-5; Maina Muiruri, "Sect Buries its Pope on top of a Holy Hill", Nairobi, 1998.

31 Barrett & Padwick, 11, 15-6, 22-4, 66.

32 Ibid., 36-7, 40-1, 74-86; World Council, 15-6, 23-4; G.I.M. Otobu, "The AICs in Nigeria", *Baragumu: The African Independent Churches Voice* 1, July 1996, 13.

The assistance of John Padwick of Nairobi in correcting some of the details of this chapter is gratefully acknowledged.

8

PENTECOSTAL AND
CHARISMATIC CHURCHES

The role of a new and rapidly growing form of African Christianity, here called "newer Pentecostal and Charismatic churches" (NPCs), is increasingly being recognized.[1] This movement, which has only emerged since 1970, is fast becoming one of the most significant expressions of Christianity on the continent, especially in Africa's cities. We can't understand African Christianity today without also understanding this latest movement of revival and renewal. Ogbu Kalu calls it the "third response" to white cultural domination and power in the church, the former two responses being Ethiopianism and the Aladura/ Zionist churches.[2] I would argue that this newer Pentecostal and Charismatic movement is not fundamentally different from the Holy Spirit movements and so-called "prophet-healing" and "spiritual churches" that preceded it in the AICs, but it is a continuation of them in a very different context. The older AICs, the "classical" Pentecostals, and the newer churches have all responded to the existential needs of the African worldview. They have all offered a personal encounter with God through the power of the Spirit, healing from sickness and deliverance from evil in all its manifestations, spiritual, social, and structural. It's for this reason that the newer Pentecostal and Charismatic churches are included in a book about AICs and indeed, they *may* be regarded as AICs. This is not to say that there are no tensions or differences between the "new" and the "old" AICs, which will be obvious here. In all reformations, the question is how far a reformation should go, and when does (or should) it stop. In a study of NPCs in north-east Zimbabwe, David Maxwell points out that many Christian movements in Africa (and, in fact, all over the world) have begun as movements of youth and women. The new churches give opportunities not afforded them by patriarchal and gerontocratic religions that have lost their charismatic power. As Maxwell points out, even the older Pentecostal churches, whether AICs or founded by western missions, "can lose their pentecostal vigor" through a process of bureaucratization and "ageing".[3]

The entrance and pervading influence of many different kinds of NPCs on the African Christian scene now makes it even more difficult, if not impossible, to put AICs into types and categories. It is becoming increasingly difficult to define "Pentecostal" precisely, and if we persist with narrow perceptions of the term, we will escape reality. In the West, "Pentecostal" usually refers to the older, "classical" Pentecostals who arose in the revivals at the beginning of this century, particularly the Azusa Street Revival in Los Angeles, 1906-8, paradoxically yet significantly presided over by an African-American, William J. Seymour. These churches characteristically understand themselves as those who believe in the "baptism with the Spirit" with the "initial evidence" of speaking in tongues. This limited, rather stereotyped and dogmatic understanding of "Pentecostal", however, fails to recognize the great variety of different Pentecostal movements in the Third World, many of which arose quite independently of western Pentecostalism. The Pentecostal and Charismatic movement is better understood as a movement concerned primarily with the *experience* of the working of the Holy Spirit and the *practice* of spiritual gifts.

In this sense, the term would include the majority of older AICs, those "classical" Pentecostals originating in western Pentecostal missions, and those independent churches, "fellowships", and "ministries" in Africa which are the focus of this chapter. It is in this sense that we refer to these various movements as "newer Pentecostals" and of course, the term "Pentecostal" would also apply to a great number of other, older kinds of AICs which emphasize the Holy Spirit in the church. The "classical" or "denominational" Pentecostals (like the Assemblies of God and the Church of God) are also a very active and growing phenomenon throughout Africa, and undoubtedly played a significant role in the emergence of some of these newer groups. But as these were founded by missionaries mostly from Britain and North America—although with more African involvement in leadership and financial independence than was the case in most of the older missionary founded churches—these "classical" Pentecostals cannot be regarded primarily as African *initiated* movements.

The Development of Newer Churches

Pentecostal churches with western origins have operated in Africa for most of the twentieth century. Most of these churches trace their historical origins to the impetus generated by the Azusa Street Revival, which sent out missionaries to fifty nations within two years.[4] The connections between this "classical" Pentecostal movement and AICs throughout Africa have been amply demonstrated in this book and elsewhere.[5] Some of these "classical" Pentecostal churches have become vibrant and rapidly expanding African churches throughout the continent, in particular the Assemblies of God, which operates in most countries of the Sub-Sahara. Throughout the history of AICs there has been a predominance of Pentecostal features and phenomena, many of which have been described in earlier chapters of this book. Harvey Cox is at least partly correct to refer to the Apostolic/ Zionist, Lumpa, and Kimbanguist churches as "the African expression of the worldwide Pentecostal movement". Not enough attention has been given to this resonance, although Gifford is also right to question whether the older AICs can be regarded as *paradigmatic* of the Pentecostal movement in Africa.[6]

In the 1970s, partly as a reaction to the bureaucratization process in established churches, independent Pentecostal and Charismatic churches began to emerge all over Africa, but especially in West Africa. Many of these vigorous new churches were influenced by the Pentecostal and Charismatic movement in Europe and North America and by established Pentecostal mission churches in Africa. However, it must be remembered that these churches were largely independent of foreign churches and had an African foundation. Many arose in the context of interdenominational evangelical campus and school Christian organizations, from which young charismatic leaders emerged with significant followings, and often the NPCs eventually replaced these former movements.[7] At first they were "nondenominational" churches, but in recent years, as they've expanded, many of these churches have developed denominational structures, several prominent leaders have been "episcopized", and some are now international churches. The process of "ageing" and the proliferation of these new movements now continue as their founders die (in at least one case) or approach old age. The African Charismatic churches or "ministries" initially tended to have a younger, more formally educated and consequently more westernized leadership and membership, including young professionals and middle class urban Africans.[8] In leadership structures, theology and liturgy, these churches differ quite markedly from both the older AICs and the western mission-founded churches, Pentecostal and non-Pentecostal. Their services are usually emotional and enthusiastic, and many NPCs use electronic musical instruments, publish their own literature and run their own Bible training centers for preachers, both men and women, to further propagate their message. These movements encourage the planting of new independent churches and make use of schoolrooms, cinemas, community halls, and even hotel conference rooms for their revival meetings. Church leaders sometimes travel the continent and inter-continentally, and some produce glossy booklets and broadcast radio and television programs. They are often linked to wider international networks of independent Charismatic preachers, some of which (but by no means all) are dominated by North Americans.

These NPCs are, like the older AICs before them, an African phenomenon, churches which for the most part have been instituted by Africans for Africans. They are also self-governing, self-propagating, and (in some cases to a lesser extent) self-supporting, and usually they have no organizational links with any outside church or denomination. In fact, they may be regarded as "modern versions" of older AICs. Although they differ from the classical AICs in that they don't try as much to offer solutions for traditional problems, yet they do address the problems faced by AICs, but offer a radical reorientation to a modern and industrial global society.[9] Asamoah-Gyadu makes the interesting point that one of the basic differences between the older AICs and the NPCs lies in the fact that in the spiritual churches, "members are the clients of the prophets who may be the custodians of powers to overcome the ills of life". In the NPCs, however, "each believer is empowered through the baptism of the Holy Spirit to overcome them."[10] It may be argued that in the spiritual churches too, provision is made for any person to become a prophet and therefore to be a custodian of spiritual power, and that the difference might not be as great as imagined.

Some of the main methods employed by the NPCs are very similar to those used by most Pentecostals—including door-to-door evangelism, meetings held in homes of interested inquirers, preaching in trains, buses, on street corners and at places of public concourse, and "tent crusades" held all over the continent.[11] Access to modern communications has resulted in the popularizing of western (especially North American) independent Pentecostal "televangelists", several of whom make regular visits to Africa and broadcast their own television programs there, public scandals notwithstanding. The strategies employed by these evangelists have been subject to criticism,[12] but have had the effect of promoting a form of Christianity that has appealed especially to the urbanized and significantly westernized new generation of Africans. Theologically, the NPCs are Christocentric but share an emphasis on the power of the Spirit with other Pentecostals, including many AICs. A particular focus on personal encounter with Christ (being "born again"), long periods of individual and communal prayer, prayer for healing and problems like unemployment and poverty, deliverance from demons and "the occult" (this term often means traditional beliefs and witchcraft), the use of spiritual gifts like speaking in tongues, and (to a lesser extent) prophecy—these features more or less characterize all NPCs.

Charismatics in West Africa

The growth of NPCs has been most dramatic in West Africa, especially in Nigeria and Ghana, where new Pentecostal churches abound in almost every neighborhood, some of which have an internationally high profile. In these countries, many new churches arose in interdenominational university student groups, notably the Scripture Union and the Christian Union. These groups later became "fellowships" that grew into full-blown denominations often led by lecturers and teachers.[13] One of the most remarkable and earliest of these movements in Nigeria is the Deeper Life Bible Church, with branches all over West Africa and inter-continentally, with over half a million members in Nigeria only ten years after its founding. William Folorunso Kumuyi (b.1941) was a former education lecturer at the University of

Lagos and an Anglican who became a Pentecostal in the Apostolic Faith Church. He began a weekly interdenominational Bible study group in 1973 that spread to other parts of Nigeria and was called Deeper Christian Life Ministry. The Apostolic Faith Church expelled him in 1975 for preaching without being an ordained minister. Kumuyi began holding retreats at Easter and Christmas, emphasizing healing and miracles and living a "holy life". His followers distributed thousands of free tracts, evangelized, and established Bible study groups all over western Nigeria. The first Sunday service held in Lagos in 1982 is regarded as the foundation date of the new church. The following year, Kumuyi sent some of his leading pastors to Yonggi Cho's Full Gospel Central Church (now, Yoido Full Gospel Church) in Seoul, Korea, after which a system of 5,000 "home caring fellowships" based on the Korean model was instituted. Unlike more recent NPCs which tend to be less prescriptive, Deeper Life emphasizes personal holiness evidenced by rejection of the "world" and the keeping of a strict ethical code—and in this respect it is more like classical Pentecostal churches and some older AICs. The church prides itself in being a wholly African church totally independent of western links, and here again it differs from many other NPCs that regularly promote western Pentecostal media. It has tended to be exclusive in its approach to other churches, but its more recent involvement in ecumenical organizations has tempered this somewhat.[14]

Other prominent Nigerian examples of this new phenomenon are the Redeemed Christian Church of God of E.A. Adeboye (who was a university teacher with a PhD in mathematics), the Christ Chapel founded by Tunde Joda in 1985, and the controversial Synagogue Church of All Nations of Prophet T.B Joshua. In 1981 Adeboye, now a prominent and respected leader in Nigerian Christianity, took over a Yoruba church that had seceded from the Aladura movement in 1958, and he transformed it into a new, multiethnic Charismatic church, now possibly the largest in the country, with monthly meetings in the

"Redemption Camp" that draws hundreds of thousands.[15] Prophet Joshua had Zambia's President Chiluba as his special guest early in 2001. David Oyedepo, a trained architect, started "Winner's Chapel" in 1981, which since 2000 has erected a 50,000 seat auditorium called "Faith Tabernacle", reputed to be one of the largest church buildings in the world, in an impressive complex of modern buildings at the 300 acre "Canaan Land". Oyedepo, "presiding bishop" of the Living Faith World Outreach claimed 200 churches in Nigeria with over 400 pastors in forty African nations in 1998.[16]

One of the first and most influential NPCs in Africa is the Church of God Mission International of Benson Idahosa (1938-98), founded in 1972. Idahosa had some 300,000 members in 1991 and a headquarters in Benin City, where a "Miracle Center" was erected in 1975 seating over 10,000 to which thousands flock every week to receive their own personal miracles.[17] Idahosa, who became one of the best-known preachers in Africa, attended the Christ for the Nations Institute in 1971, an independent Pentecostal college in Dallas, Texas. His stay there was short-lived, however, and he returned to Nigeria after three months with an increased "burden" for his people. He began the first of many mass evangelistic crusades for which he was so well known. He received considerable financial support from well-known independent Pentecostal preachers in the United States, including his mentor, Gordon Lindsay, the healing evangelist T.L. Osborne, and the now discredited televangelist, Jim Bakker.[18] As part of the Miracle Centre, Idahosa's church runs the All Nations for Christ Bible Institute, probably the most popular and influential Bible school in West Africa, from where hundreds of preachers fan out into different parts of the region, often to plant new churches. Idahosa became a Bishop in 1981 and later took the title Archbishop. He had formal ties with other NPCs throughout Africa—especially in Ghana, where he held his first crusade in 1978.[19] When Idahosa died suddenly in 1998, his wife, Margaret Idahosa, who had shared ministry and leadership with her husband since the church began, took his place as head and bishop of the Church of God Mission.

NPCs in Nigeria and in other parts of West Africa have begun to move from loose associations of "ministries" to more institutionalized denominations, and in this transition many seem to be moving away from an emphasis on "prosperity".[20] The NPCs tend to be more enthusiastic in their services than the older Pentecostals are, and they usually emphasize miracles and healings more than personal holiness and ethical legalism. A particular emphasis in West African NPCs is a stress on the need for deliverance from a whole host of demonic forces, most of which are identified with traditional deities and "ancestral curses".[21] In 1986 the Pentecostal Fellowship of Nigeria (PFN) was formed, an ecumenical association incorporating all the various "born again" movements and one of the most influential ecumenical organizations in Nigeria. In 1995, Adeboye was president of the PFN, considered the most powerful voice in the national Christian Association of Nigeria of which it is now a part. There were more than 700 churches registered as members of PFN in 1991 in Lagos State alone. In particular, the PFN sees one of its main tasks as that of uniting Christians against the perceived danger of the "Islamization" of Nigeria.[22]

Pentecostals are also prominent in Ghana, where the Church of Pentecost was the second largest denomination in Ghana after the Roman Catholics in 1993. This church has its roots in the pioneering work of Peter Anim, who invited the Apostolic Church in Britain to send a missionary, James McKeown. McKeown later differed with his church and split from the Apostolic Church in 1953.[23] The church is now entirely African, although it has a working relationship with the Elim Pentecostal Church in Britain.

Idahosa's 1978 crusade in Accra resulted in the subsequent formation of the first "charismatic ministries" there. Bishop Nicholas Duncan-Williams, formerly of the Church of Pentecost, is leader of the largest and earliest NPC founded in

1980, Christian Action Faith Ministries. Trained at Idahosa's Bible Institute, Duncan-Williams heads an association called the Council of Charismatic Ministers. Fraternization between the NPCs and the Rawlings government in Ghana led to a new church-state alliance, particularly as Duncan-Williams became virtually a national chaplain to the regime. Another rapidly growing NPC is the International Central Gospel Church founded in 1984 by former Anglican Mensa Otabil, one of the best-known Ghanaian Charismatic leaders outside Ghana. Otabil also heads an umbrella organization called Charismatic Ministries Network, and in 2000 opened a Christian university. He has become particularly well known for his brand of black consciousness propagated in his writings and preaching that takes him to different parts of Africa.[24] Other leading NPCs in Ghana are the Holy Fire Ministries of Bishop Ofori Twumasi, the International Bible Worship Centre of Sam Korankye Ankrah, Victory Bible Church of Tackie Nii Yarboi and Broken Yoke Foundation of Eastwood Anaba. The latter is an expanding organization especially active in the remote and largely rural northeast region of Ghana. NPCs in Ghana also make extensive use of home groups to effectively manage pastoral care.[25]

The NPCs are also found in several other West African countries. In Monrovia, the fastest-growing churches in Liberia in 1989 were the Transcontinental Evangelical Association Church (Transcea) founded in 1982—not a typical NPC, as it rejects speaking in tongues, drums and dancing—and the Bethel World Outreach, founded in 1986, another example of the "prosperity" type of NPC popular in several African cities.[26] In Abidjan, Ivory Coast, a rapidly growing church led by Dion Robert is called the Yopougon Protestant Baptist Church and Mission, claiming over 70,000 members in 1995, and based on a well-structured home group system.

Pentecostals and Charismatics Elsewhere

During the 1980s, rapidly growing new Pentecostal groups began to emerge in East Africa, where they were sometimes seen as a threat by older churches, from whom they often gained members. Some of these new churches were directly affected by the phenomenon in West Africa, particularly in Nigeria and Ghana. Preachers like Benson Idahosa, David Oyedepo, Duncan-Williams, and Mensa Otabil have traveled extensively in Africa. NPCs are active throughout Africa and in some countries they consist of many different smaller groups. One of the fastest growing churches in Kenya is the Winners Chapel in Nairobi, which dedicated a building in 1998 for its 3,500-member congregation after only one year of existence. This congregation was commenced by Dayo Olutayo from Oyedepo's church in Nigeria, who arrived in Kenya in 1995. The media advertising hype for the dedication service in Nairobi gushed, "Winners Chapel, Nairobi was built entirely debt free. No loans of bank borrowing and certainly no begging trips to the West!". The organization had two other "Winners Chapels" in Kisumu and Mombasa.27

Uganda, dominated by Catholic and Anglican missions over the past century, has been fertile ground for NPCs since the late 1980s. Gifford speaks of "homegrown pentecostal churches... mushrooming in luxuriant fashion" in Uganda. He describes four of the largest in Kampala: the Kampala Pentecostal Church with 5,000 members; Namirembe Christian Fellowship founded by Simeon Kayiwa, a preacher well-known for his healing and miracle ministry; the Abundant Life Church founded by Handel Leslie, a black Canadian; and the Holy Church of Christ, a church more in the prophet-healing AIC tradition, founded by Ghanaian prophet John Obiri Yeboah. Yeboah, who was in Uganda in the 1970s, returned to Ghana during Idi Amin's reign of terror and spent a further year in Uganda from 1986 until his death the following year. Several NPCs in Uganda owe their origins to him, and he organized the still-active association of Pentecostal churches called the National Fellowship of Born Again Churches and United Reformed Council.[28] Tensions in the Anglican church over spiritual gifts led to the formation of the Charismatic Church of Uganda by the former provost of the cathedral in Kampala in 1991. The NPCs in East Africa, following the emphasis of the East African Revival, preach the need for a personal experience of God in Christ through being "born again". But to this they add the Pentecostal and AIC emphasis on the power of the Spirit manifested in healing, speaking in tongues, prophecy and deliverance from demons, manifestations that the East African Revival later discouraged. It was this that brought conflict with the inheritors of the Revival legacy, the Anglicans, and added to the impetus behind the new churches.

In Malawi, young preachers in Blantyre in the 1970s propagated a "born again" message in their revival meetings that at first didn't always result in the formation of new churches. By the 1980s however, the pattern of NPCs elsewhere in Africa was emerging. These revival meetings had developed into "ministries" and "fellowships", and inevitably some were further institutionalized into new churches. One of the largest of these was the Living Water Church founded by Stanley Ndovi in 1984. As elsewhere, these Malawian movements focused on young people in schools, colleges and university.[29]

President Frederick Chiluba, a "born again" Christian with a pentecostal experience, declared Zambia a "Christian nation" two months after his landslide election victory in 1991. He appointed "born again" Christians to government posts, and regularly promotes Pentecostal evangelistic crusades and conventions, where he is sometimes featured as a preacher. Vice-President Godfrey Miyanda attends an NPC, the Jesus Worship Center led by Ernest Chelelwa. The NPCs are now in abundance in Zambia and the charismatic movement has split some "mainline" churches. A leading NPC preacher, Nevers Mumba, founded Victory Faith Ministries in 1985, and is another product of Christ for the Nations Institute in Dallas. He has a network of

Victory Bible Churches and has even formed his own political party.[30]

One of the largest denominations in Zimbabwe is the Zimbabwe Assemblies of God Africa (popularly called ZAOGA), a Pentecostal church with roots in South African Pentecostalism. ZAOGA commenced in urban areas of Zimbabwe and is led by Archbishop Ezekiel Guti. In 1959, Guti with a group of young African pastors were expelled from the AFM after a disagreement with white missionaries. The group joined the South African Assemblies of God of Nicholas Bhengu, but separated from there in 1967 to form the Assemblies of God, Africa (later ZAOGA). Guti went to Christ for the Nations Institute in 1971 just as Idahosa had done, and he too received financial and other resources from the USA. But Guti, like many NPC leaders, resists any attempts to identify his church with the "religious right" of the USA or to be controlled by "neo-colonial" interests. In a very pertinent development in 1986, leaders of twelve of the largest Pentecostal churches in Zimbabwe, including Guti, wrote a "blistering rebuttal" to a right-wing attack on the Zimbabwean state by a North American Charismatic preacher. [31] Since 1986, ZAOGA has also had churches in Britain, Zimbabwean ZAOGA missionaries went to South Africa to plant churches there in 1989, and the church also has branches in seventeen other African countries called "Forward in Faith". ZAOGA is now organized as a fully-fledged denomination with complex administrative structures headed by Guti. By 1999 ZAOGA had an estimated 600,000 affiliated members, which made it the third largest denomination in Zimbabwe after the Marange Apostles and the Roman Catholics, with over 10% of the total Christians in the country. ZAOGA itself claimed to be the largest, with one and a half million members in 1995, but this figure is disputed. Guti's leadership style and expensive overseas trips were becoming contentious issues in the late 1990s, as were the lifestyles of some of his more powerful pastors. ZAOGA has already experienced various splits, one of the most significant led by Guti's cofounder, Abel Sande.[32] There are several rapidly expanding new Pentecostal churches with branches throughout Zimbabwe, some of the largest being the Family of God founded by Andrew Wutaunashe (a former ZAOGA pastor), Faith Ministries formerly led by Ngwisa Mkandla, and the Glad Tidings Fellowship of Richmond Chiudza.

In South Africa, NPCs may not be as prominent as in other parts of Africa, but nevertheless are very significant. Kenneth Meshoe, leader of the African Christian Democratic Party, which polled enough votes in the 1999 elections to gain seven members of parliament, is an NPC pastor of the Hope of Glory Tabernacle and was formerly an evangelist in Reinhard Bonnke's Christ for the Nations organization. The Director General of President Thabo Mbeki's "Office of the President", Frank Chikane, is a "classical" Pentecostal and was still Vice-President of the Apostolic Faith Mission in 1999. Chikane is a person of considerable influence in South Africa, having one of the most powerful executive positions in the ANC government and well placed to speak on behalf of South Africa's large Christian constituency. He maintains personal relationships with the ruling ANC hierarchy and church leaders across the denominational board from NPCs to ecumenical "mainline" churches. He has the unique distinction of having been General Secretary of the South African Council of Churches during apartheid's final years, the only Pentecostal to have occupied that position, and he also spent a while in Bonnke's organization. The largest single Christian congregation in Soweto, South Africa is the Grace Bible Church led by Mosa Sono, with over 5,000 members in 1999. This church has planted new congregations in some major urban areas, including a poverty-stricken "informal settlement" (slum) area. Sono, born in Soweto in 1961, grew up in the Dutch Reformed Church, and attended the AFM Bible college in Soshanguve before leaving to attend white charismatic leader Ray McCauley's Rhema Bible Training Center near Johannesburg. He formed Grace Bible Church in 1984, and became Vice-President of the International Fellowship of

Christian Churches in 1996, the formerly white-dominated and largest association of charismatic churches in Southern Africa, whose President is McCauley. Once again, the connection between some of these NPCs and North American "prosperity" preachers is apparent, as McCauley's original inspiration and training came from the father of the "faith message", Kenneth Hagin of Tulsa, Oklahoma. But in spite of this association, Sono is much more cautious in this regard, and has repeatedly sought to distance himself from "prosperity theology" and western, white domination, and there are signs that his stance is having a positive influence on McCauley too.[33]

The latest African churches in Europe are these independent Pentecostal and Charismatic churches. They have taken western Europe by storm since the 1980s and now form the majority of African churches there.[34] A particularly prominent case is the Kingsway International Christian Centre in London. This church, founded in 1992 by a Nigerian, Matthew Ashimolowo, had over 5,000 members in 1999 and had become the largest congregation in Britain, attracting national media attention. The majority of the members are West Africans, predominantly Nigerians. Large Ghanaian churches like the Church of Pentecost, or other Nigerian ones like the Redeemed Christian Church of God and the Deeper Life Bible Church now have congregations all over western Europe and in North America. The congregations of the Church of Pentecost are directed from its central headquarters in Accra, through its International Missions Director.[35]

Indirectly related to the phenomenon of NPCs is a growing "charismatic movement" in many of the older mission-founded churches in Africa, having a profound effect on all forms of Christianity in the continent. Some of the leaders of this Holy Spirit movement in older churches have seceded in the past to form AICs and more recently, NPCs. But there are still a considerable number of people who have remained in the older churches with a charismatic form of Christianity, expressed in fellowship and prayer groups, Sunday services, and "renewal" conferences—to some extent inspired and encouraged by similar movements in other parts of the world. The older churches have responded to the NPCs with innovations that can be described as "charismatic", where a place is given to gifts of the Holy Spirit in the church. There are many examples of this throughout Africa. One of the best known was the controversial healing ministry of Zambian Roman Catholic Archbishop Emmanuel Milingo, who was removed to Rome thereafter. Other examples are a popular Anglican healing centre in Zimbabwe; the Charismatic "Legion of Christ's Witnesses" (*Iviyo*) association within South African Anglicanism led by Bishop Alpheus Zulu long before the Charismatic movement began in America; a thriving Charismatic movement among Catholics in Uganda; one among Lutherans and in the interdenominational "Big November Crusade" in Tanzania; multitudes of Ghanaian Catholic, Methodist, and Presbyterian Charismatics; and a Charismatic movement in Nigerian Anglicanism led by Professor Simeon Onibere.[36] The list could go on.

The Challenge of the Newer Churches

One of the main criticisms leveled against NPCs is that they propagate a "prosperity gospel", the "Faith" or "Word" movement originating in North American independent Charismatic movements.[37] This "health and wealth" gospel seems to reproduce some of the worst forms of capitalism in Christian guise. Paul Gifford has become a leading exponent on this subject. He suggests that the biggest single factor in the emergence of these new churches is the collapse of African economies by the 1980s and the subsequent increasing dependence of NPCs on the USA. He proposes that it is "Americanization" rather than any "African quality" that is responsible for the growth of these churches. He sees this new phenomenon as a type of neo-colonialism propagated by American "prosperity preachers", a sort of "conspiracy theory".[38]

Gifford's analysis, which he has modified to some extent more recently,[39] has been accepted in many church and academic circles. However, it seems to ignore some fundamental features of Pentecostalism, now predominantly a Third World phenomenon, where experience and practice are more important than formal ideology or even theology. As Kalu points out, the relationship between the African NPC pastor and his or her "western patron" is entirely eclectic, and the "dependency" in fact has been mutual. The western supporter actually needs the African pastor to bolster his own international image and increase his own financial resources. Kalu observes that in the 1990s, since the public disgracing of American "televangelists", the mood in Africa has changed, and NPCs are now "characterized by independence and an emphasis on the Africanist roots of the ministries".[40] Traditionally in Africa, prosperity and success are seen as signs of God's blessings, so it is no wonder that such a message should be uncritically accepted there—and this is as true for the newer AICs as it is for the older ones.[41] There *are* connections between some of the NPCs and the American "health and wealth" movement, and it is also true that some of the new African churches reproduce and promote this teaching and literature. But identifying NPCs with the American "prosperity gospel" is a generalization that particularly fails to appreciate the reconstructions and innovations made by these new African movements in adapting to a radically different context, just as the older AICs did years before.

The NPCs form a challenge to the Christian church in Africa. To the European mission-founded churches, they are demonstrations of a form of Christianity that appeals to a new generation of Africans, and from which older churches can learn. There are indications that the NPCs increase at the expense of all types of older churches, including the prophet-healing AICs.[42] To these older AICs, with whom they actually have much in common, they are consequently often a source of tension. The NPCs preach against "tribalism" and parochial denominationalism. They are often sharply critical of the older AICs, particularly in what they perceive as the African traditional component of AIC practices, which are sometimes seen as manifestations of demons needing "deliverance".[43] As a result, older AICs feel hurt and threatened by them. At a consultation of the OAIC in Nairobi in 1995, the problems posed by the NPCs for AICs was a highly sensitive subject that produced animated discussion, and AIC delegates criticized the NPCs for their exclusiveness. Bishop Nathan Magomere of the African Church of the Holy Spirit had the following lament for the NPCs:

> Remember your African roots and culture and remember that we too are your brothers and sisters in Christ Jesus. Beware of selling your cultural birthright for a bowl of soup of foreign ideologies or money. Our own faith taken from the Old and New Testaments, is strong enough and deep enough for us not to need to look elsewhere.[44]

In addition, the NPCs have to some extent embraced and externalized western notions of a "nuclear family" and individualized, urban lifestyles. This brings them into further tension with African traditional culture and ethnic ties, thereby enabling members to escape the onerous commitments to the extended family and to achieve success and accumulate possessions independently.[45] The NPCs also sometimes castigate "mainline" churches for their dead formalism and traditionalism, so the "mainline" churches also feel threatened by them. Commenting on this, Ogbu Kalu makes the salient point:

> The established churches usually react in three stages: hostility, apologetics and adaptation. Institutionalization breeds late adoption of innovations. We witnessed this pattern in the response to the Aladura challenge. It is being repeated without any lessons learnt from history.[46]

Gifford himself is aware of the problems inherent in too simplistic an interpretation of the newer African Pentecostalism. After discussing Christian fundamentalism in the USA and the "rapidly growing sector of African Christianity" closely related to it, he says that the American groups operating in Africa "find themselves functioning in a context considerably different from that in the United States".47 Perhaps Gifford has not taken this "considerably different" context seriously enough in his substantial analyses of the newer Pentecostals in Africa. The oversimplified and patronizing idea that "prosperity" churches in Africa are led by unscrupulous manipulators greedy for wealth and power doesn't account for the increasing popularity of these NPCs with educated and responsible people, who continue to give financial support and feel their needs are met there.48 Often, those who are "anti-charismatic" and resent or are threatened by the growth and influence of the newer churches are the source of these criticisms. Kalu says that in the decade after 1985, the NPCs "blossomed into complex varieties" and that in their development, "European influence became more pronounced". But he points out that that in spite of this, "the originators continued to be African, imitating foreigners, eclectically producing foreign theologies but transforming these for immediate contextual purposes".49

With reference to ZAOGA, Maxwell says that this movement's "own dominant prosperity teachings have arisen from predominantly southern African sources and are shaped by Zimbabwean concerns". He says that the "prosperity gospel" is best explained "not in terms of false consciousness or right wing conspiracy but as a means to enable Pentecostals to make the best of rapid social change". ZAOGA's teaching of the "Spirit of Poverty", for instance, "resonates with ideas of self-reliance, indigenous business, and black empowerment propounded by the ruling party and state controlled media", while at the same time it "successfully explains and exploits popular insecurities".50 Similarly, Matthews Ojo, who writes extensively on Nigerian NPCs, says that they "are increasingly responding to the needs and aspirations of Nigerians amid the uncertainty of their political life and the pain of their constant and unending economic adjustments".51 Asamoah-Gyadu believes that the "greatest virtue" of the "health and wealth" gospel of the NPCs lies in "the indomitable spirit that believers develop in the face of life's odds.... In essence, misfortune becomes only temporary".[52] It is clear, then, that NPCs are far from being simply an "Americanization" of African Christianity.

Like the churches before them, the NPCs have a sense of identity as a separated and egalitarian community with democratic access to spiritual power, whose primary purpose is to promote their cause to those outside. These churches see themselves as the "born again" people of God, with a strong sense of belonging to the community of God's people, those chosen from out of the world to witness to the new life they experience in the power of the Spirit. The cornerstone of their message is this "born again" conversion experience through repentance of sin and submission to Christ, and this is what identifies them, even to outsiders.[53] Unlike the older AICs, where there tends to be an emphasis on the prophet figure or principal leader as the one dispensing God's gifts to his or her followers, the NPCs usually emphasize the availability and encourage the practice of gifts of the Holy Spirit by all of their members. The emergence of these NPCs at the end of the twentieth century indicates that there are unresolved questions facing the church in Africa, such as the role of "success" and "prosperity" in God's economy, enjoying God *and* his gifts, including healing and material provision, and the holistic dimension of "salvation" which is always meaningful in an African context. The "here-and-now" problems being addressed by NPCs in modern Africa are not unlike those faced by the older AICs decades before, and these problems still challenge the church as a whole today. They remind the church of the age-old conviction of Africa that for any faith to be relevant and enduring, it must also be experienced.[54] These are some of the lessons for the universal church from the AICs, and the NPCs are their latest exponents.

Notes

1 David Maxwell, "Witches, Prophets and Avenging Spirits: The Second Christian Movement in North-East Zimbabwe", *Journal of Religion in Africa* 25:3, 1995, 313; Gifford, *African Christianity*, 31; Anderson, *Zion & Pentecost*, 76-79. I have opted for "newer", because some of these churches have been established for almost three decades.

2 Ogbu U. Kalu, "The Third Response: Pentecostalism and the Reconstruction of Christian Experience in Africa, 1970-1995", *Journal of African Christian Thought*, 1:2, 1998, 3.

3 Maxwell, "Witches", 316-7.

4 Hollenweger, *Pentecostals*, 22-4; Vinson Synan, *The Holiness-Pentecostal Tradition: Charismatic Movements in the Twentieth Century*, Grand Rapids & Cambridge, 1997, 84-106.

5 Allan Anderson & Gerald J. Pillay, "The Segregated Spirit: The Pentecostals", Oxford & Cape Town, 1997, 228-9; Allan H. Anderson, "Dangerous Memories for South African Pentecostals", Sheffield, 1999, 88-92; id., *Bazalwane*, 22-4.

6 Cox, 246; Gifford, *African Christianity*, 33.

7 Kwabena J. Asamoah-Gyadu, "Traditional missionary Christianity and new religious movements in Ghana", Accra, 1996; Kalu, "Third Response", 7.

8 Hackett, Rosalind I. J. "Enigma Variations: The New Religious Movement in Nigeria Today", Elkhart, 1990, 132-5.

9 C. M. Pauw, 145.

10 Kwabena J. Asamoah-Gyadu, "The Church in the African State: The Pentecostal/Charismatic Experience in Ghana", *Journal of African Christian Thought*, 1:2, 1998, 56.

11 This latest expression of African Pentecostalism is to some extent the result of the popular method of tent evangelism pioneered mainly by North Americans in the 1940s and 1950s (with roots in the nineteenth century revivals). This was continued with considerable effect by popular South African black Pentecostals Nicholas Bhengu and Richard Ngidi, and more recently by Nigerian Benson Idahosa and German evangelist Reinhard Bonnke.

12 For example, see Paul Gifford, "Reinhard Bonnke's mission to Africa, and his 1991 Nairobi crusade", Nairobi, 1992, 157.

13 Ruth Marshall, "Pentecostalism in Southern Nigeria: an overview", Nairobi, 1992, 9; Paul Gifford, *The Christian Churches and the Democratization of Africa*, Leiden, 1995, 244.

14 Matthews A. Ojo, "Deeper Life Bible Church of Nigeria", Nairobi, 1992, 137-41, 150-3; Gifford, *Christian Churches*, 135; Johnstone, 421; Marshall, 10.

15 Marshall, 17; Ruth Marshall-Fratani, "Mediating the Global and Local in Nigerian Pentecostalism", *Journal of Religion in Africa* 28:4, 1998, 298.

16 I visited these churches in south-western Nigeria in May 2001.

17 Marshall, 16; Gifford, *Christian Churches*, 254, 257.

18 Ruthanne Garlock, *Fire in his Bones: The Story of Benson Idahosa*, South Plainfield, 1981, 117.

19 Asamoah-Gyadu, "Traditional Missionary", 60.

20 Marshall, 15-6, 25.

21 Birgit Meyer, "'Make a Complete Break with the Past': Memory and Post-Colonial Modernity in Ghanaian Pentecostalist Discourse", *Journal of Religion in Africa* 28:4, 1998, 323-4; Gifford, *African Christianity*, 97-109.

22 Gifford, *Christian Churches*, 256; Marshall, 23-9.

23 Robert W. Wyllie, "Pioneers of Ghanaian Pentecostalism: Peter Anim and James McKeown", *Journal of Religion in Africa* 6:2, 1974, 109-22.

24 In particular, Otabil expounds this form of black consciousness in his *Beyond the Rivers of Ethiopia: A Biblical Revelation on God's Purpose for the Black Race*, Accra, 1992.

25 Asamoah-Gyadu, "The church", 53, 55; Gerrie ter Haar, "Standing Up for Jesus: a survey of new developments in Christianity in Ghana", *Exchange 23:3*, 1994, 225-36; Gifford, *African Christianity*, 76-109.

26 Gifford, *New Dimensions*, 33; Paul Gifford, *Christianity and Politics in Doe's Liberia*, Cambridge, 1993, 163.

27 Charles Ouko, "The Triumph of Vision", *The Sunday Nation*, Nairobi, February 15, 1998.

28 Gifford, *African Christianity*, 157-68.

29 Richard van Dijk, "Young Born-Again Preachers in post-independence Malawi: the significance of an extraneous identity", Nairobi, 1992, 55-65.

30 Gifford, *African Christianity*, 197-205, 220, 230, 233.

31 David Maxwell, "'Delivered from the Spirit of Poverty': Pentecostalism, Prosperity and Modernity in Zimbabwe". *Journal of Religion in Africa* 28:4, 1998, 357; Gifford, *Christian Churches*, 123.

32 Maxwell, "Delivered", 351-2, 366-8, 372, n. 8; Johnstone, 598; Gifford, *Christian Churches*, 121; Presler, 290.

33 Anderson, "Prosperity Message", 74-5; id.,, *Bazalwane*, 52-5; id., *Zion and Pentecost*, chapters 7 & 9; Gifford, *African Christianity*, 236-7.

34 ter Haar, *Halfway*, 97.

35 Information from Rev. Opoku Onyinah, former International Missions Director, and currently (2000), PhD candidate at the University of Birmingham.

36 Emmanuel Milingo, *The World in Between: Christian Healing and the Struggle for Spiritual Survival*, London, 1984; Stephen Hayes, *Black Charismatic Anglicans: The Iviyo loFakazi bakaKristu and its relations with other renewal movements*, Pretoria, 1990; Josiah R. Mlahagwa, "Contending for the Faith: Spiritual Revival & the Fellowship Church in Tanzania", Oxford, 296-306; Gifford, *African Christianity*, 95-6, 154, 227-8, 330; id., *Christianity and Politics*, 127, 245.

37 For a summary of this teaching, particularly found in the preaching and writings of Kenneth Hagin and Kenneth Copeland, see Anderson, "Prosperity Message", 72-83.

38 Gifford, *Christianity and Politics*, 196-9, 294, 314-5.

39 e.g. Gifford, *African Christianity*, 236-44.

40 Kalu, "Third Response", 8.

41 Daneel, *Quest*, 46; Gifford, *Christianity and Politics*, 188.

42 ter Haar, "Standing Up", 224; Marshall, 5; Meyer, 319; Gifford, *African Christianity*, 62-3, 95, 233.

43 Asamoah-Gyadu, "The church", 56; Marshall, 11; Kalu, "Third Reponse", 8.

44 John Padwick & Maurice Onyango, "Black and White Consult", *Baragumu: The African Independent Churches Voice* 1, July 1996, 4.

45 Meyer, 320; Maxwell, 354; Marshall, 21-2.

46 Kalu, "Third Response", 3.

47 Gifford, *African Christianity*, 43.

48 Marshall, 8, 24.

49 Kalu, "Third Response", 7.

50 Maxwell, "Delivered", 351, 358-9.

51   Matthews   A.Ojo,   "The   Church   in   the   African   State: The Charismatic/Pentecostal Experience in Nigeria", *Journal of African Christian Thought,* 1:2, 1998, 25.

52 Asamoah-Gyadu, "The church", 55.

53 Marshall, 9; Gifford, *Christian Churches,* 244.

54 Anderson, "Prosperity Message", 80-2; Ojo, "The Church", 25.

Part Three

LESSONS

9

RELIGION AND CULTURE

It should be abundantly evident by now that AICs are not a monolithic and homogeneous entity. The last part of this study draws lessons from the AIC reformation described in the previous chapters. But in doing so, we must be aware of the dangers of generalization in such an enormous and multifaceted movement. Nevertheless, the implications of the AIC reformation for Christianity as a whole, specifically in Africa but also universally, must be considered. In this chapter, the interaction between Christianity and African religions and culture will be examined. This has significance for contemporary issues that are particularly important to theology, like inculturation, indigenization, syncretism, and contextualization—and the formation of an African theology that is relevant to the felt needs of people, the main concern of the next chapter. In these final three chapters, I will sometimes draw on insights gained from my own research in South Africa, where issues relating to popular religious beliefs and practices have been discussed extensively.[1] Of course, in doing so we remember that what may be true in this context is not necessarily to be applied to other parts of Africa, although there are many similarities. The conclusions will be modified and the examples widened to include AICs from all over the continent. It's also necessary to distance this discussion from cultural nostalgia, any hankering back to past traditions as if they are more genuinely "African" than more "modern" practices and beliefs are. Any movement that doesn't continue to innovate and adapt to a changing context will no longer be able to thrive, and this is as true for AICs as for any other religious movements.

Innovation and Inculturation

Understanding the attitudes of AICs to older African religious beliefs, such as the ancestors, divination,[2] traditional medicine and healing, polygyny, and traditional patterns of leadership is important for understanding the process of inculturation that has occurred in these churches. At the same time, many interesting and uniquely innovative adaptations have been made to these traditional practices. The proclamation of the Christian message by AICs often results in a rejection of the traditional practices of witchcraft, divination and ancestor rituals as a means of solving problems. As we've seen, European missionaries had also rejected these practices, but for quite different reasons. Whereas missionaries generally saw the practices as ignorant superstitions to be obliterated systematically by education, AICs saw them as expressions of real social malevolence and manifestations of evil spirits and sorcery. We've seen that their appeal to the Bible gave a more radical solution, creating a "biblical-African alliance" against the more rationalistic and inflexible Christianity brought by western missionaries.[3] In the last chapter, we saw that new AICs, particularly in West Africa, have been in the forefront of proclaiming a gospel of deliverance from evil spirits, perhaps to the extent of exaggeration. This message of deliverance has always been an essential part of this African reformation throughout the twentieth century. The African spirit world abounds with troublesome spirit beings that threaten the enjoyment of life. They must be dealt with, and the fears and insecurities they represent be eliminated. This is one of the tasks taken on by AICs.[4]

The proclamation of the Christian message by AICs was presented in symbols and experiences with which ordinary people were familiar, but this was often done in diametrical opposition to practices felt to be inconsistent with this message. We've seen that some of the largest prophet-healing churches in Africa like the Kimbanguists and the Christ Apostolic Church reject key traditional practices like polygyny, traditional beer, and the use of power-laden charms. Alice Lenshina's Lumpa Church was opposed to polygyny and beer-drinking too, and had a strong anti-witchcraft message. A central feature of Zionist and Apostolic AICs in Zimbabwe is their rejection of key elements in traditional religion and culture. These AICs demonstrate, says Inus Daneel, "how the gospel is adapted to or presented in confrontation with existing indigenous customs and values". He considers this to be one of the main contributions of AICs to African theology. The AICs provide many examples of an innovative approach, whereby traditional cultural and religious ceremonies have been adapted and transformed to have Christian meanings.[5] Rituals and symbols adapted from both the western Christian tradition and the traditional African religions (and sometimes, completely new ones) are introduced. Usually these have local relevance and include enthusiastic participation by members and lively, ecstatic worship.

Divination and Prophetic Healing

One generalization that can safely be made is that AICs are almost universally opposed to traditional divination. Although now recognized as an attempt to explain African thought in western philosophical categories, Placide Tempels' description of African concepts of power as "vital force" or "life-force" is still relevant. He says that all African behavior is centered in acquiring "life, strength or vital force, to live strongly". This force or "power" is tangibly perceived and can be manipulated for either good or evil, and some may have more power than others. The power may reside in charms, amulets, beads, medicines, words, names, and various other objects. Possessing this power enables people to do extraordinary things or to prevent evil from occurring, and so everyone longs for more power. The greatest disaster possible follows the losing of life force. Illness, suffering, disappointment, exhaustion, injustice, oppression, and failure are all regarded as a lessening of power, and so everything possible is done to avoid its loss and to promote its increase. The Supreme Being is seen as the ultimate source of all power.[6] This power, however, has no dualism, for God can use his power for good or withhold it, resulting in evil. There is a personal quality about the power residing in people, intimately linked to the ancestors and the ongoing life of the community. The inter-relatedness between power and the ancestors is shown in the diviner's capacity to make "magic", ascribed to the power of the ancestors residing within. The popular view of the world is anthropocentric and personalized. In African religions, life and existence or being itself is inextricably tied up with power. To live is to have power—to be sick or to die is to have less of it. The uniqueness of a person's living power lies in the ability to strengthen or weaken another person's power directly or by the manipulation of the power of non-human things.

This is the principle behind divination. In order to obtain power, people make use of charms and medicines, and consult diviners and healers. These specialists, who have undergone a long period of training by their elders, use their power for the good of the local community, particularly in providing protection against the illegitimate use of power, the work of sorcerers and witches. Whenever the lessening of power results in problems or even a foreboding of trouble, it is usually necessary for people to consult such specialists in order to receive more power for themselves. These specialists have power to discern the wishes of the ancestors and to act as protectors of society, and this is why it's impossible to always distinguish between "magic" and "religion". Diviners must be heeded, for one who doesn't follow their instructions courts disaster. The diviner is able to diagnose the cause of the affliction, and will usually prescribe some ancestor ritual and sometimes give protective medicines and strong charms to overcome this unseen evil force. The specialist often seeks to discover the source of the trouble and *who* sends it.[7]

Traditional specialists are believed to use their power for the good of the community, and they function as doctors, counselors, and pastors at the same time. They are often the most influential people in the whole community, with an all-encompassing mandate to serve a multitude of purposes. They explain the mysteries of life and death, convey messages from the spirit world, heal sicknesses, give guidance in daily affairs, protect from dangers seen and unseen, resolve quarrels, promote fertility, act as "agony aunts" in affairs of the heart, and ensure success and prosperity in all areas of life. Sorcery and witchcraft are to be overcome by the strengthening of people through the use of more powerful medicine or magic. There are diviners in cities throughout Africa whose techniques may differ from rural diviners and who may even consider themselves Christian, although usually they're not. Their healing power is specifically *not* Christian, coming directly from guiding ancestors, although today the influence of Christianity has contributed to a syncretism in the views of many diviners and prophets regarding their source of power.

Various healing techniques and methods used by healers include using herbs, throwing bones, stones or nuts to divine, and relying on dreams or other forms of communication with guiding ancestors. To increase the power of their patients, specialists use a wide variety of objects: amulets, necklaces, powders, tattoo markings and face paintings, incantations, forked sticks, horns, calabashes, and so on. These are all symbols of power intended either to protect or promote health, happiness, and success. Many healers are also herbalists, with detailed and intimate knowledge of what in the West is termed "alternative medicine", including the medicinal use of herbs, roots and other plants as medicines to protect or restore life. In Africa it is not always possible to distinguish between a therapeutic "herbalist" and a diagnostic "diviner", because most specialists use both methods in treating patients.[8] The power resident in material substances collectively known as "medicines" is interrelated with the power resident in people and can be used to support that power. Medicines are therefore not exclusively "curative" in a western sense, but are "powerful substances" that can be used legitimately for a wide variety of beneficial purposes such as fertility, success, courtship, protection, and even the changing of personality, and they are also used to combat sorcery and witchcraft. These medicines contain power which should be used for the benefit of the community, but they are also used illegitimately to harm people or to reduce their power.[9]

There's growing recognition among churches in Africa in general and African theologians in particular, that the problems taken to diviners, whether they relate to witchcraft, evil spirits, or something else, should be recognized and responded to.[10] Oosthuizen points to increasing acknowledgement among scientists of two different types of disease in Africa. The first may be called "natural diseases", cured by "natural" means, including western medicine. The second type, usually called "African diseases" includes those that can only be "understood by Africans in the context of their cosmology", and which are only cured by "supernatural" means, by the infusion of power. The second type was the task of the diviners to solve, and their diagnoses of its source in witchcraft, sorcery, evil spirits, and spirit possession have to be taken seriously. The AIC prophets have filled the "vacuum" left in Christianity by taking over many of the vital functions of the diviner.[11]

In many AICs in southern Africa, the prophet-healer has taken over the function of the traditional healer. In these churches the use of healing symbols is one of the central and most important features of church life and shows the "direct parallels" with traditional healing methods. Daneel says that the difference between diviner-healers and prophet-healers lies in the fact that the diviners' medicines contain "an inherent magical efficacy", whereas the methods of the prophets are "symbols... representing the healing power of God".[12] The most common symbol used by prophets is water "blessed" for use by congregants, either as a healing potion itself or else in large quantities to induce vomiting, and sometimes mixed with ash, a cleansing substance traditionally regarded as purified by fire. It is only prayer that makes the symbol effective. As in traditional healing methods (at least in southern Africa), a patient must expel the "death" in the stomach to be healed, to get rid of both physical sickness and spiritual defilement. The water represents cleansing and purification from evil, sin, sickness, and ritual pollution, concepts familiar to African thought. This holy water is taken home and sprinkled as a ritual of purification or protection, or it is drunk or washed in for healing purposes. It's believed that the Holy Spirit is present with the water that has been blessed. This water may be sprinkled on people, cars, houses, schoolbooks, food and a variety of other objects. It is used to purify people or objects after they've been contaminated (such as after a funeral), to welcome visitors, for protection against sorcery and misfortune, for obtaining employment, for abundant harvests, for cooking and washing, and for the "gate test" by prophets at church services. Another common symbol is the use of ropes and strings tied in various places on the body to procure healing and ward off evil, and staffs are the hallmark of African prophets, used to drive out evil spirits and sickness. Another healing method used in southern Africa by both traditional healers and Zionist prophets is that of pricking, where a prophet prescribes that a patient be pricked in the hands, legs, or nostrils to get rid of the source of sickness and pain, impure blood. Salt is used to clean the stomach and remove excess bile through vomiting. A small piece of wood or a sheet of paper waved rapidly over a patient's body, sand from a certain river or reservoir, and the use of other objects named by the prophets are other healing customs.[13]

In assessing these symbolic healing rituals in African churches, we must not simplistically regard them as repeating divination. Traditionally, African people didn't usually distinguish between the symbolic object and what it represented. Although the *form* of prophetic healing practices might really resemble the diviner's methods, their *meaning* is often understood to be opposed to traditional practices, symbols pointing to the power of God. Nevertheless, there is a possibility of misinterpretation. For some, healing symbols become something other than symbols of God's power and are seen as having intrinsic power in themselves. This is particularly the case, as is true of all varieties of Christian expression inside and outside Africa, when with the passing of time, members observe certain rituals because they have become traditions of the church and not because they really understand their symbolic significance. In these instances the forms remain while the meaning has become obscured.[14]

There's a parallel between African healing and New Testament teaching on illness and health. In the New Testament, the health of an individual is understood to derive from a condition of cosmic wholeness, and illness is seen as a lack of wholeness, a symptom of the disrupted and broken relationships in the whole of creation. This understanding is not very different from the African view described here. But there are seemingly inherent inadequacies in the traditional worldview, like the incessant fear of the malevolent use of power and of unseen evil forces, the unpredictability of ancestors, the perpetual dilemma of a God who is at the same time near and yet remote, the lack of relationship and fellowship with such a God who may also do nothing to prevent calamity and distress, the underlying fatalistic trends, and the need for people's "this-worldly" needs to be met. In this situation people are weak and utterly dependant on power (or powers) to which there is no permanent access and which is always conditional. In short, people need power that will cater for the necessities of life and protect from its trials—a life that is full, prosperous, healthy, peaceful, and secure. This popular urge for power seems to make the Christian message of the power of the Spirit, given to a person permanently and unconditionally, an attractive option for Africans. Any reinterpretation of these concepts by AICs in the light of the biblical revelation can only be understood when such reinterpretations are seen in the light of their cosmology. A comparison and contrast of AIC practices with those of traditionalists (such as a comparison of the practices of diviners with those of African prophets) will put these prophetic movements into correct perspective. They have provided an African Christian response to the context of traditional divination that is a religiously acceptable alternative.[15]

In the AICs, there's generally more opposition to divination than to ancestor rituals. Most churches reject the use of diviners for solving problems and consider that this practice belongs to the former, pre-Christian life. Some church members who experience what are perceived as traditional African problems may see the diviner as the only solution, such as when people believe that they've been bewitched or are troubled by evil spirits. But most AICs do *not* consult diviners and are opposed to them. Many go further and claim that diviners are possessed by demons and need to be delivered. Usually, when a person joins an AIC, visits to diviners cease, as the prophet or other church leader effectively replaces the diviner.

Despite their negative attitude to diviners, prophetic therapies indicate that AICs have not left unattended those needs addressed by diviners. It's precisely because prophets fulfill the same *functions* as diviners that they're sometimes inaccurately *identified* with them. Many AICs have effectively substituted the power wielded by diviners by their message of the power of the Spirit, enabling them to treat "African" problems. Sorcery and witchcraft, evil spirits and ancestor possession are usually encountered by these churches as problems that must be overcome by the Spirit rather than by any other power. Because the source of the power of the diviners, the ancestors, is specifically not Christian, there is widespread disapproval of these methods to treat "African sicknesses". Although a minority of church members might feel that diviners are better able to help them with these problems, the predominant attitude of AICs to divination is rejection, as it's incompatible with their understanding of Christian faith. This Christianity offers solutions for these problems that are more effective and life-changing than the traditional solutions were.[16]

AICs and Ancestors

The approach of AICs to ancestors is more ambiguous than that relating to diviners.[17] The religious practices associated with the ancestors are without question the most prominent aspect of African religions in the sub-Sahara and the very heart of the African worldview. For many people, the ancestors are a reality to be given due acknowledgement. They provide for felt needs and are benevolent guardians and protectors of people. Some African Christians feel that even God is unable to do anything without the assistance of ancestors, as they are mediators giving people power to pray to God. Ancestor rituals are widely practiced in African cities, although its incidence among church members is no longer as high as it used to be.[18]

Generalizations about beliefs and attitudes of AICs to ancestors mustn't give the impression of finality, especially when dealing with such a dynamic and constantly changing movement. It's clearly important for Christians who want to be relevant in Africa to respond to the beliefs in ancestors, traditionally guardians and protectors of their surviving families and still respected by most Africans. Ancestors are believed to bring harm to those who ignore or neglect their instructions given through dreams or diviners. Their sanctions have a fearful control over people's lives, and most seem to practice ancestor rituals in order to be rid of disturbing visitations. AICs have responded to the phenomenon of ancestors in two different ways.

The first and seemingly most frequent response is *confrontation*, as many AICs reject the ancestor observances. Ancestors appear to Christians, but usually their response as believers is to reject the visitation. The "ancestors", they believe, are not ancestors at all, but demons that need to be confronted and exorcized, for they only bring further misery and bondage. They have no power over Christians, because Christians have the greater power of the Spirit, which overcomes Satan's power. These beliefs are most evident among Pentecostal churches but are also prominent in other AICs.[19] Daneel's research in Zimbabwe found that "from the outset the leaders of the prophetic movements launched an attack on all forms of ancestor 'worship'". He says that the Shona Zionists "consistently regard heathen *midzimu* (ancestors) as 'evil spirits' (*mweya yakaipa*) from whom they must break away".[20] Prophets diagnosing sicknesses and other problems as caused by ancestors or sorcery show their orientation towards the traditional worldview. But in contrast to diviners, instead of accommodating the ancestor, the spirit is branded a demon and Daneel explains:

> Its claims on the patient—especially if these involve ancestor worship—are rejected and the spirit is exorcized. Here the Holy Spirit and the ancestor spirit are usually diametrically opposed and it is a matter of confrontation rather than identification.[21]

New Pentecostal and Charismatic churches usually give an unqualified rejection of ancestors and as we've seen, they're the most confrontational of all AICs with regard to traditional beliefs. The ancestor rituals are regarded as "pagan" practices—a person who is "saved" doesn't do these things, which represent the "old life" out of which everything has become new. New Pentecostals often identify ancestors as "demons" or "evil spirits" who impersonate deceased relatives in order to receive veneration.

But there's also a second and more ambiguous response, one of *accommodation* and concession. For some AICs, especially in South Africa, ancestors still play an important role and are to be respected and obeyed. They are mediators for God, sometimes revealing God's will and sometimes inspiring African prophets. They may be identified as angels, witnesses in heaven, or mediators between people and God, but however they're regarded, the function of ancestors as protectors and benefactors of their progeny is preserved. This more tolerant and ambivalent attitude confirms what some earlier researchers discovered. A publication by South African AIC leaders said the following:

> The customary way of commemorating and making contact with the spirits of our ancestors is a family affair, not a religious service... in most cases our leaders do encourage the commemoration of our ancestors in our homes.[22]

But even in these AICs, the principle is usually to modify the traditional custom so that the Christian God and not the ancestors are central to worship and prayer.

But accommodation is not the predominant reaction to ancestor rituals among AICs. On the contrary, a Spirit-inspired confrontation with the ancestor observances has usually replaced traditional beliefs with Christian alternatives. The AICs, less inhibited by dogma, may have a greater awareness of the African spirit world and therefore make a greater contribution to contextualization in this area. Many AICs have effectively reduced dependence on ancestors in the lives of their members, although some believe that ancestors reveal themselves to African prophets and must be respected. AIC leader Paul Makhubu points out that although AICs in South Africa believe in the existence of ancestors and "honor and respect" them, "they do not worship them". He says that those AICs who do "mix Christian religion with ancestor worship" are "a very small minority".[23] AICs do not universally confront traditional beliefs about ancestors, although most seem to have little need for ancestor rituals. This is mainly because AICs generally, especially in their prophetic therapy and prescriptions, provide the protection and guidance formerly sought from ancestors. Isaiah Shembe, leader of one of the most traditionally oriented AICs of all, the amaNazaretha, while recognizing the ancestors, did not give any place to ancestor veneration in his teachings and practices, in spite of what some have suggested to the contrary.[24] The OAIC summarized their convictions about ancestors in 1996 in a paragraph that illustrates how AICs have transformed traditional beliefs without denying them, and have made a significant shift away from practices inconsistent with the Christian message:

> *Communion of Saints*—the relationship between the living and the dead enrich our churches as the living nurture the memory of our predecessors who are still influencing our own lives by their contributions to the welfare of our communities while they were still alive.[25]

Burial and mourning customs in AICs, as well as in other churches, suggest that many traditional practices still prevail in Christian funerals, as they do indeed in other parts of the Christian world. Some of these practices are vestiges of ancestor rituals, especially the practice of ritual killings, draping the coffin with the hide of a beast, and the home-bringing rites. Most of these practices are found to some degree among different AICs in southern Africa. Since a funeral is mainly a community and family affair in which the church is but one of several players, the church doesn't always determine the form of the funeral. And so many Christian funerals are accompanied by traditional rites, including people who may not be Christians sending messages through the deceased to other deceased relatives. Many AICs, however, don't usually participate in rituals perceived as being associated with ancestors or divination. Some traditional customs have really been transformed and given Christian meanings to which both Christians and those with traditional orientation can relate. Sometimes there are signs of confrontation and the changing and discontinuance of old customs to such an extent that they're no longer recognizable. And yet, AIC funerals continue to be true to the African worldview in which they're immersed. This is a community affair in which the whole community feels the grief of the bereaved and shares in it. The purpose of the activities in the days preceding the funeral, especially the night vigils, is to comfort, encourage, and heal those who are grieving. Thereafter, the churches see to it that the bereaved family makes the transition back to normal life as smoothly and quickly as possible. This transition during the mourning period is sometimes accompanied by cleansing rituals by which the bereaved are assured of their acceptance and protection by God. Behind the rejection of some of the traditional mourning customs is the firm conviction that the resurrection of the Christian dead to eternal life in God's presence must be confessed to the community. The funeral therefore also becomes an opportunity to evangelize and declare Christian faith.[26]

Indigenization and African Pentecostalism

At several points in this book, the close connection between the AIC movement and Pentecostalism has been demonstrated. The prophet-healing and "Spirit" AICs, as well as other Pentecostal and Charismatic churches are an expression of Pentecostalism in Africa. Their reformation of missionary Christianity went much further than the "Ethiopian" and "African" churches had done. The expansion of the Pentecostal message in the twentieth century in Africa can be attributed, at least partially, to cultural factors. Walter Hollenweger sees the "oral structures" of Pentecostalism, like Christianity itself, to be the reason for its initial growth. His list of characteristics of these oral structures includes oral liturgy, narrative theology and witness, reconciliatory and participant community, the inclusion of visions and dreams in worship, and understanding the relationship between body and mind revealed in healing by prayer and liturgical dance.[27] He points out that spontaneity and enthusiasm in Pentecostal worship, rather than leading to an absence of liturgy, produce flexible oral liturgies memorized by the congregation. The most important element of these liturgies is the active participation of every member in the congregation.28 Pentecostal liturgy has social and revolutionary implications in that it empowers marginalized people, takes as acceptable what ordinary people have in the worship of God and thus overcomes "the *real* barriers of race, social status, and education".29

Many observers consider the free African liturgy of music and dance in the AICs to be their most obvious demonstration of their indigenization or "African-ness".30 The emphasis on "freedom in the Spirit" has rendered the Pentecostal movement inherently flexible in different cultural and social contexts, and Africa's no exception. This flexibility has made the transplanting of its central tenets more easily assimilated. Many older missionary churches arose in the western contexts of written liturgies, set theologies, highly educated and professional clergy, and church structures with strongly centralized control. This often contributed to the feeling in Africa that these churches were "foreign" and that people first had to become westerners before becoming Christians. In contrast, the Pentecostal emphasis on immediate personal experience of God's power by the Spirit was more intuitive and emotional, and it recognized charismatic leadership and indigenous church patterns wherever they arose. Even in most Pentecostal churches with western missionary involvement, leadership wasn't kept long in the hands of missionaries, and the proportion of missionaries to church members was usually much lower than that of the older missions.

Preaching a message that promised solutions for present felt needs like sickness and the fear of evil spirits, pentecostal AIC preachers were heeded and their message readily accepted by ordinary people. Churches were rapidly planted in African cultures, and Africa took on its own, different expressions of Pentecostalism. We've seen that the AICs are mostly churches of a pentecostal type that have contextualized and indigenized

Christianity. Although Cox's generalization may not tell the whole story, AICs are "the African expression of the worldwide Pentecostal movement" because of both their Pentecostal style and their Pentecostal origins.[31] One of the outstanding features of pentecostal and prophet-healing AICs is their religious creativity and spontaneously indigenous character, a characteristic held as an ideal by missionary scholars for over a century. The "three self" formula for indigenization of missionary leaders Henry Venn and Rufus Anderson in the mid-nineteenth century—self-governing, self-supporting and self-propagating—was automatically and effortlessly achieved by AICs long before this goal was realized by European mission churches.[32] The AIC movement represents "a kind of Christianity that has the trademark of African culture".[33] Contrary to what some have suggested in the past, AICs are not "tribally based" religions. Many have programs for recruiting new members that transcend national and ethnic divisions. This belief in the movement's universality and message for the whole world is a radical departure from ethnically based traditional religions. Most of the biggest AICs in Africa, like the Christ Apostolic Church, the Zion Christian Church, the Marange Apostles, and the Kimbanguists, as well as several of the largest new Pentecostal and Charismatic churches, have transcended these parochial limitations and have become international and multiethnic African movements, forming new voluntary organizations to replace traditional kinship groups.

Thriving indigenous churches, established in Africa without the help of foreign missionaries, were founded in innovative initiatives unprecedented in the history of Christian missions. They were motivated by a compelling need to preach and even more significantly, to *experience* a new message of the power of the Spirit. Cox suggests that for any religion to grow today, it must demonstrate two vitally important and underlying capabilities. First, the religion "must be able to include and transform at least certain elements of preexisting religions which still retain a strong grip on the cultural subconscious". Secondly, "it must also equip people to live in rapidly changing societies". He finds these two "key ingredients" in Pentecostalism.[34] The question is, have pentecostal forms of Christianity in Africa adapted to and transformed their cultural and religious environment, or are they a foreign, western imposition? I think more obviously the former, but this doesn't mean that foreign influences are entirely absent. Pentecostal AICs are in constant interaction with the African spirit world, western culture, and the Christian message. Those who censure them for their alleged "syncretism" often fail to see that parallels with traditional religions and cultures in AIC practices are also often continuous with the biblical revelation. Western Pentecostals do not have to look very far to see the same cultural influences in their own forms of Christianity—one glaring example being the capitalistic emphasis on prosperity and success, the "American dream", which pervades many, perhaps most, Pentecostal activities in the western world. Furthermore, AICs usually define their practices by reference to the Bible and not to traditional religions, and they see their activities as creative adaptations to the local cultural context. At the same time, some African Pentecostals might need to have a greater appreciation for the rich diversity of their cultural and religious past and not feel the need to bow to the cultural hegemony of western Christianity. Demonizing the cultural and religious past does not help explain the present attraction of Pentecostalism for African peoples, even though it might help in the religious competition that is a feature of pluralist societies today.

Harvey Cox sees the largely unconscious interaction of Pentecostalism with indigenous religions as helping people recover vital elements in their culture that are threatened by modernization. Pretorius and Jafta speak of "the intrinsic affinity between traditional African conceptions and Pentecostal religiosity".[35] African Pentecostals have found in their own context, both culturally and biblically acceptable alternatives to and adaptations from the practices of their ancient religions, and they are seeking to provide answers to the needs inherent there. Any religion that doesn't offer at least the same benefits as the old religion does will probably be unattractive. Christianity, particularly in its Pentecostal emphasis on the transforming power of the Spirit, purports to offer more than the traditional religions did. In Africa, Pentecostal AICs have changed the face of Christianity because they have proclaimed a holistic gospel of salvation that includes deliverance from all types of evil oppression like sickness, barrenness, sorcery, evil spirits, unemployment, and poverty. This message may not have engaged always effectively with the more structurally oppressive political and economic monopolies, but the needs of Africa have been addressed more fundamentally than the rather spiritualized and intellectualized legacy of European and North American missions. The good news in Africa, AIC preachers declare, is that God meets all the needs of people, including their spiritual salvation, physical healing, and other material necessities. The phenomenon of mass urbanization results in AICs providing places of spiritual security and personal communities for people unsettled by rapid social change. The more relevant the church in Africa becomes to its cultural and social context, the more prepared it will be to serve the wider society.

Syncretism and Contextualization

The question of "syncretism" is a vexing one for researchers of AICs, often with negative connotations resulting from hasty generalizations. We should take utmost care to avoid evaluating African movements according to western criteria. What's more, we can't evaluate a religious movement like an AIC as if in its final, static form. Theologies today seek to be "contextual", expressing God's concerns in a particular human context. Robert Schreiter asks whether the AIC movement should be seen as "the ultimate outcome of contextualization rather than as some aberration". This he says is one of the "hard questions" to be faced regarding the relationship between "syncretism" and contextualization. Because contextualization is concerned with getting to the heart of a culture, then Christianity that is truly contextualized will indeed, he says, "look very much like a product of that culture". This doesn't imply syncretism in any negative sense like "impure". AICs to a large extent have achieved an instinctive and automatic contextualization from which the rest of Christianity can learn.[36] Daneel says that contextualization isn't "a simplistic adaptation to traditional thought", but rather "an adaptation that, while displaying parallels with traditional religion, essentially implies a continuing confrontation with and creative transformation of traditional religion and values".[37] The AICs provide many examples of innovative approaches whereby traditional cultural and religious ceremonies are adapted and transformed to have Christian meanings.

AICs raise many questions concerning the central theological issue of the relationship between Christianity and other religions, particularly because of their emphasis on the Spirit. Chinese-American Pentecostal theologian Amos Yong says that the experiences of the Spirit common to Pentecostals and Charismatics demonstrate "indubitable similarities across the religious traditions of the world". This fact opens the way for a constructive Pentecostal theology of religions that explores "how the Spirit is present and active in other religious traditions".[38] In an attempt to apply scientific principles to human cultures and languages, more conservative forms of western theology assumed that there was a pure "Message" free of cultural constraints, and that when the "purity" of the gospel was affected in some way by cultural adaptations, the result was "syncretism". The word "syncretism" was often used in a negative way to suggest that the "gospel" had somehow been corrupted by culture. But as Chilean Pentecostal theologian Juan Sepúlveda points out, "the concern for preserving the "purity" of the Gospel has always been stronger than the desire to incarnate (or "inculturate") the Gospel in a particular situation". He says that we can't "grasp any meaning without the help of our precious cultural categories", and so "'purity' is not given to us. Some sort of syncretism *is* inevitable."[39] And so, Pentecostalism in its African expressions, like Christianity everywhere, is inherently "syncretistic". Because of the way that AICs proclaim the Christian message, however, a selective rejection of some religious practices as a means of solving problems takes place. The syncretizing tendencies are seen in the rituals and symbols adapted and introduced in AICs from both the western Christian and the African religious traditions. Sometimes completely new ones appear, usually with local relevance and including enthusiastic participation by members and lively worship.

AICs proclaim a pragmatic gospel that seeks to address practical and contextual issues like sickness, poverty, unemployment, loneliness, evil spirits, and sorcery. In varying degrees and in their many different forms, and precisely because of their inherent flexibility, these churches are able to offer answers to some of the fundamental questions asked in their own context. A sympathetic approach to local culture and the retention of certain cultural practices are undoubtedly major reasons for their attraction, especially for those millions overwhelmed by urbanization with its transition from a personal rural society to a more impersonal urban one. At the same time, AICs confront old views by declaring what they're convinced is a more powerful protection against sorcery and a more effective healing from sickness than either the existing churches or traditional rituals had offered. Healing, guidance, protection from evil, and success and prosperity are some of the practical benefits offered to faithful members of their churches.

Whenever Christianity, unencumbered by its various cultural expressions, encounters another living religion as it does in AICs, a transformation takes place in both directions. The Christian message challenges, confronts, and changes whatever seems incongruous or inadequate in African religion, and African religion transforms and enriches the Christian message so that it's understandable and relevant within the worldview in which it's submerged. And so the Christian message becomes more appropriate and comprehensible to both those to whom it's proclaimed and to those who proclaim it. At the same time, the Christian community throughout the world discovers new depths in its message that it would not have discovered except for this encounter with African religion.

I have previously outlined the parallels between the African concept of "power" and the biblical ones, making the Christian concept of spiritual power easier to assimilate.[40] It's this biblical message of the power of the Spirit that finds familiar ground in Africa. This is possibly one of the main reasons for the rapid growth of pentecostal AICs. Ancient African beliefs have been transformed in these churches so that Christianity is presented as an attractive and viable African alternative. AICs encounter African religions and provide answers to a host of perplexing questions that seem to be inherent there. Although my analysis is not exhaustive, at least from my particular Christian perspective at the moment it appears that traditional African religions are inadequate on several fronts. The supreme being seems often distant and unfathomable, the human ancestors appear sometimes fickle and unpredictable, and the diviners seem limited by the omnipresent fear of powers that might be greater than their own. The solutions offered in traditional religions, at least from this Christian viewpoint, seem to be seldom completely satisfying and leave people uncertain, threatened, and fearful. "African" problems caused by a loss of power and life through the malicious workings of sorcery, magic, and witchcraft, and through capricious spirits who often demand more than people can provide, demand a Christian response.[41]

The great attraction of AICs is that they *do* offer answers to these problems. In their encounter with African religions they have themselves been challenged and enriched concerning the content of their message, which would have been impoverished and "foreign" without this encounter. Their message of the power of the Spirit challenges evil powers and what are roundly declared to be the work of Satan. In many AICs, the ancestors are confronted as impersonating demons from which people need deliverance, and evil spirits are exorcised in the name of Jesus Christ. Sorcerers, witches, and even diviners are declared to be agents of the devil. AICs acknowledge all these various African forces as realities and not as "ignorant superstitions" from which people need "enlightenment". A problem doesn't disappear by pretending that it's not there. The AICs offer realistic solutions by accepting these problems as genuine, conscientiously attempting to provide authentic explanations, and expecting to resolve the problems through faith in God. Christians don't need to fear these things because they have received the power of the Spirit enabling them to overcome any onslaughts against them. The AIC response involves prayer to an almighty God for deliverance from the evil, protection from its possible future occurrences, and the restoration of that well being found in Christ. The methods by which this deliverance is effected may differ and the use of symbols vary greatly, but the outcome is the same: God is glorified as demonstrably more powerful than other "gods".

Notes

1 Greater detail on this subject is found in Anderson, *Zion & Pentecost,* 175-218.

2 "Divination" refers here to the practices of traditional African doctors and healers, those who throw bones and those that do not, as well as traditional herbalists.

3 Hastings, *The Church,* 529.

4 Anderson, *Zion & Pentecost,* chapter 6.

5 Daneel, *Quest,* 26; id., *Old & New 2,* 309-347.

6 Placide Tempels, *Bantu Philosophy,* Paris, 1959, 44-46, 98; Anderson, *Moya,* 58, 65.

7 Anderson, *Moya,* 67; John S. Mbiti, *African Religions and Philosophy,* London, 1969, 167; Laurenti Magesa, *African Religion: The Moral Traditions of Abundant Life,* New York, 1997, 194.

[8] Magesa, 209, 212.

[9] Axel-Ivar Berglund, *Zulu Thought Patterns and Symbolism*. London, 1976, 256-7, 346; Magesa, 210, 213.

[10] Aylward Shorter, *Jesus and the Witchdoctor: An Approach to Healing and Wholeness*. Maryknoll, 1985, 8.

[11] G.C. Oosthuizen, "The Interpretation of and Reaction to Demonic powers in indigenous Churches", Pretoria, 1987, 63-5; id., *The Healer-Prophet in Afro-Christian Churches*, Leiden, 1992, 165.

[12] Daneel, *Old and New 2*, 232, 338.

[13] Daneel, *Old and New 2*, 302-6; Anderson & Otwang, 75, 79.

[14] Daneel, *Old and New 2*, 338.

[15] Anderson, *Moya*, 69.

[16] Anderson, *Zion & Pentecost*, chapter 7.

[17] In this book, the unsatisfactory word "ancestor" has been used rather than others like "shade" and "living dead", just because it is the word most frequently used. There's no accurate English word to describe the relatives who have died and now occupy a position of revelation, protection, and direction for their surviving families.

[18] Anderson, *Zion & Pentecost*, chapter 6.

[19] Many younger people in AICs have no experience of ancestors, which may be evidence of a greater westernization and secularization— although traditionally, the youth are excluded from participation in ancestor rituals. As they grow older and are included in religious observations, they begin to assimilate traditional religious values.

[20] Daneel, *Old & New 1*, 462; id., *Quest*, 233.

[21] Daneel, *Quest*, 261.

[22] Institute for Contextual Theology, *Speaking for Ourselves*. Johannesburg, 1985, 24; B.A. Pauw, *Christianity and Xhosa Tradition*, Cape Town, 1975, 302.

[23] Makhubu, 60.

[24] Anderson, *Zion & Pentecost*, chapter 6; M.C. Kitshoff, "Isaiah Shembe's View on the Ancestors in Biblical Perspective", n.d.

[25] Pobee & Ositelu, 71.

26 Anderson, *Zion & Pentecost*, chapter 16; Makhubu, 60.

27 Anderson & Hollenweger, chapter 1; Hollenweger, *Pentecostalism*, 23.

28 Hollenweger, *Pentecostalism*, 269-71.

29 Ibid., 274-5.

30 Pobee & Ositelu, 26; Ayegboyin & Ishola, 151.

31 Cox, 246; Hollenweger, *Pentecostalism*, 52.

32 David J. Bosch, *Transforming Mission*. Maryknoll, 1991, 331-332.

33 Ayegboyin & Ishola, 150.

34 Cox, 219.

35 Cox, 228; Pretorius & Jafta, 217.

36 Robert J. Schreiter, *Constructing Local Theologies*, New York, 1985, 145, 150.

37 M. L. Daneel, "Exorcism as a means of combating wizardry", *Missionalia* 18:1, 1990, 56.

38 Amos Yong, "'Not Knowing Where the Wind Blows...': On Envisioning a Pentecostal-Charismatic Theology of Religions", *Journal of Pentecostal Theology* 14, 1999, 85-7, 99-100.

39 Juan Sepúlveda, "To overcome the fear of syncretism: a Latin American perspective", Frankfurt, 1997, 167.

40 Anderson, *Moya*, 113-5.

41 Ibid., 67-8.

10

THEOLOGY IN PRACTICE

ICs seldom have an elaborately worked-out theology such as is found in most "mainline" churches. Nevertheless, in their inculturation of Christianity, they *do* have a distinct and considerable contribution to make to African Christian theology. This inculturation, as we saw in the previous chapter, has been done in an intense and far-reaching way. Daneel considers that the main significance of AICs lies in their "spontaneous indigenization of Christianity, uninhibited by direct Western control" and in their unique erection of "bridgeheads between the Christian gospel and traditional thought forms".[1] Although AICs have little formalized theology, they have what Hastings terms a "praxis and a spirituality in which a theology is profoundly implicit".[2] In a 1996 article on "AIC Contributions to the World Church", the OAIC said, "We may not all be articulate in written theology, but we express faith in our liturgy, worship, and structures".[3] Theology is our human response to God's Word. The African pastors, bishops, or prophets who lay hands on the sick and lead their congregations in rituals of worship are enacting theology. Members of AICs have responded to God's word to them in a particular way. Their interpretation of the working of the Spirit as emphasized in the daily life and practices of their churches is real theology. And in this respect they have an extremely significant part to play in formulating African theology. Indeed, says Justin Ukpong:

> The main goal of African theology is to make Christianity attain African expression... to become a way of life to Africans, Christianity must be made relevant to and expressive of the way they live and think.[4]

This is precisely what the AICs have done, if largely unconsciously. Probably more than any other form of Christianity in Africa, the pentecostal, "Spirit" AICs have given a uniquely African character to their faith. In certain respects, they have attained the goals towards which formal African theology still struggles. Because theology is our human response to God's word, Christianity must be expressive of everyday life or be in danger of becoming inconsequential. Barrett says that the emphases of the AICs have resulted in a "sufficient creative reinterpretation of the Christian faith" that can be seen as an "emergent African theology". In particular, he describes the contribution of AICs to the development of a theology of the church as community within African society, through its emphasis on "brotherly love". He thinks that this is where AICs are making their strongest appeal.[5]

Some African theologians, mainly with western theological orientation, have pointed rather hesitatingly to the contribution of AICs to African theology. For instance, Fashole-Luke sees them as the "raw material" of African theology and points out that a careful and critical study should be made of AICs to assess their value for the development of African theology. Burgess Carr says that African theology "comes to life" in the music, prayers, liturgy, church structures, and community life of AICs. Carr speaks of the AICs' freedom from imperialistic structures that perpetuate slavery, and of their discovery that the Christian faith is one of joyful celebration.[6] In this they've achieved an implicit liberation theology by their rejection of western ecclesiastical domination. This contribution has not been sufficiently recognized, because of the preoccupation of liberation theology with socio-political analyses, not the main concern of AICs. In attaining organizational liberation, AICs have also achieved a liturgical transformation and have been able to re-evaluate African culture and religion. And so, Daneel speaks of the "religiocultural liberation" of AICs. John Mbiti says that AICs are "ultimately an expression of theological protest", and it is the formalistic, rationalistic, and often irrelevant theology imported to Africa from the West that AICs implicitly challenge. Pobee and Ositelu say that AICs are "a protest movement, principally against the model of the church imposed by the North Atlantic captivity of the Christian faith".[7]

AICs take seriously the African worldview and the Christian response to it. Healing, exorcism, and other manifestations of the Spirit illustrate what Daneel calls "the relativity, if not futility, of our neat Western theories when confronted, in practice, with the belief systems and stark pastoral realities of Africa". Healing and deliverance from evil are essential parts of the life of AICs, because these problems affect the whole church community. They are not simply regarded as the private domain of an individual relegated to pastoral care—often the approach to these problems in western churches. African experience is the crucible in which African theology is made. AICs have what Daneel describes as an "enacted theology", which is "a vitally significant component of a developing African Christian theology".[8] Shenk says that AICs teach us that "theology may be constructed in modes other than Hellenistic philosophical categories", and that "theology is a dynamic, living, growing interpretation of the faith in response to a changing environment".[9] The continuing dialogue between AICs and popular culture and religion helps clarify the Africanization process that's essential to the realization of African theology. In the healing rites of AICs in particular, a psychological liberation from the terrors and insecurities inherent in African experiences of evil powers and sorcery is also achieved.

Hermeneutical Perspectives

The dynamic, enacted theology found in AICs is based on their interpretation of the Bible, or their hermeneutical perspectives. For the great majority of AICs, the Bible is central to their beliefs and practices.[10] In his definition of hermeneutics, Severino Croatto speaks of "three aspects of interpretation". In addition to the "privileged locus" of "the interpretation of *texts*", the first aspect, hermeneutics must also take into account that "all interpreters condition their reading of a text by a kind of *preunderstanding* arising from their own life context", the second aspect. The third aspect is that "the interpreter *enlarges* the *meaning* of the text being interpreted".[11] Carlos Mesters says that when the "common people" read the Bible a "dislocation" occurs and "emphasis is not placed on the text's meaning *in itself* but rather on the meaning the text has *for the people* reading it".[12] For most AICs, who rely on an oral rather than a literate understanding of the Bible, it doesn't make sense to discuss the interpretation of the "pure" text.[13] AICs enlarge the meaning of the Bible for themselves, out of their own context with its inherent presuppositions. AICs generally do not have a philosophical articulation of theological beliefs. Nevertheless, as is true of all Christians, their interpretations of the Bible are undoubtedly conditioned by presuppositions arising out of their life situation, and their understanding of how the Bible speaks into their life context inevitably enlarges its meaning.

Most AICs may be said to have a literalistic or "concordistic" approach to hermeneutics.[14] The biblical literalism found in many of these churches, however, cannot simply be equated with fundamentalism. The Bible is sometimes read as an ethical rulebook, and many AICs have definite, sometimes dogmatic opinions on biblical ethics. However, AICs may be said to have a concordistic approach to the Bible in that they take the Bible as it is and look for common ground in real life situations. On finding these "correspondences" they believe that God is speaking. The gospel therefore has immediacy and becomes relevant to life experiences, focusing on divine intervention in daily life situations, through a constant emphasis on the so-called "supernatural". Most AICs usually interpret the Bible in a way that makes use primarily of the normal or customary understanding of the literal words, and in so doing most use an African vernacular translation. The translation of the Scriptures into the vernacular has reinforced the conviction that in the Bible there is "a spontaneity, a vitality, and a dynamic which was apparently lacking in the rigid structures of the missionary agencies".[15] Implicitly, AICs are constantly seeking to relate the Bible to their daily experience. Although this may be a "pre-critical" method of reading the Bible common to "ordinary readers" who are not "trained in critical methods",[16] this shouldn't be seen necessarily as a disadvantage. It isn't slavish literalism either, because the Bible is usually read and understood in the context of a real-life community and a real situation in AICs.[17] Many members of AICs are underprivileged, poor, and functionally illiterate. In keeping with the strong sense of community among African people, members usually read or rather, *hear* the Bible in the community of the faithful, during celebrations of communal worship, where it is often directly related to real problems encountered by that community. This oral interpretation of the Bible as it is prayed, sung, danced, and preached in the worship of these churches implies a hermeneutics from the underside of society. There, ordinary African people, like the people Mesters describes in the basic ecclesial communities of Brazil, have "found the key and are beginning again to interpret the Bible ... using the only tool they have at hand: their own lives, experiences, and struggles".[18] Itumeleng Mosala says that AICs in South Africa developed "new ways of interpreting the Bible, which included trying to interpret the Bible in terms of African culture, and in terms of the black experience of suffering, insecurity, and oppression".[19]

One presupposition that conditions this hermeneutical perspective is the emphasis on the experience of the Spirit common to prophet-healing and pentecostal AICs. The Bible is used to explain the experience of the working of the Spirit in the church with "gifts of the Spirit", especially healing, exorcism, speaking in tongues, and prophesying. But the significance of this hermeneutic is that a reciprocal relationship between the Bible and the Spirit occurs. Not only does the Bible explain the experience of the Spirit, but also perhaps more importantly, the experience of the Spirit enables people to better understand the Bible. This emphasis on experiencing the power of the Spirit is a common characteristic of these churches, where the Holy Spirit is the agent of healing and deliverance. In this regard, the experience of the Spirit becomes a self-authenticating key in the hermeneutical process. In these churches therefore, the experience of the Spirit becomes an essential and perhaps the most important key in the hermeneutic. It might even be said that this experience of the Spirit is the dominant theme of the gospel as understood by pentecostal AICs. The gifts of the Spirit are proof that the gospel is true and the confirmation of the written word of the Bible.

This AIC hermeneutical perspective means that probably above all other considerations, AIC members believe that their churches provide biblical answers for "this worldly" needs like sickness, poverty, hunger, oppression, unemployment, loneliness, evil spirits, and sorcery. This usually happens through what is seen as the intervention of God through his Spirit, including the use of agents of the Spirit: prophets, pastors, and other gifted church leaders. All of these experiences are often backed up, either implicitly or explicitly, by scriptural support. The Bible in this way becomes a source book of answers to human need. Most AICs don't separate their understanding of the gospel from their personal experience of the events the Bible describes. In their liturgy, the telling of stories or "testimonies" is very important, where people are able to relate their experiences of divine intervention in order that the congregation may further participate in the hermeneutical process.[20] The assumption of the possibility of continuity between the Bible and contemporary experience is fundamental to AIC hermeneutics. The Bible, however, is also understood in some prophet-healing AICs, particularly Southern African Zionists, to be a rationale for practices that might not be considered biblical by most other AICs. Although some may have difficulty with the way that the Bible is used to support essentially African traditional religious practices, the fact of the "African-ness" of this hermeneutic and that African people contextualize the Bible themselves is very significant. These churches are specifically geared to fulfill African aspirations and meet African needs, and in this sense they have "enlarged" the meaning of the Bible to include this African-ness.

We may describe certain trends and common characteristics in AIC hermeneutics in terms of the three aspects of Croatto's model.[21] The authority of the biblical text and its interpretation, the first aspect, is literal and assumed, but not emphasized. The preunderstanding that influences the hermeneutical process includes a high view of the Bible overshadowed by the experience and interpretation of the African context on the one hand, and the power of the Spirit on the other. This uniquely African and biblical experience is taken back to the text and new and relevant meanings are found there which enlarge the meaning of the Bible for us all. In prophet-healing and pentecostal AICs, the Bible is interpreted holistically to include all of life's problems, which is particularly relevant in societies where disease is rife and access to basic health care is a luxury. The prevalence of sickness and affliction therefore becomes a hermeneutical key with which the Bible is interpreted. Healing is part of the biblical revelation and reference is made to Old Testament prophets, Christ himself, and New Testament apostles who practiced healing. This healing offered to people usually relies heavily upon various symbols, which becomes another hermeneutical key with which the treasures of the Bible are unlocked for ordinary people. Symbolic healing practices are also referred back to the Bible, where Jesus used mud and spittle to heal a blind man, Peter used cloths to heal the sick, and Old Testament prophets used staffs, water, and various other symbols to perform healing and miracles. People join AICs because felt needs are met, which includes healing from physical sickness and discomfort. Despite the political liberation of Africa from colonialism, the majority is still underprivileged, which means *inter alia* that efficient medical facilities are scarce and expensive. The fact that people believe themselves to be healed in AICs means that their unique understanding of the Bible is a potent remedy for their experience of affliction. AICs believe that the Bible reveals an omnipotent and compassionate God who is concerned with all the troubles of humankind. Bishops, prophets, ministers, evangelists, and ordinary church members exercise the authority that has been given them by the God of the Bible. This authority is reinforced by the power of the Spirit to announce the good news that there is deliverance from sin, from sickness and barrenness, and from every conceivable form of evil.

A discussion of hermeneutics in AICs must reckon with the very important fact of African prophets, who are seen as continuing the biblical prophetic tradition, particularly that of the Old Testament. These prophets are an interesting example of the hermeneutical aspect of interpreting the Bible through the grid of presuppositions arising from the context. African prophets have arisen in the situation of the felt needs of African people, and provide an innovative alternative to traditional healers. It is believed that the prophets are the ones to whom God reveals his will and through whom he manifests his power. Their pronouncements are accepted as revelations from God, but are not usually accorded the authority of Scripture, and they are subject to the leadership of the church. An illustration of this was given during an AIC service I attended, when superior church officials chided a prophet for prophesying to me, a visitor, without permission. Although sometimes Southern African prophets reveal the will of ancestors, most believe the source of revelation to be the Holy Spirit. He is the one who gives the prophets the power to heal sickness and overcome evil generated by deep-seated fears and insecurities. This understanding of the present dynamic of the Holy Spirit, common to pentecostals everywhere, presupposes that there is a personal and omnipotent power assisting in the hermeneutical process, bearing witness to the word of God. In this regard, African prophets with their pronouncements of the Spirit enlarge the meaning of the biblical text. As revealers of God's will from the Scriptures and dispensers of God's power through his Spirit to meet human needs, the African prophets become agents of salvation.

Emphasis on the Spirit

The *sine qua non* of pentecostal and "spiritual" AICs is the power of the Spirit.[22] He is the one to whom credit is given for almost everything that takes place in church activities. Pobee and Ositelu place first in their list of "main characteristics" of AICs, "their emphasis on receiving a conscious experience of the Holy

Spirit".[23] The Spirit causes people to "receive" power, to prophesy, speak in tongues, heal, exorcize demons, have visions and dreams, and live "holy" lives—generally he directs the life and worship of the church. Most AIC researchers find this the most obvious feature of this type of church, and AIC leaders also acknowledge it themselves. A South African AIC ecumenical organization, in *Speaking for Ourselves* stated, "if our theology has one central focal point then it is the *Holy Spirit*".[24] In a consultation between the WCC and AICs in 1996, an Aladura leader spoke of the "prime emphasis on the charismatic gifts of the Holy Spirit" that singled out AICs from other churches.[25]

In the previous chapter, we discussed the Tempels theory that all African behavior is centered in the single value of acquiring power, tangibly perceived and manipulated, with some having more of it than others.[26] The African spirit world is a "personal", inter-related universe in which an individual as a living force is dependent upon all other forces for existence. The emphasis on receiving the power of the Spirit, a power greater than any power that threatens this existence is really good news. Because all things are a present material-spiritual unity, the "spirit" (or in a Christian context, the "Spirit") pervades all things. In the pentecostal and "spiritual" AICs in particular, the all-embracing Spirit is involved in every aspect of individual and community life, particularly evident in the person of the prophetic or charismatic leader, pre-eminently a man or woman of the Spirit. The rather dualistic, rationalistic theology of western "mainline" churches simply didn't meet the need of Africans for holistic involvement in religion. David Bosch points out that the first European missionaries in Africa were "children of the Enlightenment" who "tended to deny the existence of supernatural forces located in human beings as well as the reality of spirits in general and the "living-dead" in particular".[27] The results were either that traditional spirituality went underground or that a syncretism emerged in the encounter between African and western worldviews. African members of "mainline" churches experienced an identity crisis as they sought to relate their Christianity to their existential needs. When they discovered that help wasn't offered for "African" problems, they were forced to turn to "outside" assistance, either from traditional healers or from the newer "spiritual" churches. These AICs often combined African and "western" Christian elements in order to provide solutions for these problems, but didn't always thereby seek contextualized and biblical Christian answers. Those that did were often misunderstood and accused of being "syncretistic"— in the sense of "not really Christian".

But in the early twentieth century, new AICs discovered that the biblical doctrine of the Holy Spirit was not as detached and uninvolved as western theology had often supposed, and the African need for religious involvement was met here. The tendency to oppose or discount the emotional in religion made western forms of Christianity unattractive to a great many Africans. The pervading Spirit in the AICs gave Christianity new vibrancy and relevance. The biblical concept of the Spirit, as outlined in my earlier study,[28] in fact makes an experience of divine involvement possible for Christians in real terms. This experience absorbs the whole person, and not just the "spiritual" part of Christian life. This often results in a release of emotion too, a catharsis that has a purifying effect. Criticisms of AICs and their emphasis on the Spirit with its emotionalism are often therefore irrelevant, not only in an African context but also in a biblical one. AICs, like many "mainline" churches, are naturally limited by their humanness and for this reason they need biblical correction. But many western observers have probably misunderstood not only the African worldview with its seeming strange and somewhat unnerving spirit manifestations, but many have also missed the essential, dynamic nature of "spiritual" and biblical Christianity and have crowded it out with theoretical theologizing. The AICs have demonstrated that it is at least as important to practice theology as it is to theorize about it. In Africa there are a myriad of needs that will seldom be met by old-fashioned, rational, and rather impotent, philosophical Christianity. The innovative African Christianity of many AICs takes seriously the African worldview with its existential needs. It's important for anyone doing Christian theology in Africa to look at the contribution of pentecostal and prophet-healing AICs closely. In the process, the shortcomings of western theology and even of that African theology based on western presuppositions might also be revealed. It is specifically in the various manifestations of the Spirit in these churches that the valuable contribution to theology is seen.

The central place given to the Spirit in AICs hasn't gone unchallenged by western theologians, and although the debate has long been abandoned, it has left such an indelible mark on AIC studies that it needs to be revisited. Early missionary studies of AICs suggested at least two problems with what had apparently been judged as exotic, heterodox sects. The first problem was that AICs were thought to think of the Holy Spirit as an "impersonal force" that could be "possessed" and "given" at random by human will, whenever needed. Influenced by Tempels, these critics said that the Holy Spirit had become a manipulable, "morally neutral" force like the supposed traditional idea of "life-force" or "vital force".[29] In fact, later studies established that AICs don't see the Holy Spirit as an impersonal, manipulable force at all. To the contrary, when the Spirit comes on prophets, instead of people "manipulating" the Spirit, it often appears that the prophets are seized by the Spirit and have little control of their actions or utterances. It's usually believed that the Spirit has "possessed" them, not vice versa. Whatever they do is believed to be the work of the Spirit, and the Spirit cannot be controlled by anyone, not even by the leader of the church. Furthermore, the presence of the Spirit in a person's life can hardly be conceived as being "morally neutral" when the Spirit's possession of people in AICs not only results in evidence of power, but also in sometimes stringent changes in ethical standards. Many of these evaluations seem to stem from an overemphasis on theological theory and an unfortunate insensitivity to African experience.[30]

The western approach to the African worldview categorized "life-force" as an impersonal controllable force. Africans, on the other hand, had no such dualistic categorization that labeled "impersonal" something often and at the same time "personal". Perhaps the biblical "power" made available to Christian believers through the Spirit is closer to the African concept of "life-force" than many would admit. In my brief study of the significance of biblical words for "Spirit" in Africa, I pointed out that African concepts of power, like the biblical ones, were of forcefulness, strength, and ability. These concepts carried the idea of dignity, authority, and power over oppression; they also meant power in action, and had their ultimate source in God. African "power" couldn't therefore be said to be at variance with the biblical concept of power, but it was strikingly similar to it. This was the power sought for and claimed through the Spirit in so many different ways in pentecostal and "spiritual" AICs.[31]

The missionary observers saw a second danger in the emphasis on the Spirit. Some suggested that the traditional concept of ancestor had simply been transferred to the "Holy Spirit" in AICs. Oosthuizen, for example, wrote a chapter in his *Post Christianity in Africa* entitled, "The Misunderstanding of the Biblical Meaning of the Holy Spirit in the Independent Movements". In his view, this was "the most difficult theological problem in Africa, namely, the confusion that exists with regard to the ancestral spirits and the Holy Spirit".[32] Sundkler pointed out that Zionists were careful to point out the discontinuity between their practices and those associated with ancestors, but spoke of the role of the "Angel", who "not only brings a message from the ancestral spirit" but *is* the "ancestral spirit".[33] African experiences of the Spirit need to be interpreted in the light of the biblical revelation, the African spirit world, and pentecostal Spirit experiences the world over. Although at times some AICs see the ancestors as fully compatible with Christian beliefs, they do not replace faith in God. The activities of the AICs, instead of being a bridge back to ancestor veneration, are actually "characterized by confrontation and change".[34] These rather outdated opinions were mostly based on unsubstantiated theological presuppositions and may no longer be held by these observers. The fact that the Holy Spirit has taken over some of the functions of the ancestor does not mean that the Spirit has thereby *become* the ancestor. We should rather consider that the theology of the Spirit has become relevant in this important African context. Far from being a resurgence of ancestor possession, the revelations of the Holy Spirit in AICs point to a realistic encounter between the new Christian faith and the old beliefs, by which Christianity attains an African character.

Clearly, many AICs are founded on this emphasis on the Holy Spirit. This distinguishes them in their own estimation from other churches. A demonstration of God's power through his "pervading" Spirit embracing all of life will often convince people that God is really more powerful than the surrounding evil forces and therefore worthy of worship, faith, and service. The power of the Spirit, whether through an anointed leader or through the whole congregation in worship or prayer, can effectively meet existential needs in the African worldview. Without the power of the Spirit, African Christians can easily revert to traditional religions more "powerful" than the rather sterile, rational Christianity imported to Africa from the West. Africans discover in their own context that God is really all-powerful and that this God manifests his presence through the Spirit working graciously and actively in the church. Theology must be applicable to the experiences of life, and the pneumatology enacted in these AICs is a contextual pneumatology that usually remains consistent with the biblical revelation. This is a dynamic Christian response to the very real possibilities in Africa of a revival of traditional spiritualism on the one hand, and the emergence of a syncretism that is neither true to African religions nor to the Christian message, on the other.

For these fundamental reasons the pneumatology of AICs must be seriously considered. Far from being Sundkler's bridge back to the "heathen past",[35] when we carefully assess this African pneumatology, it will be seen to meet existential needs more effectively than the somewhat impotent and "foreign" theology from the western world. We see the enacting of pneumatology in the various and multiplied manifestations of the Spirit. Sometimes there is spurious play-acting and manipulation through a bogus "manifestation of the Spirit"—but this is not peculiar to AICs. Christianity throughout the world is plagued with "false prophets" and people who use religious sanctions to enforce their human will. In the AICs there are checks and balances against such manipulation, which might not always be obvious. In the perceptions of these churches, it is the Spirit who controls people and people cannot manipulate the Spirit, who takes the initiative and does a sanctifying work in God's people so that they desire to live moral lives in keeping with the Christian revelation.

The Place of Christ

It wasn't only in the realm of pneumatology that AIC theology was criticized. Western missionary observers also said that because of a perceived "overemphasis" on pneumatology, AICs had a "weak Christology", where Christ was hardly mentioned and had been superseded by a paramount leader holding the keys to heaven, a mediator in whom the Holy Spirit works pre-eminently.[36] This criticism struck to the heart of theology and if accepted, would result in hundreds of AICs being judged "not quite Christian" or "post Christian" sects. AICs see themselves as Christian churches and part of the universal church, and so this is really a serious charge. Quite apart from the fact that the judgment overlooked the centrality of healing rites usually performed "in the name of Jesus" and the emphasis on sacraments with clear Christological meaning, most AICs recognize that it is Christ who heals. A related question in the study of AICs is whether they have "messianized" their leaders. Some missionary researchers, perhaps following Swedish missionaries Efraim Andersson and Bengt Sundkler, created a category "messianic" to describe some movements. Oosthuizen spoke of "post Christian" movements no longer recognizable as Christian churches, and Martin said that they exhibited a "false Christology", giving Kimbanguism in the Congo and the Zion Christian Church in South Africa, the two largest AICs in Africa, as examples.[37] The ZCC in South Africa is a movement for which these allegations proved unfounded,[38] and Martin repudiated her own earlier view of Kimbanguism as a result of working closely with this movement. The same about-face happened to both Sundkler and Oosthuizen as their understanding deepened, showing again how wrong conclusions often follow superficial observations.[39]

For Sundkler, the fundamental Christological question was one of mediatorship: who stands at the gates of heaven to admit Christians there? It is alleged that AIC leaders like Simon

Kimbangu, Isaiah Shembe, or Engenas Lekganyane have taken over Christ's mediating position. In the amaNazaretha, Shembe admits his followers to Heaven and turns away whites who have already received the good things in this life.[40] However, a fundamental distinction must be made between the mediation of Christ and that arising in an African context. A mediator's position is not to *admit* people, but rather to *introduce* them to a superior who may not be approached directly. An African "mediator" does therefore not negate Christ's central function, and perhaps this term shouldn't even be used. Some have had to re-evaluate their positions in the light of later research. Sundkler, for example, reassessed his conclusions as he spent more time with AICs, suggesting that the term "iconic leadership" might be more appropriate than "messianism".[41] The leader is an African concretization and reflection of Christ rather than one who has taken the place of Christ.

A clear Christological emphasis in AICs is found especially in the observance of the two sacraments of baptism and Holy Communion, both of which are central to the life of most AICs, at least in West Africa and Southern Africa. Both sacraments speak of the centrality of the cross and the atonement of Christ for sins. Baptism, often celebrated in AICs by immersion in rivers, identifies believers with Christ in his own baptism, which itself was a portent of his coming death and resurrection. In baptism, believers die to the old life, and are washed from their sins because of the sacrificial death of Christ. They rise from their burial under the water in newness of life, as Christ too was resurrected from the tomb. Members are then reminded of the significance of the death of Christ when they partake of the Communion. This becomes an occasion for self-examination and cleansing through the work of Christ on the cross. The joyful mass celebrations of these sacraments in AICs have demonstrated the presence of Christ in his cross and resurrection as central to their worship.

Most AICs acknowledge a God who has come near in the person of Christ, of whom the Holy Spirit bears abundant witness. "Iconic" leadership in AICs simply represents a respected church leader with which African people can more easily identify, and not a deficient Christology. Christ manifests his presence through the Holy Spirit working actively in the church and endowing people with various gifts of grace, especially the gift of healing. These gifts make it possible for a person to have a dynamic relationship with God. They provide for the universal need for solutions to life's felt problems. They make Christ relevant to and practical in all of life. The Bible is the measuring rod by which most AIC theology is conceived and continuously modified, and for this reason churches bear witness to Christ. The honor given to heads of churches must be understood in the African context of respect that is traditionally accorded leaders, and it can't usually be assumed that this has gone beyond this sense of esteem. The reverence for the principal leader of an AIC to the extent that he or she may have appeared on the surface to have overshadowed Christ, may in fact be an attempt on the part of followers to achieve "the closest possible *identification* with biblical figures and the *re-enactment* of biblical events", observed Daneel.[42] Martin modified her earlier judgment of Kimbanguism, the ZCC, and other "messianic movements" with the following comments:

> In the light of what we have observed among the Kimbanguists, the tendencies of the various "messianic movements" in Southern Africa would have to be studied afresh every few years. What still appeared yesterday to be a messianic movement may today already be becoming a church of Jesus Christ on the basis of the ever-renewing Spirit of God.[43]

Robert Schreiter observes that what today may appear to be an aberration of Christianity or "syncretism" from a "foreign" perspective may in fact be at a stage on the way to total conversion:

> The conversion process... is much slower than we had first thought.... what appears to be syncretism... may be but reflective of the stages in the conversion process.... the firm foundations we experience today were not easily achieved. No doubt they may have looked like a dangerous syncretism to an earlier generation.[44]

This "total conversion" is probably a goal that western Christianity itself has not yet attained. Anyone trying to evaluate African phenomena from outside the cultural matrix in which those phenomena are found, may be making "foreign" evaluations which don't accurately account for the realities. To assume that the rapidly moving, fluid phenomenon of the AICs is static and in its final form is to start with a false premise.

Soteriology, Healing, and Exorcism

Just as the pneumatology of pentecostal and prophet-healing AICs plays a pivotal role in the formation of a contextualized African theology, so does their holistic theology of "salvation", or soteriology, which may be regarded as a pneumatological soteriology. "Salvation" in Africa needs to be related to more than an esoteric idea of the "salvation of the soul" and the life hereafter. It must be oriented to the whole of life's problems as experienced by people in their cities and villages. Christianity in Africa must give hope of deliverance and protection from evil in all its present forms, including evil spirits and sorcery, misfortune, natural disasters, disease, poverty, and socio-economic deprivation and oppression. The AIC message of deliverance from sickness and oppression by evil spirits and especially the promise of receiving the power of the Holy Spirit to help people cope in a predominantly hostile spirit world, was really welcome "good news". Many AICs see "salvation" not exclusively in terms of salvation from sinful acts and from eternal condemnation in the life hereafter (the salvation of the soul), but also in terms of salvation from sickness (healing), from evil spirits (exorcism), and from other forms of misfortune.

In particular, the church life and worship of many AICs portrays Christ as the powerful Conqueror over sickness and affliction, for which potent answers are always sought in Africa. People want to celebrate life to the full and triumph over prevailing adversity, particularly disease, poverty, and injustice. Sickness and affliction prevent the fullness of life that Christ came to bring, and like "leprosy" in biblical times, they isolate people from full participation in the community and disturb the social equilibrium. AICs offer solutions seemingly more powerful than those offered either by traditional means or by western Christianity, and they claim in the name of Christ deliverance from this adversity. European missionaries founded hospitals to alleviate suffering but by doing so, they unwittingly secularized healing, removing it from its religious context. As Pobee and Ositelu observe, "In Africa ministry will be judged deficient if it does not treat healing as a function of religion".[45] Cécé Kolié observes that all African rites, including healing rites, were either demonized or branded "pre-rational".[46] AICs reacted to this misjudgment, restoring the place of healing in the liturgy of the church with their warm, demonstrative rites that were often celebrated in smaller, more human communities. AIC rituals also abound in public demonstrations of healing that are a central part of their liturgy. Not only do the AICs themselves see their "penchant for healing and exorcism" as one of their "main characteristics", but they also see "spiritual healing" (or better, "healing by the Spirit") as "the principal focus of our worship and liturgical practices, being the main cause of our impressive growth".[47]

It's very important to understand the role of prophets and prophecy in AIC soteriology. As those who reveal God's will and dispense God's power to meet human needs, African prophets become agents of salvation in many churches. The source of their power is usually believed to be the Holy Spirit, who gives them revelations and the ability to overcome many African problems, including sickness and all kinds of evil. This becomes salvation from pain, fear, and suffering for many people. Daneel speaks of the "moralistic gospel" of western missionaries to Africa, which failed to "spell out convincingly the salvation of the entire man [sic]" and was "insufficiently related to the perplexities caused by illness and misfortune".[48] In almost all prophet-healing churches in Africa, prophets have immense importance. They are messengers who hear from God and proclaim his will to people. They are seers, people with divine power to "see" the revelations of God pertaining to the complaints of the enquirers, especially with regard to sickness. AIC prophets direct their attention towards holistic healing, linking physical healing with social healing, or the restoration of disturbed relationships. Like diviners, they seek to maintain the social equilibrium and are usually expected to "see" the complaints before the sufferers utter them. They are healers *par excellence*, the ones to whom the faithful must go when they or their loved ones are sick or afflicted in any way. In these churches, prophets are always closely associated with healing and this seems to be their most important function. Their healing practices are expected to be effective and actually to bring healing to their patients. They are the ones who must pray for and dispense the holy water that is so often used in healing rites in these churches, and they use other symbolic healing objects as the need arises. Like diviners, they are also expected to give direction and counsel for all kinds of problems, particularly those relating to bad luck and misfortune, sorcery and witchcraft, family conflicts and secret sins. In a few AICs in Southern Africa, prophets are also people who declare the will of the ancestors, which feature has enormous theological implications.

In spiritual and prophet-healing churches throughout Africa, to "prophesy" is to pass on to others revelations or messages based upon what has been seen or heard through the special work of the Holy Spirit. Much of this prophesying serves a distinct pastoral function of providing advice or exhortation.[49] In Zionist and Apostolic churches in Southern Africa, prophecy of a personal and predictive nature frequently appears. This is particularly the case where prophetic activity has much to do with helping people overcome traditional and deep-seated fears of witchcraft and sorcery. For many AIC church members, prophetic healing practices represent at the same time a Christian and an African approach to the problem of pain and suffering. If Christianity rejects the work of divination, as many assume, then it should address the question of what functions it can "take over" from divination. In one sense, as Oosthuizen has observed, the prophets have "compensated" for the role of diviners, filling "the vacuum which the loss of the diviner has left".[50] Yet it is more than mere "compensation" for lost traditional practices. Kiernan convincingly argues that the "faith healing" practices of Zionist prophets and their preoccupation with sorcery give the impression of a "semblance of syncretism", but their healing practices in fact "severed" them from traditional culture and created a "synthesis...

clearly at odds with the prevailing religious ethos of established or mission Christianity", and yet "firmly within the broad parameters of Christian tradition".[51]

One of the main differences between newer Pentecostal churches and most older "spiritual" churches is the use of symbolic objects in healing. Many Pentecostals reject their use as unbiblical and a return to the traditional past. The symbolic objects are seen to replace traditional charms given by a diviner to ward off trouble. For this reason, a person who joins these churches from spiritual churches is often expected to destroy these symbols, usually by burning them, a kind of religious "one-upmanship". For these Pentecostals, it's sufficient for a believer to "lay hands" on the sick in faith, trusting Christ's promise that the sick will recover. Nevertheless, for most spiritual churches, the use of these symbols is one of the central and most important features of church life. As we've seen in the previous chapter, the most common symbol used in these churches is water, blessed or prayed for by a bishop or prophet. The water represents cleansing and purification from evil, sin, sickness, and ritual pollution, concepts carried over from traditional thought. Sometimes the place from where the water is drawn is also important—as in baptisms, in some churches the water must be "living" or running water, and seawater or rainwater gathered during a thunderstorm is thought to be particularly powerful.[52] This belief in holy water is prominent in almost all Zionist and Apostolic churches in southern Africa, and in most Aladura and spiritual churches in West and East Africa. In these churches, holy water and other symbolic objects are used for purification, protection, prosperity, success, and healing, and are seen as visible manifestations of God's power to heal. But without faith in this power of God, the symbols are useless.

One of the central features of the "spiritual" AICs churches is the practice of the prophets. Although newer Pentecostal and Charismatic churches don't emphasize prophecy as much as the spiritual churches do, the basic understanding of prophecy as divine revelation given primarily to meet human needs is the same among all AICs. Prophets are the messengers of God who declare God's revelation to people. The source of the revelation of the prophets is the Holy Spirit. He is also the one who gives the prophets power to heal sickness and overcome the evil generated by deep-seated fears and insecurities inherent in the African worldview. African prophetic practices mustn't only be seen to overcome the *results* of evil; they must also answer Africa's question "Why?", revealing and removing the *cause* of evil. Sometimes the revelation of the cause by itself is sufficient to guarantee the alleviation of the problem, and the supplicant is satisfied. Diagnostic prophecy is the most common form of prophecy found in these churches. These revelations by the Holy Spirit become one of the major causes of attraction for outsiders seeking answers to their particularly African problems, an effective form of pastoral therapy and counsel, a moral corrective and an indispensable facet of Christian ministry. It can become an expression of care and concern for the needy and in countless cases, it really does bring relief.

One of the most difficult questions resurfacing in the new Pentecostal and Charismatic churches, particularly in West Africa, is the role of exorcism there. First of all, it must immediately be said that this is not a new thing in Africa. Exorcism from evil spirits was always one of the primary tasks of traditional diviners, it appears in the New Testament as a practice of the early church, and it occupies a central role in the ministry of AICs of the prophet-healing/spiritual type as well as in the newer Pentecostal churches. This is part of the ministry of the Spirit in the church. Some feel that an overemphasis on this practice in some churches brings an unhealthy focus on evil and the power of Satan. As one who has personally heard and recorded many "testimonies" of "deliverance" from evil spirits in African churches, I cannot honestly fail to acknowledge the reality of the help received there. To suggest that the exorcisms reinforce the sufferer's preoccupation with the African spirit world and the fear of evil spirits ignores the fact that for many Africans, exorcism provides certain relief from psychological stress.[53] Daneel's case study of AIC Bishop Nyasha's ministry of exorcism in Zimbabwe illustrates that the correct Christian response should be to confront beliefs in witchcraft "with the message of the one Scapegoat, Christ, and exorcize the invading spirits as part of the solution to a tradition-based problem, despite the risk of misinterpretation in certain quarters".[54] The appeal to the African worldview and the offer of protection from evil spirits speak to the fears and insecurities of vast numbers of ordinary Africans. Pobee and Ositelu plead for understanding the place of exorcism in the life of AICs. Because "calamities are attributed to personal forces of evil", it's important that religion "help free humanity from the tyranny of those forces", and it's pointless debating whether they are real or not.[55] The AICs themselves had this to say about their "contributions to the world church":

> *The renewal of the Holy Spirit* is continuous with and greater than the spirits around us. Our dependence on the Holy Spirit for protection from evil forces has liberated us to share with others our freedom from fear, a very enticing proposition in the African context, as well as in the rest of the world.[56]

Salvation in AICs therefore, is fundamentally a holistic concept that embraces not only the theoretical salvation of the soul but also the practical here-and-now expression of healing from sickness and deliverance from all types of evil forces and misfortune.

The Importance of AIC Theology

It's extremely difficult and probably unwise to make a theological assessment of AICs, not least of all because the movement has so much variety and is constantly adapting and changing. Theological evaluations have usually come from outsiders' perspectives and are often based on sweeping generalizations, made without thorough investigation. An evaluation is attempted here, not only because of the significance of AICs for the mission of the universal church, but also because of the interaction between Christianity and a living religion that is its focal point. The attitudes of both the older mission-founded churches and the newer Pentecostal churches will be affected by whether AICs are regarded as Christian churches or as "syncretistic sects". If they are seen as being more concerned with preserving traditional religion than proclaiming the Christian message, they become the "objects of mission".[57] Deciding whether a particular AIC can be regarded as a "Christian" church or not is a dangerous and subjective pursuit that depends on what criteria are used and who is making the evaluation. One may impose an arbitrary theological grid that determines the role given to the Bible (both Old and New Testaments), the understanding of the Trinity, and the use of sacraments. Although the great majority of AICs would be considered "Christian" according to these criteria, this is not a totally satisfactory measure in Africa, where consideration should also be given to the extent to which a Christian transformation of traditional practices has taken place. Some churches may have obscured the Christian message according to these criteria, but this doesn't justify calling them "neo-pagan" or "post-Christian". In any case, most AICs consciously use the Bible as a standard and corrective against error.

Countless exceptions and qualifications will always modify any evaluation of AICs. A church which has consciously "deified" or "messianized" its leader (and these concepts can't be used without modifications) may be evaluated as outside the category of "Christian". These movements also leave us with questions as to the adequacy of western Christology. The life and ministry of Christ needs to be reinterpreted in the light of these movements, where so-called "orthodox" Christology is clearly inadequate. The distinctions made between "true" and "syncretistic" religion by outside observers of African phenomena are only valid if applied to churches throughout the world, and not only to those that come under suspicion because they were founded by Africans.[58] The emphasis on the Spirit in the AIC movement means that we should consider whether traditionally western concepts of revelation are adequate. What theological value should be given, for example, to direct "revelation" (prophecy) given to individuals, or to visions and dreams? The prominence of healing in AICs also forces us to consider a theology of healing. Any theological reflection that is done in this type of study should be made with extreme caution and tentativeness and can never be definitive when the phenomena under discussion are dynamic and under a constant process of change.

It might be appropriate, finally, to repeat a word of

caution sounded in my earlier book.[59] If there is a criticism often justifiably leveled at Pentecostals and Charismatics, it is that they have sometimes expounded a theology of success and power at the expense of a theology of the cross. This is particularly true of the popular western fringes of the Pentecostal movement where emphasis is placed on "health and wealth" through faith in God. But at the same time this crude form of North American Pentecostalism needs to be separated from its African counterpart. The emergence of new Pentecostal churches in Africa at the end of the twentieth century indicates that there are unresolved questions facing the church. But there are not always instant solutions to life's vicissitudes. Spirituality is not to be measured merely in terms of success. People are not only convinced by the triumphs of Christianity but also by its trials. The history of the church in Africa is clear evidence of that. A one-sided pneumatology is a danger to all of us, whether in Africa or elsewhere. The Spirit is also a gentle dove, a Spirit of humility, patience and meekness, of love, joy, and peace. The Spirit is the tender Comforter, the one who comes alongside to help and strengthen us whenever we encounter trials and problems. This comforting ministry of the Spirit also needs to be emphasized in an Africa plagued with famine, poverty, economic and political oppression, and disease. Overemphasizing the power of the Spirit in terms of outward success often leads to bitter disappointment and disillusionment when that power is not evidently and immediately manifested. Christian pneumatology must not only provide power when there is a lack of it—it must also be able to sustain through life's tragedies and failures, especially when there is no visible success.

Notes

[1] M.L. Daneel, "Christian Theology of Africa", Pretoria, 1989, 54.

[2] Hastings, *African Christianity*, 54.

[3] Pobee & Ositelu, 70.

[4] Justin S. Ukpong, "Current Theology: The Emergence of African Theologies", *Theological Studies 45*, 1984, 520.

[5] Barrett, *Schism*, 169-70.

[6] E. Fashole-Luke, "The quest for African Christian theologies", New York, 1976, 144, 148, 162; Burgess Carr, "The relation of union to mission", New York, 1976, 160-1.

[7] Daneel, "Christian Theology", 59; John S. Mbiti, 1976. "Contextualising Theology", New York, 16; Pobee & Ositelu, 42.

[8] Daneel, "Exorcism", 221.

[9] Wilbert R. Shenk, "The Contribution of the Study of New Religious Movements to Missiology", Elkhart, 1990, 194.

[10] This section is adapted from Allan Anderson, "The Hermeneutical Processes of Pentecostal-type AICs in South Africa", *Missionalia 24:2*, 1996, 171-85; and id., *Zion and Pentecost*, 133-7.

[11] Severino Croatto, *Biblical Hermeneutics*. New York, 1987, 1 (italics in original).

[12] Carlos Mesters, "The Use of the Bible in Christian Communities of the Common People", New York, 1993, 14 (emphasis mine).

[13] Gerald West, *Biblical Hermeneutics of Liberation*. Pietermaritzburg, 1995, 195.

[14] Croatto, 6.

[15] Daneel, *Quest*, 84-5.

[16] Gerald West, 198.

[17] Mesters, 7.

[18] Ibid., 9.

[19] Cited in Gerald West, 54.

[20] Pobee & Ositelu, 41.

[21] Croatto, 1.

[22] Anderson, *Moya* (1991) was devoted to a study of pneumatology in Africa, particularly as manifested in pentecostal churches. Some of what follows in this section is gleaned from there and from Anderson, *Zion and Pentecost*, 237-57.

[23] Pobee and Ositelu, 40.

[24] Sundkler, *Bantu Prophets*, 242; Institute for Contextual Theology, 26, italics in original.

[25] World Council, 51.

[26] Tempels, 44-5.

[27] David J. Bosch, "The Problem of Evil in Africa", Pretoria, 1987, 42.

[28] Anderson, *Moya*, 113-20.

[29] Sundkler, *Bantu Prophets*, 244; Martin, *Messianism*, 113.

[30] Anderson, *Bazalwane*, 113-20; Anderson & Otwang, 113.

[31] Anderson, *Moya*, 115; id., "Pentecostal Pneumatology and African Power Concepts: Continuity or Change?" *Missionalia* 19:1, 1991 (65-74).

[32] Oosthuizen, *Post Christianity*, 120.

[33] Sundkler, *Bantu Prophets*, 247, 250.

[34] Daneel,*Old & New 3*, 117.

[35] Sundkler, *Bantu Prophets*, 297.

[36] Anderson, *Moya*, 36-7.

[37] Andersson, *Messianic*; Oosthuizen, *Post Christianity*, xiv; Martin, *Messianism*, 161.

[38] Anderson, "The Lekganyanes".

[39] Anderson & Otwang, 101-2; Martin, *Kimbangu*, 14.

[40] Sundkler, *Bantu Prophets*, 321.

[41] Sundkler, *Bantu Prophets*, 297; id., *Zulu Zion*, 304-5, 309-10.

[42] Daneel, *Old and New 3*, 300.

[43] Martin, *Kimbangu*, 171.

[44] Schreiter, *Local Theologies*, 158.

[45] Pobee & Ositelu, 49.

[46] Cécé Kolié, "Jesus as Healer?", London, 1992, 143.

[47] Pobee & Ositelu, 40, 71.

[48] M.L. Daneel, "Communication and Liberation in African Independent Churches", *Missionalia* 11:2, 1983, 58.

[49] Oosthuizen, *Healer-Prophet*, 16, 33-4.

[50] Ibid., 17.

[51] Jim Kiernan, "Variations on a Christian Theme: The Healing Synthesis of Zulu Zionism", London & New York, 1994, 74, 82.

[52] Oosthuizen, *Healer-Prophet*, 45.

[53] Anderson, *Zion & Pentecost,* 258-76; Shorter, 197; M.C. Kitshoff, "Exorcism as Healing Ministry in the African Independant/ Indigenous Churches", n.d.

[54] Daneel, "Exorcism", 227, 246-247.

[55] Pobee & Ositelu, 29; Ayegboyin & Ishola, 151.

[56] Pobee & Ositelu, 71.

[57] Daneel, *Quest,* 246.

[58] MacGaffey, 3.

[59] Anderson, *Moya,* 72-3.

11

REFORM AND RENEWAL

This book has looked at the enormous contribution that AICs have made to world Christianity and has only been able to give a rather introductory survey of the many issues raised. Because the writer is a theologian, the last chapter will try to draw together some of the implications of this "African reformation" for the mission of the church. Some of the major questions raised here can only be hinted at, obviously needing further extensive research. The AICs are a major force in Christianity and a manifestation of the rapidly changing nature of world Christianity in the twentieth century. The fact is that more people in several parts of Africa belong to churches originating in African initiative than to churches originating in western missions. In the past three decades the percentage of people belonging to the "mainline" churches has declined quite considerably, which raises disturbing questions, among others, about the content and relevance of theological training and the curricula of theological institutions in Africa. AICs hardly ever feature in these institutions of higher learning, either in terms of curriculum content or in student intake.

The greater inclusion of AICs in these seminaries and in the people educated there will make the churches more relevant to the majority of African Christians who read the Bible literally and use their own experience as the main hermeneutical tool with which to understand it.[1] There are ways of expressing theology other than those familiar to westerners. AICs teach us how to do theology in oral narrative and experience. African theologians must examine the AIC contribution in their attempt to provide a meaningful Christian theology in Africa.[2]

Innovations in African Christianity

The remarkable growth of AICs and the corresponding decline in membership among older churches means that the mission methods of AICs should be examined. There must be something that they are "doing right" from which all Christians can learn in the ongoing task of proclaiming the gospel. And conversely, there must be something that western missionaries failed to do or did wrongly which resulted in such a huge response. Without rehearsing all the discussion of chapter 2, there *was* sometimes a close identification between missionaries and colonizing Europeans, and sometimes African clergy were discriminated against. Part of the reasons for the emergence of AICs can be attributed to these factors, as we have seen. But there were also times when missionaries protested against injustice and oppression by the colonizing powers. Reflecting on the mistakes of missionaries in the past shouldn't let us overlook the enormous, often self-denying contribution that they made to alter the face of world Christianity. Nevertheless, the fact that AICs continue to gain strength at the expense of older churches has implications for these churches, and it no longer has much to do with the mistakes of European missionaries. It doesn't help to deride AICs or accuse them of "sheep-stealing", for as one AIC leader once cogently remarked to me, "We don't steal sheep; we plant grass"!

Important questions are raised about the relevance of the faith and life of older churches in Africa. If teachings and practices are perceived by people as powerless to meet their everyday felt needs, then these churches can't continue with "business as usual" in the face of such obvious shortcomings. The OAIC published a manifesto in 1996 that is worth quoting in part here, where "one main reason" for the drift away from "mission churches" was spelt out:

> The Western God was spiritually inadequate and irrelevant to deal with the reality of many aspects of our lives. The result was a Christian faith and conviction which were only "skin-deep" or superstitious, in spite of the successful spread of Christianity on the continent. There was and is still the question of how deep the Christian faith really is when so many of its affiliates still continue to visit the caretakers of the African traditional religions. [3]

This penetrating remark by AICs themselves challenges older churches in Africa with the need to rethink their entire mission strategy. Without such a serious reappraisal, their decline will probably continue and may be terminal.

AICs raise important questions concerning the relationship between the gospel and culture, as we've seen in chapter 9. Are we dealing with cultural variations of the Christian faith in AICs, or is there only one "gospel"? Furthermore, ethical questions arise from the interaction of western Christianity and African cultures, such as questions of polygyny and marriage goods, patriarchalism and the seeming oppression of women in society and church, and the practice of other traditional social customs. In missiology, we are partly concerned with processes of church growth. This study of AICs pays attention to historical developments and other factors contributing to the origin and expansion of these movements. A rapidly growing religious movement demands our attention, whether we agree with its theology or not. In seeking to find out *why* AICs are growing we must know how to relate to and learn from them. Part of the reason for their growth may be that they have succeeded where western founded churches often failed—to provide a contextualized Christianity in Africa. AICs give us therefore "an alternative model for understanding how the church grows". [4] The phenomenon is essentially of *African* origin, and has its roots in a marginalized and underprivileged society struggling to find dignity and identity in the face of brutal colonialism and oppression. In some parts of Africa, it expanded initially among people who were neglected, misunderstood, and deprived of anything but token leadership by their white ecclesiastical "masters". But despite these important social and historical factors, fundamentally it's the ability of AICs to adapt to and fulfill *religious* aspirations that continues to be their main strength. Research should more precisely define these aspirations, to help answer the question of whether older churches are addressing these needs today. Turner suggested that AICs offer solutions to problems existing in all Christianity, "a series of extensive, long-term, unplanned, spontaneous, and fully authentic experiments from which [Christianity] may secure answers to some of its most difficult questions".[5]

There are several other examples of these unanswered missiological questions, such as those concerning the widespread use of ritual symbolism in AICs. We might ask what symbols found in older Christian traditions are retained by the newer movements, and what symbols are borrowed from traditional religion and culture—and *why* these symbols are retained while others are discarded. Why, for example, do most prophet-healing AICs in Southern Africa prefer adult baptism by immersion? Why do AICs all over the continent use an abundance of symbolic liturgy, especially the sacramental use of water in healing and purification rituals, and episcopal leadership? There are surely more than historical explanations for these features. Why is traditional divination mostly rejected, and why (and how) have the prophets so effectively replaced diviners? Why do some AICs oppose ancestor observances while others are ambivalent about them, and still others accommodate them? And then, the widespread use of dreams and visions as a vehicle of revelation in AICs is also a biblical practice, but one regarded of little significance in western Christianity. The contribution of these African forms of spirituality is of great importance to the mission of the universal church and its effective proclamation of the gospel. As Turner has observed, the AICs help mission studies to understand "the overriding African concern for spiritual power from a mighty God to overcome all enemies and evils that threaten human life and vitality, hence their extensive ministry of mental and physical healing". He points out how different this is from "the Western preoccupation" with theoretical and rather esoteric theological issues.[6] All these questions in turn raise further questions concerning the problem of continuity and discontinuity, the intercultural communication of the Christian gospel, and the encounter between Christianity and another living religion. The historical section of this book has raised many questions about the post-colonial history of African Christianity. The AICs have created a new Christian identity for themselves that is seen to be free of "foreign" intrusions, but is it really, and who determines whether it is or not? A sympathetic and sensitive study of AICs can give us a new understanding of the meaning of history, and will help us begin to answer many of these and other important questions.

An African style of worship and liturgy and a holistic Christianity that offers tangible help in this world as well as in the next together form a uniquely African contextualization of Christianity. It's argued here that this contextual Christianity meets needs more substantially than the often sterile Christianity imported from the West. If older churches are to return to the cutting edge of the Christian mission they'll have to address and remedy these shortcomings. If not, they may continue to minister to a decreasing membership content either to practice Christianity side by side with African traditional religions, or succumb to a secular society and no longer practice Christianity at all. AICs provide what Turner calls "a salvaging or rescue function" in relation to "mainline" churches, by "preventing dissatisfied members from reverting to paganism [sic] by providing a recognizably Christian and easily available alternative spiritual home".[7] At the same time, AICs are challenged to recognize that their cultural context in an increasingly technological and urbanized society is a rapidly changing one. In order for them to change with society and thereby avoid becoming archaic and irrelevant, the contextualization process must continue. This is a lesson that the whole Christian church must learn.

African Mission Initiatives

AICs were founded in innovative African initiatives unprecedented in the history of Christianity. They were driven by a compelling need to preach, and especially to *experience,* a new message of the power of the Holy Spirit. The effectiveness of this AIC mission was based on this unique message, which was both the motivation for the thousands of grassroots emissaries and their source of attraction. These mission initiatives were often the work of ordinary members, lay people who, as Barrett observes, accomplished their evangelism "through the movements of the laity in the normal course of their secular occupations".[8] All the widely differing pentecostal and spiritual AICs have several important common features. They proclaim and celebrate a salvation (or "healing") that encompasses all of life's experiences and afflictions. They offer power to provide a sense of dignity and coping mechanism for life. Their mission is to share this all-embracing message with as many people as possible, and to accomplish this, African preachers traveled far and wide.

The astonishing journeys in 1914 of Wade Harris through the Ivory Coast to western Ghana, one of the most remarkable evangelistic campaigns ever seen, resulted in tens of thousands of conversions to Christianity.[9] Garrick Braide in the Niger Delta area of Nigeria conducted a similar crusade with thousands becoming Christians, and was barred from the Anglican church because of his practice of healing the sick and his tolerance of polygyny—and because he called himself a prophet. Later, prophets like Joseph Babalola in Western Nigeria and Johane Marange in Zimbabwe set off on similarly remarkable journeys resulting in thousands of conversions. Much more recently, Nigerian pentecostal preachers like William Kumuyi and Benson Idahosa have changed Christianity in their country. These and many other African missionaries demonstrated their proclamation of the manifestation of divine power through healing, prophecy, speaking in tongues, and other pentecostal phenomena. African societies welcomed the message of receiving the power of the Spirit to meet human needs, where a lack of power was keenly felt on a daily basis. These preachers preached a radical healing message that often rejected medicine, whether western or African, and some, like the Christ Apostolic Church in Nigeria, later seceded from western pentecostal missionaries who were not as radical in their healing practices.[10]

The impact of the AICs must be assessed primarily in terms of this proclamation rather than as a reaction to western missions.[11] Nevertheless, because western cultural forms of Christianity were often regarded as superficial and out of touch with many realities of African life, it was necessary for a new indigenous and culturally relevant Christianity to arise. This was a reformation of Christianity in Africa indeed. Although AIC mission initiatives *were* in some ways an indirect response to the inadequacies of western mission, they were not discontinuous with those initiatives. African missionaries went out just as European missionaries had done to proclaim the message of the Bible, to appeal to the Christian scriptures as their authority for doing so, and to call people to repentance, conversion, and especially to baptism. But this proclamation was fundamentally different in that it was more radical in its orientation to the African worldview than that of the western missionaries had been. Furthermore, as we've seen, although western missionaries believed in the *content* of the Bible, they didn't usually see any *continuity* or connection between the biblical context and the present African one, a feature that African missionaries were quick to discover and proclaim. Although having some validity in the case of the earliest movements, the tendency to regard the growth of AICs mainly as a reaction to western missions and colonialism detracts from an important fact. Long after the initial secessions, AICs went on growing and changing the face of African Christianity without any reference to western missions whatsoever. Because western forms of Christianity were often regarded as superficial and out of touch with many realities of African life, it was therefore necessary for a new, truly African mission initiative to arise with a powerful message to penetrate Africa's soul. The strength and attraction of these churches, observes Daneel, should be seen in "their original, creative attempts to relate the good news of the gospel in a meaningful and symbolically intelligible way to the innermost needs of Africa".[12]

Healing and protection from evil are the most prominent features of the proclamation and worship of these AICs, and are probably the most important factors in their evangelism and church recruitment. In Africa, the problems of disease and evil affect the whole community and are not simply a private domain relegated to individual pastoral care. As Cox observes, the AICs "provide a setting in which the African conviction that spirituality and healing belong together is dramatically enacted".[13] African communities were always to a large extent health-oriented communities, and in the traditional religions, rituals for healing and protection were the most prominent ones. AIC missionaries responded to what they experienced as a void left by a form of Christianity that had unwittingly initiated what amounted to the destruction of African spiritual values. AICs were able to declare a message reclaiming biblical traditions of healing and protection from evil, they demonstrated the practical effects of these traditions, and by so doing became the heralds of a Christianity with an implicit yet really meaningful theology. African missionaries proclaimed that the same God who saves the "soul" also heals the body, delivers from evil forces, and provides answers to other human needs. This message went a long way towards meeting the physical, emotional and spiritual needs of people, and it offered solutions to life's problems and ways to cope in a seemingly threatening and hostile world.[14]

We can't isolate the fact of the remarkable growth of AICs in twentieth century Africa from the fact that this is a "people movement",[15] a massive turning of African people to Christianity from traditional religions on an unprecedented scale. This revival movement was set in motion by a multitude of factors for which western missions were unprepared at the time. In fact, when these movements first arose a century ago, very little "mission" work had been carried out among the African peoples in most of the places where the movements originated.[16] The charismatic leaders tapped into the times and so became catalysts of what Hastings has called a "primary movement of mass conversion".[17] Many of the "spiritual" AICs arose in the first three decades of this century, but of course, there have been numerous secessions and new movements created since. The early African missionary initiators were followed by a new generation of leaders, learning from and to some extent patterning their ministries on those who had gone before them. The talented administrator Edward Lekganyane, for example, consolidated his charismatic father's work after the setbacks of Engenas' death and a major schism in the church in 1948, and the Zion Christian Church became the largest AIC in South Africa by the time of Edward's death in 1967.[18] Of course, when new charismatic leaders arose, each with their own sense of divine call and commission, the possibilities of fission were heightened enormously, because it is a well-known premise that "charismatic authority militates against stable institutionalization".[19]

The Reformation of African Christianity

We come back to the question with which we began this study: to what extent can the AIC phenomenon be considered an "African Reformation"? Critics have pointed to so-called "dubious" theology and practices, and have said that this was simply a sectarian movement of secession and not a reformation at all. Some have gone further and have questioned the very "Christian-ness" of the AIC movement. As Barrett points out, it depends on the observer's point of view. If we're trying to understand the movement from the perspective of the AICs themselves, then it is certainly a reformation of continental proportions and international significance. Pointing to the "errors" of this African reformation only needs the hindsight of history to realize that these same "errors" (and worse) were found in the European Reformation, at least to the same extent.[20] One of the abiding legacies of the AICs is that they've provided an approach to African religion and culture that is more innovative and responsible than that of almost all other forms of African Christianity. Instead of thinking of this as their reinterpretation of Christianity in the light of African religion, it's probably more correct to say that their unique contribution to the gospel and culture debate is that they have selectively reinterpreted African tradition in the light of their radical reformation of Christianity.

One feature of this fundamental reformation of African Christianity is what has been described as the "democratization" of leadership. In contrast to the traditional deposit of authority for leadership in older men, many AICs were founded by young men and women. Because pentecostal and spiritual AICs place such strong emphasis on the role of the experience of the Spirit, the Spirit is given to every believer without preconditions. One of the results of this is that it ensured that the rigid dividing line between clergy and laity, young and old, and between men and women did not develop early on in these churches.[21] In addition, leaders tended to come from lower and formally uneducated strata of society, and as soon as their gifts and calling emerged, they were trained in apprentice-type training, where their charismatic leadership abilities were encouraged. Of special importance was the fact that women were effectively mobilized into service, and some became founders of significant churches. Women pioneers of church movements like Christina Nku of the St. John Apostolic Faith Mission in South Africa and Christianah Abiodun of the Cherubim and Seraphim in Nigeria were two of the better-known ones, but it wasn't only the women *founders* who were significant. The use of women with charismatic gifts is widespread throughout the AIC movement, and women make up the great majority of their membership. The ministry of women accorded well with the traditional prominence of women in African religious rituals and contrasted with the prevailing practice of older churches, most of whom barred women from entering the ministry or even from taking any part in public worship.

We shouldn't think that the impact of the AIC reformation was mainly a result of the efforts of a few charismatic leaders— nothing could be further from the truth. The proliferation of the movement wouldn't have occurred without the tireless efforts of a vast number of ordinary women and men. They networked across regional and ethnic boundaries proclaiming the same message they'd heard their leaders proclaim, which had sufficiently altered their lives to make it worth sharing wherever they went. The most obvious example of this is one of the largest AICs of all, the Kimbanguist church, emerging while its main leaders were in prison or had been detained and deported, and it did not rely on particular charismatic leaders for its growth. The mass involvement of the "laity" in the AICs was undoubtedly one of the main reasons for their success. There was little need for a theologically articulate clergy, because cerebral and clerical Christianity had, in the minds of many Africans, already failed them. What was needed was a demonstration of power by people to whom ordinary people could easily relate. In spite of the autocratic leadership style of some AIC leaders, this *was* the democratization of Christianity. Henceforth, the mystery of the gospel would no longer be reserved for a select privileged and educated few, but would be revealed to whoever was willing to receive it and pass it on. These itinerant preachers were encouraged by the regular pilgrimages they made to the church headquarters, the new "Zion" or "Jerusalem" (or, recently, "Canaan Land" or "Miracle Center"), the holy city from which they would receive fresh inspiration from their paramount leader to continue their mission. This place of pilgrimage becomes at once a place of magnetic attraction to which converts flock to realize their new Christian identity and dignity, and sometimes, to find the ultimate source of empowerment in the person of the prophetic leader. The significance of these "holy cities" can't be underestimated.

The new Pentecostal and Charismatic churches at the end of this century seem to be increasing at the expense of all types of older churches. Like the older AICs before them, these churches have a sense of identity as a holy and separated community, whose primary purpose is to promote their cause to outsiders. These are the "born again" people of God, with a strong sense of belonging to the community of God's people, chosen from out of the world to witness to the new life they experience in the power of the Spirit. This latest expression of the AIC reformation has had the effect of popularizing a new form of Christianity appealing especially to the urbanized and significantly westernized new generation of Africans.

Another significant feature of the AICs is that the dichotomy often found in western forms of Christianity (including Pentecostalism) between "evangelism" and "social concern" does not exist. African spirituality, as Turner points out, "concerns the whole man [sic], and therefore the healing of his sicknesses and the prosperity of his family and affairs".[22] This African holism, a concern for the whole of life and not just the "spiritual" part of it, is to a great extent a biblical holism and a dimension that the church needs to rediscover in its mission to the world. At the same time, we must ask ourselves questions about the content of our message. If there is really good news in the gospel of Jesus Christ, if we believe that there is "no other name" by which humankind can be saved, and if we believe in the ability of God through his Spirit to liberate people from every conceivable kind of human problem—whether physical, emotional, mental, social, personal, or any other—then our mission is both to proclaim and to practice this good news. The mission of the church includes of necessity both the *proclamation* of the gospel and the *demonstration* of its power. The gospel involves a message of an all-inclusive salvation from evil in all its forms, whose power is demonstrated when people perceive our message to actually work in bringing deliverance to the whole of life as they experience it. The message must also include a clear pneumatology, where God's salvation is seen in different manifestations of his abiding presence through his Spirit, divine revelations which assure us that "God is there" to help us in every area of need. The AICs urge all Christianity to seriously reconsider the effectiveness, the content, and the relevancy of its mission. We must be humble enough to learn from this example, which makes full use of African opportunities to proclaim the gospel. Whether at night vigils, where the whole community gathers to comfort and be comforted, or during church conference celebrations of the Eucharist, AICs use these and many other occasions to zealously evangelize, resulting in the growth of the church.

Holistic, ecstatic, and experiential religious practices are found in Christianity throughout the world today. The antiphonal singing, simultaneous and spontaneous prayer, dance and motor behavior found throughout worldwide Pentecostalism, all of which are also essentially African practices, emphasize the freedom, equality, community, and dignity of each person in the sight of God. The experience of the power of the Spirit can be a unifying factor in a global society that is still deeply divided, and it can be the catalyst for the emergence of a new society where there is justice for all and hope for a despairing world. But it dare not become an escape mechanism to flee from the harsh realities of life today. The Spirit should liberate us from prejudice, arrogance, isolationism, and ethnocentrism—in short, all our abominable selfishness. We should be brought to the place where God can truly bring His dominion to bear on all facets of life as we experience it—that His kingdom may come, and His will be done throughout the earth, and especially in Africa, as it is done in heaven.

Nkosi Sikelel' iAfrika!

Woza Moya oyingcwele!

("Lord, bless Africa! Come, Holy Spirit!")[23]

Notes

[1] Anderson, "Hermeneutical Processes", 171-2.

[2] Allan Anderson, "Challenges and prospects for research into AICs in Southern Africa", *Missionalia 23:3*, 1995, 288; Anderson & Otwang, 25.

[3] Pobee & Ositelu, 68.

[4] Shenk, 198.

[5] Turner, *Religious Innovation*, 209.

[6] Ibid., 210.

[7] Ibid., 19.

[8] Barrett, *Schism*, 173.

[9] Hastings, *History*, 67.

[10] Hastings, *Church in Africa*, 445-6, 514.

[11] Hastings, *History*, 69.

[12] Daneel, *Quest*, 101; Hastings, *Church in Africa*, 527, 531; id., *History*, 69-71.

[13] Cox, 247.

[14] Anderson & Otwang, 32.

[15] This term is commonly found in the "church growth" school within North American Evangelicalism.

[16] Kiernan, 72.

[17] Hastings, *Church in Africa*, 530-1.

[18] Anderson, *Bazalwane*, 99; id., "The Lekganyanes".

[19] Comaroff, 186.

[20] Barrett, *Schism*, 164.

[21] Willem A. Saayman, "Some reflections on the development of the Pentecostal mission model in South Africa", *Missionalia* 21:1, 1993, 43.

[22] Turner, *Religious Innovation*, 195.

[23] From the South African national anthem.

SELECT BIBLIOGRAPHY

Adogame, Afeosemime U. *Celestial Church of Christ,* Studies in the Intercultural History of Christianity 115. Frankfurt am Main: Peter Lang, 1999.

Allen, Tim, "Understanding Alice: Uganda's Holy Spirit Movement in Context". *Africa* 61 (3), 1991 (370-99).

Anderson, Allan, *Moya: The Holy Spirit in an African Context.* Pretoria: University of South Africa Press, 1991.

— *Bazalwane: African Pentecostals in South Africa.* Pretoria: University of South Africa Press, 1992.

— with Otwang, Samuel, *Tumelo: The Faith of African Pentecostals in South Africa.* Pretoria: University of South Africa Press, 1993.

— & Pillay, Gerald J. "The Segregated Spirit: The Pentecostals", Elphick & Davenport (eds.), *Christianity in South Africa,* Oxford & Cape Town, 1997 (227-41).

— & Hollenweger, Walter J. (eds.), *Pentecostals After a Century: Global Perspectives on a Movement in Transition.* Sheffield: Sheffield Academic Press, 1999.

— "Dangerous Memories: South African Pentecostals", Anderson & Hollenweger (eds.), *Pentecostals After a Century,* Sheffield, 1999 (89-107).

— "The Lekganyanes and Prophecy in the Zion Christian Church", *Journal of Religion in Africa,* 29:2, August 1999.

— *Zion and Pentecost: The Spirituality and Experience of Pentecostal and Zionist/ Apostolic Churches in South Africa.* Pretoria: University of South Africa Press, 2000.

Anderson, David M. & Johnson, Douglas H. (eds.), *Revealing Prophets: Prophecy in Eastern African History,* London: James Currey, 1995.

Andersson, Efraim, *Messianic Popular Movements in the Lower Congo*, Uppsala: Studia Ethnographica Upsaliensia 16, 1958.

Asamoah-Gyadu, Kwabena J. "Traditional missionary Christianity and new religious movements in Ghana", thesis, Accra: University of Ghana, 1996.

— "The Church in the African State: The Pentecostal/Charismatic Experience in Ghana", *Journal of African Christian Thought*, 1:2, December 1998 (51-7).

Ayegboyin, Deji & Ishola, S. Ademola, *African Indigenous Churches: An Historical Perspective*, Lagos: Greater Heights Publications, 1997.

Baëta, G. C. *Prophetism in Ghana: A Study of some "Spiritual" Churches*, London: SCM, 1962.

Barrett, David B. *Schism and Renewal in Africa: An Analysis of Six Thousand Contemporary Religious Movements*. Nairobi: Oxford University Press, 1968.

— (ed.) *African Initiatives in Religion*. Nairobi: East African Publishing House, 1971.

— Kurian, George T. & Johnson, Todd M. (eds.) *World Christian Encyclopedia*, 2nd Ed, 2 vols. Oxford & New York: Oxford University Press, 2001.

— & Padwick, T. John, *Rise Up and Walk! Conciliarism and the African Indigenous Churches, 1815-1987*. Nairobi: Oxford University Press, 1989.

Barrett, Stanley R. "All Things in Common: The Holy Apostles of Western Nigeria (1947 onwards)". Isichei (ed.), *Varieties of Christian Experience in Nigeria*, London, 1982 (149-62).

Becken, Hans-Jürgen, "Die Wasserkirche — St John's Apostolic Faith Mission", in *Neue Zeitschrift für Missionswissenschaft*, 42(2), 1986.

Behrend, Heike, *Alice Lakwena & the Holy Spirits: War in Northern Uganda 1986-1995*. Oxford: James Currey, 1999.

Bond, G., Johnson, W. & Walker, S. S. (eds.), *African Christianity: Patterns of Religious Continuity*, New York: Academic Press, 1979.

Bond, George C., "A Prophecy that Failed: The Lumpa Church of Uyombe, Zambia". Bond, Johnson, & Walker (eds.), *African Christianity*, New York, 1979 (137-60).

Bosch, David J. *Transforming Mission*. Maryknoll: Orbis, 1991.

Callaway, Helen, "Women in Yoruba Tradition and in the Cherubim and Seraphim Society", Kalu (ed.), *The History of Christianity in West Africa*, London & New York, 1980 (321-32).

Clarke, Peter B. *West Africa and Christianity*, London: Edward Arnold, 1986.

— *Mahdism in West Africa: The Ijebu Mahdiyya Movement*. London: Luzac Oriental, 1995.

Comaroff, Jean, *Body of Power, Spirit of Resistance: The Culture and History of a South African People*. Chicago & London: University of Chicago Press, 1985.

Cox, Harvey, *Fire from Heaven: The rise of pentecostal spirituality and the reshaping of religion in the twenty-first century*. London: Cassell, 1996.

Croatto, Severino, *Biblical Hermeneutics*. New York: Orbis, 1987.

Dada, S. A., *J. K. Coker: Father of African Independent Churches*, Ibadan: AOWA Printers and Publishers, 1986.

Daneel, M. L. (Inus) *Old and New in Southern Shona Independent Churches. Vol. 1*. The Hague: Mouton, 1971.

— *Old and New in Southern Shona Independent Churches. Vol. 2*. The Hague: Mouton, 1974.

— *Quest for Belonging*. Gweru, Zimbabwe: Mambo Press, 1987.

— *Old and New in Southern Shona Independent Churches. Vol. 3*, Gweru: Mambo Press, 1988.

— *Fambidzano: Ecumenical Movement of Zimbabwean Independent Churches*, Gweru: Mambo Press, 1989.

De Gruchy, John W. *The Church Struggle in South Africa*. Grand Rapids: Eerdmans & Cape Town: David Philip, 1986.

De Villiers, P.G.R. (ed.), *Like a Roaring Lion: Essays on the Bible, the Church and Demonic Powers.* Pretoria: University of South Africa, 1987.

Dillon-Malone, Clive M. *The Korsten Basketmakers: A study of the Masowe Apostles, an indigenous African religious movement,* Manchester: Manchester University Press, 1978.

— "The 'Mutumwa' Churches of Zambia", *Journal of Religion in Africa* 14:3, 1983, 204-22.

Elphick, Richard & Davenport, Rodney (eds.), *Christianity in South Africa: A Political, Social & Cultural History,* Oxford: James Currey & Cape Town: David Philip, 1997.

Fernandez, James W. "The Idea and Symbol of the Saviour in a Gabon Syncretistic Cult", *International Review of Mission* 211: 53, 1964 (281-9).

Garlock, Ruthanne, *Fire in his Bones: The Story of Benson Idahosa,* South Plainfield: Logos, 1981.

Gerloff, Roswith, *A Plea for British Black Theologies: The Black church movement in Britain in its transatlantic cultural and theological connection with special reference to the Pentecostal Oneness (Apostolic) and Sabbatarian movements,* 2 Vols., Frankfurt: Peter Lang, 1992.

Gifford, Paul (ed.), *New Dimensions in African Christianity,* Nairobi: All Africa Conference of Churches, 1992.

— *Christianity and Politics in Doe's Liberia,* Cambridge: Cambridge University Press, 1993.

— (ed.), *The Christian Churches and the Democratization of Africa,* Leiden: E.J. Brill, 1995.

— *African Christianity: Its Public Role.* London: Hurst, 1998.

Githieya, Francis Kimani, *The Freedom of the Spirit: African Indigenous Churches in Kenya,* Atlanta: Scholars Press, 1997.

Grenfell, F. James, "Simâo Toco: an Angolan prophet", *Journal of Religion in Africa* 28:2, 1998 (210-26).

Hackett, Rosalind I. J. (ed.), *New Religious Movements in Nigeria*, Lewiston, NY, 1987.

— "Enigma Variations: The New Religious Movement in Nigeria Today", Walls & Shenk (eds.), *Exploring New Religious Movements*, Elkhart, 1990 (131-42).

Haliburton, Gordon MacKay, *The Prophet Harris: A Study of an African Prophet and his Mass Movement in the Ivory Coast and the Gold Coast 1913-1915*. London: Longman, 1971.

Hastings, Adrian, *A History of African Christianity 1950-1975*, Cambridge: Cambridge University Press, 1979.

— *The Church in Africa 1450-1930*, Oxford: Clarendon, 1994.

Hayward, Victor E.W. (ed.), *African Independent Church Movements*, London: Edinburgh House Press, 1963.

Hexham, Irving & Oosthuizen, G. C. (eds.) *The Story of Isaiah Shembe: History and Traditions Centered on Ekuphakameni and Mount Nhlangakazi*, Lewiston: Edwin Mellor Press, 1996.

Hinfelaar, Hugo F. "Lumpa and Reconciliation", *AFER* 26(5), 1984 (292-6).

— "Women's Revolt: The Lumpa Church of Lenshina Mulenga in the 1950s", *Journal of Religion in Africa* 21:2, 1991 (99-129).

Hodgson, Janet, "Ntsikana — A Precursor of Independency?", *Missionalia* 12:1, 1984 (19-33).

Hoehler-Fatton, Cynthia, *Women of Fire and Spirit: History, faith and gender in Roho religion in Western Kenya*, Oxford: Oxford University Press, 1996.

Hollenweger, Walter J., *The Pentecostals*, London: SCM, 1972.

— *Pentecostalism: Origins and Developments Worldwide*, Peabody: Hendrickson, 1997.

Institute for Contextual Theology, *Speaking for Ourselves*. Johannesburg, 1985.

Isichei, Elizabeth (ed.), *Varieties of Christian Experience in Nigeria*, London: Macmillan, 1982.

— *A History of Christianity in Africa: from antiquity to the present,* London: SPCK, 1995.

Johnson, W. "The Africanization of a Mission Church: The African Methodist Episcopal Church in Zambia". Bond, Johnson & Walker (eds.), *African Christianity,* New York, 1979 (89-107).

Johnstone, Patrick, *Operation World,* Carlisle: OM Publishing, 1993.

Jules-Rosette, Benetta (ed.), *The New Religions of Africa,* Norwood, NJ: Ablex, 1979.

— "Women as Ceremonial Leaders in an African Church: The Apostles of John Maranke", Jules-Rosette, (ed.), *The New Religions of Africa,* Norwood, 1979 (127-44).

— "Prophecy and Leadership in the Maranke Church", Bond, Johnson & Walker (eds.), *African Christianity,* New York, 1979 (109-36).

Kalinga, Owen J. M. "Jordan Msumba, Ben Ngemela and the Last Church of God and his Christ 1924-1935", *Journal of Religion in Africa* 13:3, 1982 (207-18).

Kalu, Ogbu U. (ed.), *The History of Christianity in West Africa,* London & New York, 1980.

— "The Third Response: Pentecostalism and the Reconstruction of Christian Experience in Africa, 1970-1995", *Journal of African Christian Thought,* 1:2, 1998 (3-16).

Kiernan, Jim, "Variations on a Christian Theme: The Healing Synthesis of Zulu Zionism", Stewart & Shaw (eds.), *Syncretism/ Anti-Syncretism,* London & New York, 1994.

Kileff, Clive & Kileff, Margaret, "The Masowe Vapostori of Seki: Utopianism and Tradition in an African Church", Jules-Rosette, (ed.), *The New Religions of Africa,* Norwood, 1979 (151-67).

Lukhaimane, E. K. "The Zion Christian Church of Ignatius (Engenas) Lekganyane, 1924 to 1948: An African Experiment with Christianity", MA thesis, Pietersburg: University of the North, 1980.

MacGaffey, Wyatt, *Modern Kongo Prophets: Religion in a Plural Society*, Bloomington: Indiana University Press, 1983.

Magesa, Laurenti, *African Religion: The Moral Traditions of Abundant Life*, New York: Orbis, 1997.

Makhubu, Paul, *Who are the Independent Churches?*, Johannesburg: Skotaville Publishers, 1988.

Maimela, Simon S. "Salvation in African traditional religions". *Missionalia* 13:2, 1985 (63-77).

Mala, Sam Babs, "African Instituted Churches in Nigeria: the quest for unity, education and identity", Shank (ed.), *Ministry in Partnership with African Independent Churches*, Elkhart, 1991 (22-39).

Marshall, Ruth, "Pentecostalism in Southern Nigeria: an overview", Gifford, *New Dimensions*, Nairobi, 1992 (7-32).

Marshall-Fratani, Ruth, "Mediating the Global and Local in Nigerian Pentecostalism", *Journal of Religion in Africa* 28:4, 1998 (278-315).

Martin, Marie-Louise, *The Biblical Concept of Messianism and Messianism in Southern Africa*, Morija, Lesotho: Sesuto Book Depot, 1964.

— "The Mai Chaza Church in Rhodesia", Barrett (ed.), *African Initiatives in Religion*, Nairobi, 1971 (109-21).

— *Kimbangu: An African Prophet and his Church*, Oxford: Basil Blackwell, 1975.

Maxwell, David, "Witches, Prophets and Avenging Spirits: The Second Christian Movement in North-East Zimbabwe", *Journal of Religion in Africa* 25:3, 1995 (309-35).

— "Rethinking Christian Independency: The Southern African Pentecostal Movement ca. 1908-1960". Unpublished paper, 1997.

— "'Delivered from the Spirit of Poverty': Pentecostalism, Prosperity and Modernity in Zimbabwe". *Journal of Religion in Africa* 28:3, 1998 (350-73).

Mesters, Carlos, "The Use of the Bible in Christian Communities of the Common People", Gottwald & Horsley (eds.), *The Bible and Liberation*, New York, 1993.

Meyer, Birgit, "'Make a Complete Break with the Past': Memory and Post-Colonial Modernity in Ghanaian Pentecostalist Discourse". *Journal of Religion in Africa* 28:4, 1998 (316-349).

Milingo, Emmanuel, *The World in Between: Christian Healing and the Struggle for Spiritual Survival,* London, 1984.

Mlahagwa, Josiah R. "Contending for the Faith: Spiritual Revival & the Fellowship Church in Tanzania", Spear & Kimambo, *East African Expressions of Christianity,* Oxford, 1999 (296-306).

Ndiokwere, Nathaniel, *Prophecy and Revolution: The role of prophets in independent African churches and in biblical tradition,* London: SPCK, 1981.

Njeri, Philomena, "The Akurinu Churches: A Study of the History and Some of the Basic Beliefs of the Holy Ghost Church of East Africa", MA thesis, University of Nairobi, 1984.

Nussbaum, Stan (ed.), *Freedom and Independence,* Nairobi: Organization of African Instituted Churches, 1994.

Obafemi, Olu, *Pastor S.B.J. Oshoffa: God's 20th Century Gift to Africa,* Lagos: Pathway Publishers, 1986.

Ogunranti, Ayokunnu, "Pastor and Politician: Isaac Akinyele, Olubadan of Ibadan (1862-1955 [sic])". Isichei (ed.), *Varieties of Christian Experience in Nigeria,* London, 1982 (131-40).

Ojo, Matthews A. "Deeper Life Bible Church of Nigeria", Gifford (ed.), *New Dimensions,* Nairobi, 1992 (135-56).

— "The Church in the African State: The Charismatic/ Pentecostal Experience in Nigeria", *Journal of African Christian Thought,* 1:2, 1998 (25-32).

Omoyajowo, Akin, *The Cherubim and Seraphim Church in Relation to Church, Society and State,* Ibadan: Claverianum Press, 1975.

Oosthuizen, Gerhardus C. *The Theology of a South African Messiah,* Leiden: Brill, 1967.

— *Post Christianity in Africa,* London: Hurst, 1968.

— *The Healer-Prophet in Afro-Christian Churches,* Leiden: E.J. Brill, 1992.

Opoku, Kofi A. "Changes within Christianity: the case of the Musama Disco Christo Church". Kalu (ed.), *The History of Christianity in West Africa*, London & New York, 1980 (309-20).

Oshun, Christopher O. "Christ Apostolic Church of Nigeria: A Pentecostal Consideration of its Historical, Theological and Organisational Developments, 1918-1978", PhD thesis, University of Exeter, 1981.

Otabil, Mensa, *Beyond the Rivers of Ethiopia: A Biblical Revelation on God's Purpose for the Black Race*, Accra: Altar International, 1992.

Pauw, C. M. "Independency and Religious Change in Malawi: a new challenge for the church", *Missionalia* 21:2, 1993 (138-51).

Peel, J. D. Y. *Aladura: a Religious Movement among the Yoruba*, Oxford: Oxford University Press, 1968.

Peires, J. B. *The Dead Will Arise: Nongqawuse and the Great Xhosa Cattle-Killing Movement of 1856-7*. Johannesburg: Ravan Press, 1989.

Pobee, John S. & Ositelu II, Gabriel, *African Initiatives in Christianity: The Growth, Gifts and Diversities of Indigenous African Churches — A Challenge to the Ecumenical Movement*, Geneva: WCC, 1998.

Poewe, Karla (ed.), *Charismatic Christianity as a Global Culture*, Columbia: University of South Carolina Press, 1994.

Presler, Titus L. *Transformed Night: Mission and Culture in Zimbabwe's Vigil Movement*, Pretoria: University of South Africa Press, 1999.

Pretorius, H. L. *Ethiopia Stretches Out her Hands unto God: Aspects of Transkeian Indigenous Churches*. Pretoria: University of Pretoria, 1993.

Pretorius, Hennie & Jafta, Lizo "'A Branch Springs Out': African Initiated Churches", Elphick & Davenport (eds.), *Christianity in South Africa*, Oxford & Cape Town, 1997 (211-226).

Price, L., Sepúlveda, J. & Smith, G. (eds.), *Mission Matters*, Frankfurt: Peter Lang, 1997.

Ranger, Terence O. "Christian Independency in Tanzania", Barrett, (ed.) *African Initiatives in Religion*, Nairobi, 1971 (122-45).

Rasmussen, Ane Marie Bak, *Modern African Spirituality: The Independent Spirit Churches in East Africa, 1902-1976*, London & New York: British Academic Press, 1996.

Saah, Richard B. "African Independent Church studies", *Church History in East Africa* 7:3, 1991 (46-57).

Saayman, Willem A. "Some reflections on the development of the Pentecostal mission model in South Africa", *Missionalia* 21:1, 1993 (43-57).

Sandgren, David, "Kamba Christianity: From Africa Inland Mission to African Brotherhood Church", Spear & Kimambo (eds.), *East African Expressions of Christianity,* Oxford, 1999 (169-95).

Sanneh, Lamin, *West African Christianity: The Religious Impact,* London: Hurst, 1983.

Schoffeleers, Matthew, "Ritual Healing and Political Acquiescence: The Case of the Zionist Churches in Southern Africa", *Africa* 60 (1), 1991 (1-25).

Schreiter, Robert J. *Constructing Local Theologies,* New York: Orbis, 1985.

— (ed.), *Faces of Jesus in Africa.* London: SCM, 1992.

Schwartz, Nancy, "Christianity and the Construction of Global History: The Example of Legio Maria", Poewe (ed.), *Charismatic Christianity as a Global Culture,* Columbia, 1994.

Serbin, Marie-Jeanne & Catherine Simon, "Alice, la grande prophetesse Ougandaise", *Africa International,* 203, March 1988 (45-7).

Sepúlveda, Juan, "To overcome the fear of syncretism: A Latin American perspective", Price, Sepúlveda & Smith (eds.), *Mission Matters,* Frankfurt, 1997.

Shank, David A. (ed.), *Ministry in Partnership with African Independent Churches,* Elkhart: Mennonite Board of Missions, 1991.

Shenk, Wilbert R. "The Contribution of the Study of New Religious Movements to Missiology", Walls & Shenk (eds.), *Exploring New Religious Movements,* Elkhart, 1990 (179-205).

Shorter, Aylward, *Jesus and the Witchdoctor: An Approach to Healing and Wholeness.* Maryknoll: Orbis, 1985.

Sinda, M. *Le Messianisme Congolaise et ses Incidences Politique: Kimbanguisme — Matsouanisme — Autres Mouvements,* Paris: Payot, 1972.

Spear, Thomas, & Kimambo, Isaria N. (eds.), *East African Expressions of Christianity*, Oxford: James Currey, 1999.

Stewart, C. & Shaw, R. (eds.), *Syncretism/ Anti-Syncretism: The Politics of Religious Syncretism.* London & New York: Routledge, 1994.

Sundkler, Bengt G. M. *Bantu Prophets in South Africa.* Oxford: Oxford University Press, 1961.

—*Zulu Zion and Some Swazi Zionists*, London: Oxford University Press, 1976.

Swiderski, Stanislaw, *La Religion Bouiti*, Tome I Histoire, Ottawa: Éditions de l'Université d'Ottawa, 1985.

Synan, Vinson, *The Holiness-Pentecostal Tradition: Charismatic Movements in the Twentieth Century.* Grand Rapids & Cambridge: Wm. B. Eerdmans, 1997.

Tasie, G.O.M. "Christian Awakening in West Africa 1914-18: a study in the significance of native agency", Kalu, (ed.), *The History of Christianity in West Africa*, London & New York, 1980 (293-306).

— "The Prophetic Calling: Garrick Sokari Braide of Bakana", Isichei, *Varieties of Christian Experience in Nigeria*, London, 1982 (99-115).

Taylor, J. V. & Lehmann, D. A. *Christians of the Copperbelt: The growth of the church in Northern Rhodesia.* London: SCM, 1961.

Tempels, Placide, *Bantu Philosophy*, Paris: Presence Africaine, 1958.

Ter Haar, Gerrie, "Standing up for Jesus: a survey of new developments in Christianity in Ghana", in *Exchange 23:3*, 1994, (221-40).

— *Halfway to Paradise: African Christians in Europe*, Cardiff: Cardiff Academic Press, 1998.

Thompson, T. Jack, "African Independent Churches in Britain: An Introductory Survey", Towler (ed.) *New Religions and the New Europe*, Aarhus, 1995 (224-31).

Towler, R. (ed.) *New Religions and the New Europe*, Aarhus: Aarhus University Press, 1995.

Tshelane, Sipho, "The Witness of the African Indigenous Churches in South Africa", *International Review of Mission* 83: 328, January 1994.

Turner, Harold W. *History of an African Independent Church (1) The Church of the Lord (Aladura),* Oxford: Clarendon, 1967.

— *Bibliography of New Religious Movements in Primal Societies. Vol. 1: Black Africa.* Boston: G. K. Hall, 1977.

— *Religious Innovation in Africa.* Boston: G. K. Hall, 1979.

Van Binsbergen, Wim M. J. *Religious Change in Zambia: Exploratory studies.* London & Boston: Kegan Paul International, 1981.

Van Dijk, Richard (Rijk), "Young Born-Again Preachers in post-independence Malawi: the significance of an extraneous identity", Gifford, *New Dimensions,* Nairobi, 1992 (55-65).

— "Pentecostalism, Cultural Memory and the State: Contested Representations of Time in Postcolonial Malawi", Werbner (ed.), *Memory and the Postcolony,* London & New York, 1998 (155-81)

Walker, Sheila S. "The Message as the Medium: The Harrist Churches of the Ivory Coast and Ghana", Bond, Johnson & Walker (eds.), *African Christianity,* New York, 1979 (9-64).

— "Women in the Harrist Movement". Jules-Rosette (ed.), *The New Religions of Africa,* Norwood, 1979 (87-97).

— *The Religious Revolution in the Ivory Coast: The Prophet Harris and the Harrist Church,* Chapel Hill, N. C.: The University of North Carolina Press, 1983.

Walls, Andrew F. & Shenk, Wilbert R. (eds.), *Exploring New Religious Movements.* Elkhart, Indiana: Mission Focus, 1990.

Wamba-dia-Wamba, Ernest, "Bundu dia Kongo: A Congolese Fundamentalist Religious Movement", Spear & Kimambo (eds.), *East African Expressions of Christianity,* Oxford, 1999 (213-28).

Webster, James B. *The African Churches among the Yoruba 1888-1922,* Oxford: Clarendon, 1964.

Welbourn, F. B. *East African Rebels: A Study of Some Independent Churches,* London: SCM, 1961.

— & Ogot, B. A. *A Place to Feel at Home.* London: Oxford University Press, 1966.

Werbner, Richard (ed.), *Memory and the Postcolony: African Anthropology and the Critique of Power*, London & New York: Zed Books, 1998.

West, Gerald, *Biblical Hermeneutics of Liberation*, Pietermaritzburg: Cluster Publications, 1995.

West, Martin, *Bishops and Prophets in a Black City*, Cape Town: David Phillip, 1975.

World Council of Churches, "Consultation with African Instituted Churches, Ogere, Nigeria, 9-14 January 1996", Geneva: World Council of Churches, 1996.

Wyllie, Robert W. "Pioneers of Ghanaian Pentecostalism: Peter Anim and James McKeown", *Journal of Religion in Africa*, 6:2, 1974 (109-22).

Yong, Amos, ""Not Knowing Where the Wind Blows...": On Envisioning a Pentecostal-Charismatic Theology of Religions", *Journal of Pentecostal Theology* 14, 1999 (85-100).

ABBREVIATIONS

AACC	All African Conference of Churches
AACJM	African Apostolic Church of Johane Marange
AFM	Apostolic Faith Mission
AICN	African Israel Church Nineveh
AICs	African Initiated/ Instituted/ Indigenous Churches
AIPC	African Independent Pentecostal Church
ABC	African Brotherhood Church
ACCS	African Christian Church and Schools
ACHS	African Church of the Holy Spirit
AGOC	African Greek Orthodox Church
AME	African Methodist Episcopal Church
ANC	African National Congress
AOC	African Orthodox Church
BCS	Brotherhood of the Cross and Star
BMS	Baptist Missionary Society
C&S	Cherubim and Seraphim
CAC	Christ Apostolic Church
CCA	Church of Christ in Africa
CCC	Celestial Church of Christ
CLA	Church of the Lord (Aladura)
CMS	Church Missionary Society

EJCSK	Church of Jesus Christ on Earth through the Prophet Simon Kimbangu (French)
HSCEA	Holy Spirit Church of East Africa
IPC	International Pentecost Church
KKEA	Kikuyu Karing'a Educational Association
KISA	Kikuyu Independent Schools Association
KOAB	Society of the One Almighty God (Ganda)
LMS	London Missionary Society
MDCC	Musama Disco Christo Church (Fanti)
NPCs	New Pentecostal and Charismatic Churches
OAIC	Organisation of African Instituted Churches
PFN	Pentecostal Fellowship of Nigeria
UNIP	United National Independence Party
WCC	World Council of Churches
ZAOGA	Zimbabwe Assemblies of God Africa
ZCC	Zion Christian Church

INDEX